Islands
of
Women

Islands of Women

Eileen A. O'Hara

BOOKLOGIX
Alpharetta, Georgia

This is a work of fiction. Names, characters, businesses, places, and events are either the products of the author's imagination or are used in a fictitious manner. Any resemblance to actual persons, living or dead, or actual events is purely coincidental.

Copyright © 2023 by Eileen A. O'Hara

All rights reserved. No part of this book may be reproduced or transmitted in any form or by any means, electronic or mechanical, including photocopying, recording, or any information storage and retrieval system, without permission in writing from the author.

ISBN: 978-1-6653-0606-5 - Paperback
ISBN: 978-1-6653-0607-2 - Hardcover
eISBN: 978-1-6653-0608-9 – ePub

Library of Congress Control Number: 2023904464

These ISBNs are the property of BookLogix for the express purpose of sales and distribution of this title. BookLogix is not responsible for the writing, editing, or design/appearance of this book. The content of this book is the property of the copyright holder only. BookLogix does not hold any ownership of the content of this book and is not liable in any way for the materials contained within. The views and opinions expressed in this book are the property of the Author/Copyright holder, and do not necessarily reflect those of BookLogix.

Printed in the United States of America   0 4 2 0 2 3

♾This paper meets the requirements of ANSI/NISO Z39.48-1992 (Permanence of Paper)

Cover Design by Dylan Stevens Photography,
dylanstevensphotography@gmail.com

On the Shore

She sits on the shore.
Pockets filled with stones she
Took time and care to select.
Stones full of color, all the
Colors her life has lost.

She leans into the wind.
Hugging her knees, she
Sighs and closes her eyes.
Blown sand scrapes and scours,
As abrasive as her emotions.

She sinks into the coast.
Waves pounding on the beach,
Echo the throbbing of her heart.
Gull cries overhead, match hers,
As tears run down her cheeks.

She feels herself facing.
Yet for this singular moment,
She can and will endure.
The sand's damp coldness,
Embodies the chill of her emotions.

She has, is, nothing.
No family, no lover,
No friend who cares.
Standing, she makes her
Decision and moves forward . . .

Gina Dyer

Chapter One

Penelope Worth limped to a stop and dropped her rear onto the glistening white sandy path. Lifting a bone-thin, tanned leg, the nine-year-old plucked a sand burr from the sole of her bare foot. Leaping to her feet, she continued her run toward the shore paying no mind to ragged weeds along the path snagging her faded, frayed blue dress.

A glitter along the edge of the path caught Penelope's eye. Skidding to a stop, she circled the area and carefully combed through broken shells in search of whatever treasure might have washed up from an incoming tide.

Penelope loved anything that sparkled. She would stare up at the stars twinkling on a clear night. As they reflected off the Gulf, she imagined millions of diamonds floating on the water. She dreamed of a pink dress trimmed in lace and adorned with sparkly jewels ... just like the princess's gown in a tattered and worn story book she kept hidden under her bedroom pillow.

The shiny object turned out to be a silver-colored button, its center broken away. Dropping it into the pocket of her dress, Penelope resumed her run, her long, straight, flaxen hair whipping around her face.

In the hot August air currents from the west, flocks of gulls screeched and glided over the Florida Gulf coast island of Pine Cove Key. A trio of pelicans descended and landed somewhere beyond a dune of wispy sea oats.

As Penelope approached the shoreline, Sanderlings scurried out of her way. From another part of the beach, a dog's incessant barking brought Penelope to a halt again. Bell could get excited over a dead fish washed up on shore, but she seemed especially excited now. Oblivious to the steamy, scorching heat, Penelope retraced a few steps, annoyed that her mongrel pet interfered with the job at hand.

"Bell! Come here, girl!" Penelope yelled.

Over a wave of dunes, flashes of burnt red fur charged through the sea oats. The dog bounded toward Penelope sending sprays of powder-fine white sand into the air and continued her urgent barking and jumping.

"Stop it, you ding dong! I can't play now!" Penelope tried to run past Bell, but the dog persisted. "Bell, stop it! I said I ain't playin' now! Go! Go on and leave me be! I got work ta do!"

Penelope waved her arms at the dog and ran to the top of the dune. Shielding her watercolor-blue eyes from sunlight reflecting off brilliant aqua-green water, she spotted three white buoys bobbing in the calm inlet. She ran to the shoreline and waded into the surf, eager to see how many crabs might be snagged in the traps. If there were even a couple, the hotel's cook, Molly Harper, might swap Penelope's crabs for a few bowls of soup.

Maybe even some chocolate cake.

Penelope's mouth watered. She loved chocolate cake more than anything in the world. She dreamed of the day when she could have all the chocolate cake her tiny tummy could hold.

Molly told Penelope often, "Jus' keep on dreamin', child. Someday, you'll have all the chocolate cake and whatever else you want ta eat. Don't let nobody tell you diff'ernt."

Perched on a stool in the hot hotel kitchen, as she slurped a bowl of fish chowder or chicken vegetable soup, Penelope would nod her head. "I will, Miss Molly. I will."

Squinting as she waded further into the dazzling, warm water, Penelope muttered, "Please don't be empty. Please don't be empty."

If the chicken neck bait was still there, well, she would figure out something. Penelope's father, Jasper Worth, would be back from his trip up the Suwannee soon.

Maybe Pa'll have somethin' in the buckboard ta tide us over. Maybe another watermelon.

The week before, Jasper gave Penelope one of two watermelons he had brought home along with two bags of nearly rotten oranges from last year's season. Her only clue to the disappearance of the other was a pile of rinds tossed among a couple of empty liquor bottles rolling around the floor in her father's bedroom. He had left again a few days later with no word as to when he might return.

Penelope lugged her watermelon to the hotel. She rolled the giant oval ball down the hallway and into the kitchen where Molly split it with a butcher knife. For over an hour, Penelope gorged herself on the ripe, juicy red fruit. She hoped her father would bring her another one day, but she would never dare to ask. She learned simply to be grateful for whatever he brought home.

Jasper thought nothing of leaving his waif of a daughter to fend for herself. He claimed he had business to tend to and had no need of help from anyone. Sometimes he would be gone a couple of days, sometimes a week. He never said what he was doing up the Suwannee . . . or wherever he went. Sometimes he brought home food of one kind or other—usually fish, some gator meat, or a dead rabbit that he almost always traded at the hotel bar for liquor. Jasper's horse-drawn wagon left Pine Cove Key empty and most times returned that way. The town's residents chose to keep their distance from Jasper and his drunken tirades, so no one knew or ventured to guess how he had money to live on.

As for Penelope, Jasper had been fiercely disappointed she was not born a boy. Because "girls ain't worth a gawd-damned plug nickel," he was determined to name her "Penny." Her young mother, Adelaide, intimidated by her blustery husband fifteen years her senior, did not want her daughter to grow up feeling worthless. Adelaide felt enough of that for the two of them. She did not win many arguments with Jasper, but she was finally able to get him to agree to "Penelope."

"Do what ya want with her," Jasper grumbled. "She's all your'n. Nothin' but Penny ta me!"

Adelaide did her best to protect Penelope from Jasper's harsh temperament. But then Adelaide disappeared . . . died, according to Jasper, in a river accident when the three were returning from a trip up the Suwannee. Everyone in Pine Cove puzzled over Jasper's account of the accident, and a few attempted a search. With the town folks' own struggles to survive following the 1896 hurricane ten years before that wiped out the cedar industry, the matter simply drifted away like the small island's outgoing tide.

Not yet five years old, with only a neglectful father in her life, Penelope was forced to learn basic survival skills on her own. Climbing onto a rickety chair she pulled next to the rain barrel behind the Worth's shack in Hungry Bend, she would scoop a drink from the roof run-off. Scampering behind the hotel right after the breakfast, lunch, and dinner hours, she might find discarded, half-eaten biscuits, crumbles of bacon, and bones, sometimes with meat still on them. She shared those with Bell. Before long, with nothing but survival on her mind, Penelope's memory of her mother faded.

The women of Pine Cove, despite their own hardships, did their best to see that Penelope was taken care of . . . or at least fed. Her favorite person to see for tasty leftovers was Glory Bee Porter, housekeeper for the island's elderly matriarch, Winifred Peck, or "Birdie" to the towns' folk. Like a stray kitten, with her hair all a-tangle and hunger in her eyes, Penelope would appear at the Peck's back porch door.

Glory Bee would whisper through the rusted screen, "I'll be makin' a chicken pot pie later. Stop by tomorra' an' I'll have some fer ya," or "I'll be stewin' some 'maters an' okra an' might can spare a bowl fer ya."

It was a hand-to-mouth existence, but Penelope had learned how to weather the unpredictable storms that plagued her life on the island.

Bell had bounded after Penelope into the water then turned and ran back to the beach. Again and again, she rushed into the water, barking wildly. She would then run a little further up the beach where she barked more urgently than ever.

Penelope stopped short of the buoys, her dress floating around her like a cloud. She scowled at Bell. "What's the matter, girl? What'd you find?"

The tide would not be in for a little while. Deciding the crab traps could wait a bit, Penelope waded back to the shore. She ran after Bell, who was still barking and running ahead of her, away from the inlet and out to the open beach. Knowing Bell as she did, Penelope figured it had to be something good to be this excited . . . nothing like a dead animal or a dead fish. They and their stink were everywhere. It had to be something really important, like a big conch, or maybe a manatee or a sea turtle.

Up ahead, Penelope spotted something in the shallows. "Sure don't look like a manatee. Ain't no conch or turtle neither," she muttered.

She ran closer . . . then slowed . . . then stopped. Inhaling sharply, Penelope slapped her hand over her mouth, her eyes growing large with disbelief.

"Good Lordy," she whispered. Struggling to comprehend what her eyes knew, she whispered again. "Good Lordy."

Less than twenty feet away, a body lay sprawled face down. Entangled in rope-like lengths of seaweed, it looked like a sea monster might have washed up from the deep.

Bell whimpered and shoved her nose against Penelope's leg nudging the girl on. Penelope tiptoed forward, her flesh suddenly chilled. Salt water dripped off the edge of her dress and puddled in the sand around her.

A few feet away from the body, Penelope dropped onto all fours and squinted her eyes to get a better look. "It's a lady!" she whispered. "An' she's nek'ed."

Penelope struggled to see the woman's face through the mass of matted hair and seaweed. She looked for any signs of life, but the only movement was the sway of the woman's legs from the ebb and flow of the waves.

Life on Pine Cove Key seemed to stop altogether. Gulls and pelicans disappeared from the sky. Clumps of sea oats stood motionless. Even the wind seemed to hold its breath as Penelope studied the lifeless body.

The dog inched on her belly toward Penelope. Whimpering, she nuzzled the girl's leg again and rested her head on her thigh. Patting Bell's head, Penelope whispered: "Good girl. Yer a good girl."

Penelope looked around and noticed a battered, hinged board several yards away entangled in more seaweed. She combed this beach daily and knew it had not been there the day before. Shielding her eyes, she scoped the horizon for a boat or any other debris. Nothing.

Water sloshed around the woman's feet and legs, inching its way to her hips. The tide was coming in.

"I think she's dead, Bell," Penelope whispered.

Penelope was not repelled with the thought of touching the body. Having come across dead manatees, sea turtles, rabbits, and endless kinds of fish, she had learned to take death in stride.

Pushing Bell's head off her lap, Penelope scooted forward a little, oblivious of the wet gritty sand digging into her knees. Reaching out slowly, she pulled some of the slimy seaweed from the woman's outstretched arm. Although sunburned, the skin was cold to the touch.

"Cold as a dead fish," she muttered.

Penelope scanned the beach and the horizon once more. No one was about. Picking up the woman's hand, she slid green slime from her slender, cold fingers then laid the woman's hand back onto the warm sand.

Realizing the danger of the incoming tide, Penelope knew she needed to alert someone about her discovery. But something about the woman's pretty, gentle-looking face nudged Penelope's subconscious and caused her to hesitate. Unnerved by unsettling thoughts and feelings, Penelope backed away. She became confused by stirrings deep within her so strong as to cause her breath to quicken.

Long-stored slivers of foggy memories, like smudged pictures cut into pieces, brightened and began to merge and engage . . . of a dark-haired woman combing Penelope's hair, bathing her, playing together in the water, running through the pine woods . . . her pine woods. Disturbing images, while only glimpses, began to surface . . . of the woman screaming and running, of a man, Penelope's father, yelling, and of herself crying.

"Oh, sweet Jesus," Penelope murmured. Wrapping her thin arms around herself, she backed further away and stared. "Oh, sweet Jesus," she muttered again, rubbing her hands up and down her arms. Adrenalin raced through Penelope's body. "Ohmigod."

A faint moan stunned Penelope. With a gasp, she reeled back, landing on her bottom. Bell jumped up and began whining again. Unsure if the sound came from the woman's mouth or maybe suction of water under the body, Penelope scolded, "Be still, Bell!"

Again, a distinct moan undoubtedly came from the woman's mouth. Astonished, Penelope backed up a dune. She whispered, "She's alive!"

Water sloshed further up the woman's body and she moaned again. The tide was coming in faster. Gulls reappeared in the sky, squawking, diving, and skimming the water. Pelicans soared and plunged, scooping up mouthfuls of water and fish. The sea oats danced in a renewed stiff breeze.

Untangling the wet, sand-coated dress fabric from around her legs, Penelope scrambled off the dune. With Bell on her heels, barely able to breathe, she ran for the path yelling at the top of her lungs. "Glory Bee! Come quick! It's Mama! I found my Mama! An' she's alive!"

Chapter Two

Streams of sweat escaped from under Glory Bee Porter's head wrap. Wiping her thick, black arm across her forehead, she glanced up at the kitchen ceiling's peeling paint. A kettle of water boiled on the cast iron stove as steam dripped off the ceiling and down the once-white walls now yellowed with age and neglect.

Glory Bee had cautioned the home's owner several times. "That ceiling's gotta' get fixed or there's gonna' be paint peelin's landin' in the soup."

Towering above more humble residences in Pine Cove, the once lavish, once white Victorian house with its cracked ornate scrollwork stood as evidence of the deteriorating spirit of the entire town. The roof leaked and the front porch sagged, its weathered floor missing a few boards. Several railing posts had rotted away like missing teeth. The entire house, inside and out, needed patching and painting. Without funds to pay for them, those repairs had remained untouched for several years.

Glory Bee picked up a threadbare dishtowel from the kitchen table and swatted a few flies buzzing around a bowl of biscuit dough. "Go do yer buzzin' somewhere's else," she mumbled.

In the relentless heat both inside the house and out, flies clung for their lives to the screen on the kitchen door leading to the back porch.

Overhead, floorboards creaked and groaned. As predictable as the sun rising in the east, on cue, Glory Bee began scooping out ladles of dough and dropping them into the cast iron skillet sizzling with melted lard. Once filled, she covered the skillet with a lid and wiped her hands on her apron that covered her generous girth.

In another smaller cast iron skillet, Glory Bee broke two eggs into more melted lard. Grease spattered onto her leathery dark hands. From the shelf over the sink, she lifted a plate and cup, chipped from years of use, and placed them on a worn wooden tray. She filled the cup with weak black coffee then slid the eggs out of the skillet and onto the plate. Lifting the lid on the larger skillet, she scooped out two biscuits, split them open, and drizzled grease left over from the eggs onto each one. She then added three thick, bright red tomato slices from a bowl she brought out from the larder.

The floorboards above creaked in the opposite direction. Glory Bee picked up the tray and headed toward the worn carpeted stairs at the front of the house. "I'm a'comin', I'm a comin'," she muttered as she made her way slowly up the stairs. "One more time, Lawd. One more time."

When Glory Bee reached the upstairs landing, she stopped long enough to catch her breath. She then set the tray on the floor in front of a closed bedroom door and knocked twice. Returning to the staircase, feeling the strain of her weight-laden bones, she gripped the banister and began the slow trek back down the stairs.

With few exceptions, it was a routine Glory Bee had carried out for the last twenty-seven years as a housemaid . . . right along with that of her daily walk from and return to her own house on Lizey's Hill, a small island community of Colored families.

Back in the kitchen, out of breath, Glory Bee wiped her brow with her apron. "I thank ya fer keepin' me goin', Lawd," she muttered. She then cackled. "But I be prayin' you got somethin' up yer sleeve before I go tumblin' down those stairs."

Glory Bee helped herself to a biscuit from the skillet and dunked it into grease left over from the eggs. Sitting down at the table, grateful to relieve the strain in her back and legs, she nibbled on the biscuit and pondered how she would spend the day after cleaning up the mess in the kitchen.

Silver ought ta be polished agin befo' the next Bible study. Prob'ly ought ta check the tablecloth and napkins fer stains. Dust the parlor. Need ta ask Miz Peck what kind o' cake ta make this time.

A dog's bark and a child's yell in the distance distracted Glory Bee from musing over her household tasks. Rising from the table, she pushed open the screen door, swatting away the never-ending swarm of flies. Hoping for even a slight breeze to cool her, she stepped onto the back porch. Before she had time to sit down in the weathered wicker chair that had seen better days, from around the corner of the house, Bell bounded and leaped onto the porch, nearly knocking Glory Bee off her feet.

Grabbing hold of the wobbly chair, she steadied herself. "Good gracious me! What you think you doin'?!"

Within moments, Penelope followed, gasping for air. "Glory Bee! Ya gotta come quick! Before she drowns!" Penelope scampered up the steps and pulled on Glory Bee's hands. "Come on! It's Mama! On the beach! I found my Mama!"

Stunned by Penelope's abrupt arrival, not to mention what the child could possibly mean, Glory Bee pulled away her hands. Exasperated, she scowled and shooed a fly from her face. "What you mean, child? You know yer Mama ain't comin' back nohow!"

Glory Bee opened the screen door to return to her duties in the kitchen. Realizing she might have been a bit too stern, she turned back to Penelope. "I know ya want ta believe yer Mama is gonna come back someday. But like I told ya before an' I'm gonna keep tellin' ya cuz I don't want ya ta keep gittin' yer hopes up. Jus' like yer Pa said, yer Mama likely dead, an' I'm sorry as I can be I have ta keep tellin' ya that."

Penelope shook her head, her eyes as round and pale as a full blue moon. "No!" she shouted, grabbing Glory Bee's hands again. "Yer wrong! She ain't dead! I found her! Layin' on the beach! Ya gotta come and help! And we hafta' take a blanket or somethin' 'cause she's nek'ed!"

Before Penelope could say another word and before Glory Bee could further react to Penelope's startling story, another figure sauntered around the corner of the house. Forty-year-old Nathan Walker, born and raised on the island, came from a long line of seafarers. Lanky and tanned from work on the docks and weeks at sea, Nathan would pop in now and then. In exchange for a fish or two, he was always happy to relieve Glory Bee of any available breakfast leftovers.

"Mornin', Glory Bee." Approaching the porch, he handed Glory Bee a fish wrapped in newspaper. "Caught it this mornin'."

"Mornin', Mr. Nathan," Glory Bee said as she took the wrapped fish. "Mighty nice of ya."

Dropping down onto the sagging weathered porch steps, Nathan stretched out his legs. Dark stains covered his worn tan trousers, the result of months—or maybe years—of cleaning fish and repairing nets. Under the floppy brim of his equally stained and worn hat, shaggy blond hair framed his lean face, subtly lined and tanned from years of Florida sunshine.

Nathan reached out and pulled Penelope to him. "Come here, urchin. So what's all the fuss about? I could hear you down the street."

Penelope pushed against Nathan's shoulder and wiggled away. She loved "Mr. Nathan" like a brother, or like a father to replace the one she had. At that moment, though, all she could think about was the lady lying on the beach—and the tide rushing toward her. She jumped off the porch, grabbed hold of Nathan's hand, and pulled.

"Quick! Ya hafta' come quick or she'll drown!"

Nathan tugged back and frowned. "Who'll drown?"

"The lady!" Her agitation growing, Penelope yanked on Nathan's arm as she turned to Glory Bee. "I told you! There's a lady on the beach and she moaned. I heard her moan, so I know she's alive, but you got ta come now! And bring somethin' . . . Glory Bee, I need somethin' to cover her up with. She don't have any clothes on an' she's cold, so we have ta cover her up."

Nathan and Glory Bee both knew the child would not make up such a story. Glory Bee hurried into the house. Within moments, she returned with a folded bed sheet, only to find that Nathan and Penelope had already disappeared around the corner of the house.

Hobbling down the steps, she followed Bell's barks and Penelope's shouts, the heat of the scorching Florida sun baking her skin. Perspiration found its way into the folds of Glory Bee's neck and streamed down her back as she hurried as fast as she could toward the water. Sand worked its way over the tops of her old, worn shoes and ground its way under the soles of her feet.

"Laws a mercy, Lawd," she grumbled. "I'm a'comin', ya'll! I'm a'comin'." Glory Bee's stout legs strained as she huffed and puffed up the town's steepest grade. "Bad 'nough that trek up and down Lizey's Hill ever' day," she mumbled. "I ain't no spring chicken, ya know."

Glory Bee stopped to catch her breath before continuing toward the sparkling Gulf water. At the top of the hill, she caught sight of Penelope's blue dress as the child ran down the far side of a sand dune. Nathan was out of sight apparently having run ahead.

Glory Bee wadded the sheet tighter, tucked it under her arm, and hustled down the slope toward the beach. In the back of her mind, she grew anxious about Penelope's insistence that she had found her Mama. She knew the child believed her hostile father had driven her mother away and that she would return someday. Sadly, Glory Bee was convinced otherwise. No matter the level of abuse Jasper Worth inflicted on his wife, she knew Adelaide Worth never would have abandoned her little daughter. She was dead and everyone in Pine Cove knew it. As to how she died, they likely would never know.

By the time Nathan reached the beach and discovered the woman's body, the tide had indeed advanced far enough to threaten to wash her back out to sea. Water sloshed heavily around her bare legs and torso and was close to reaching her face.

Despite the effects of the sun and sea on much of her body, Nathan determined her to be quite young—perhaps in her twenties or thirties. He placed his hand gingerly on the woman's sunburned shoulder, the touch cold and gritty with sand. Parts of her body that had not been burned by the sun were so white, like the underbelly of a fish, that he could not believe she was alive. And like Penelope, he was startled when he heard a soft moan.

"Let's get you out o' this water before we lose ya." Nathan placed his hands under her arms and gently pulled her out of the surf and further up onto the warm sand.

With Bell on her heels, barking incessantly, Penelope had retreated up the dunes to be sure Glory Bee would know where to find them. Waving her arms, she yelled, "Down here, Glory Bee! We're down here!"

She ran back and knelt next to Nathan. Eager to help, she went to work pulling more of the slimy, cold seaweed from the woman's body.

When Glory Bee reached the beach, she could not believe her eyes. "What in the name of . . .?" she muttered.

With the seaweed removed, as more moans escaped the woman's swollen, salt-caked lips, Glory Bee covered her and tucked the sheet snugly around her. Nathan then expertly rolled her onto her side and carefully picked her up, cradling her like a newborn, her head resting against his chest.

All the way back to town, no one spoke a word. None of the

three questioned where they would take the woman, nor the likely reaction of a stranger occupying a bedroom. Glory Bee, however, could not quell the nagging, worrisome apprehension bombarding her thoughts.

Lawd, give me strength. Please Lawd, fer once, let that woman show some mercy.

Bell nuzzled her nose into Penelope's free hand and whimpered. With her tail hanging limp, even she seemed to understand the gravity of the moment.

Chapter Three

Winifred Roberta "Birdie" Peck had eaten her breakfast and was ready for the porcelain pitcher of water Glory Bee brought to her every morning. On this particular day, Birdie lost count of the number of times she walked from bedroom to bedroom to bedroom signaling with the squeak of the floorboards she was ready for her toilette.

Birdie shouted from the stair landing, "Glory Bee, where in God's name are you?!"

In the suffocating heat rising steadily, perspiration dripped from Birdie's double chin and trickled down her fleshy back and between her large breasts. She wiped moisture from the back of her neck with the sleeve of her once white, threadbare cotton dressing gown. Random dark curls coiling through shoulder-length silver hair, dampened from the moist air, hinted at its once sable color.

Returning to her bedroom, Birdie dropped into a stuffed chair upholstered in saucer-size faded pink roses. Her patience, like her dressing gown, had worn thin.

Birdie could not imagine descending the stairs before garbing herself in full attire . . . corset, whichever one of her three remaining dresses that fit, and complementary jewelry. After styling her hair into a severe bun, she would apply generous layers of makeup that only slightly masked her fleshy face's deepening wrinkles and age spots steadily darkened by the harsh Florida sun.

Returning to the top of the stairs, Birdie bellowed: "Glory Bee!"

When no answer came, she shuffled back to her bedroom and slammed the door. The walls shuddered. Shoving up the bedroom window to its full height, she leaned over the sill. "Glory Bee! Where are you?" she yelled. When no answer came, Birdie paced the room a few more times before dropping back into her chair.

Anger and irritation sprung quickly in Birdie. They seemed ingrained in her nature. Before he died seven years before, her husband, Walter Peck, got the brunt of it. When the hurricane of 1896 wiped out the cedar industry leading to the demise of the pencil factory, the railroad, and the turpentine industry, Walter's thriving accounting business suffered as well. He became withdrawn and depressed over his failing business. Every afternoon, after locking up his office, he would amble along the boardwalk and into the bar at the hotel.

Mortified at her husband's changed behavior, Birdie's sharp tongue sharpened even more. "Don't you realize the whole town is talking about you, Walter?" Birdie would scold. "What's come over you? You're embarrassing me!"

"The whole town?!" Walter would shout. "There's nobody left!"

Flailing his arms, he would rant. "Anybody with any sense who wasn't killed in that damnable hurricane has left this God forsaken island! Jacksonville, Tallahassee, Tampa!" Slouching over his dinner, he would mumble. "We should've done the same thing."

When Birdie's lavish spending habits that had seen no limits came to an end, she blamed Walter. "If you knew how to run a business, we wouldn't be having these problems."

As the town's population continued to decline, the few remaining struggling business owners handled their accounting needs themselves. Consequently, the Peck's income suffered along with everyone else's. With no other skills beyond his knowledge of accounting, Walter further succumbed to the bottle. In a few short years, Walter was dead.

The Peck's two-story Victorian home, perched at the top of the highest hill on the town's main street, diminished to a joyless shrine to what had been. Birdie was left to scratch for income through occasional piano lessons and a pittance from the church for accompanying the choir on Sunday mornings. The parlor no longer glowed at night with flames of countless candles, lanterns, and newly installed electric light fixtures. The sounds of laughter and the spirited music of Birdie's fingers over the piano keys no longer rippled through the open parlor windows. The only occasion for which her silver, crystal stem ware, and delicate China graced the dining room table was the Bible study she hosted every Wednesday evening.

As her waistline increased, Birdie's spirit and her health declined. No amount of scolding from Dr. Bartlett, who came weekly from nine miles away in Otter Creek to tend the island residents' medical needs, made a difference in her eating habits.

Every Wednesday afternoon, he would climb the stairs to Birdie's bedroom for a consultation. "Maybe you ought to stay home Sunday evenings instead of attending the church suppers. I know you love fried chicken and fried okra, but all that fat's clogging up your arteries, Birdie. You need to eat fresh fruits and vegetables. Glory Bee brings all kinds from Tom's and her garden and fruit trees. There's no excuse for what you're doing to yourself."

"Hogwash," Birdie would retort. "Besides, what I eat is my own business. Now please close the door on your way out. And tell Glory Bee to make the icing on the cake for tonight thicker. Last week's was very sparse."

Back in the kitchen, Dr. Bartlett would shake his head at Glory Bee. "I might as well be talking to the wall. Nothing more I can do if she isn't willing to cooperate. And I know she doesn't make life easy for you, Glory Bee. Cooking, cleaning, laundry." He raised his arms in defense. "Oh, I know you've got your reasons for puttin' up with her miserable disposition. All's I can say is God bless you."

***

Glory Bee's chest heaved with the exertion of trudging the arduous ascent from the beach back to Birdie Peck's house. "Much as I dread it, only place ta take her is ta Miz Peck's house," she gasped.

"She ain't gonna' like it," Nathan panted. Perspiration poured down his face, and his arms ached from carrying the unconscious woman. He squinted against the blinding sunlight. "You know good as me, Glory Bee. Miz. Peck's gonna' blow a gasket."

Glory Bee managed a barely discernible reply. "Jus' let me handle it."

Penelope clasped the woman's limp hand that had slipped out from the sheet and toyed with the cold, slender fingers. The child could not take her eyes off the woman's face . . . the woman she wanted so badly to believe was her mother. "When will she wake up?"

Finally reaching the front of the Peck's house, Glory Bee dropped her rear onto the first step and mopped her sweating face with her apron.

"Child, I don't reckon I know what ta tell ya 'bout that. We jus' got ta give it time." She loosened the laces of her cracked leather high-top shoes to relieve the swelling of her ankles. "Docta' B is comin' tomorra' so we'll know more afta' he takes a look at her."

Nathan had climbed the few steps to the porch, waiting for Glory Bee to open the door. Though grateful to be out of the scorching sunlight, his chest heaved from the exertion of carrying the woman's dead weight.

"I'm a'comin', Mr. Nathan." Glory Bee gripped the wobbly, paint-chipped railing and pulled herself up. Lifting her ankle-length skirt to avoid tripping, she slowly maneuvered the last few steps that groaned under her weight.

Penelope gazed up at Glory Bee. "Can I come, too?"

Knowing the risk she was taking in letting the child . . . or any uninvited individuals . . . in the house, Glory Bee could not get past Penelope's imploring face. "You can come, but we got ta be real quiet, you hear?"

Penelope bobbed her head and smiled, her disheveled, white-blond hair fluttering around her face. She had never been inside the Peck's house and had only heard about all the beautiful things throughout. Picturing a castle like the one in her picture book, her heart pounded as she climbed the porch steps and followed Glory Bee and Nathan in the house.

Closing the door quietly behind them, Glory Bee pointed up the staircase a few feet in front of them. Placing a foot on the first step, Nathan rested the woman's torso on his knee and took a deep breath. He then hefted the woman in his aching arms once again. With Glory Bee in the lead, they began the climb up the stairs.

Having brushed sand off her bare feet on the porch, Penelope tiptoed behind . . . but not before gaping at the dining room to the right of the staircase. A crystal chandelier glittered above a shiny mahogany table surrounded by chairs covered in deep maroon velvet. Lost in the dazzle of the room, it took a moment before Penelope heard Glory Bee's "Psssst," and she scampered up the steps.

At the top of the stairs, Glory Bee pointed Nathan and Penelope toward a spare bedroom to the left of the landing. Once in the room, Nathan laid the woman on the narrow bed while Penelope fussed with the sheet. His arms and legs shook, and he could not resist dropping down onto a wood chair on the opposite side of the room.

As quiet as they were coming into the house, climbing the

stairs, and making their way into the bedroom, nothing could hide the squeak of the well-worn floorboards.

Glory Bee rushed to the bedroom door. "Ya'll got ta go now. Quick!"

Nathan and Penelope made it as far as the staircase when another bedroom door on the opposite side of the landing suddenly opened. Birdie Peck, still clad in her threadbare gown and dripping with perspiration, stood in the doorway in evident shock. Her high-pitched shriek could have awakened the dead before she ducked behind the door and slammed it shut.

"Lawd'a mercy! Go now. I got some explainin' ta do." Glory Bee nudged the two down the stairs then hurried back to the spare bedroom.

Having no idea if the jostling while being carried from the beach might have helped eliminate seawater in the woman's lungs, Glory Bee did the only thing she knew to do. She gently turned the woman's limp body onto her side then checked her pulse, which seemed normal. Raising the window sash, she savored for a brief moment the moist breeze spreading throughout the bedroom. She then left the room and closed the door behind her.

Wiping perspiration from her face with her apron, she slowly walked to Mrs. Peck's bedroom door, cleared her throat, and knocked. "Miz Peck?" A rustling sound from the other side of the door alerted Glory Bee to her mistress's movements.

Birdie pulled open the door a crack and peeked through the small opening. She glared at Glory Bee with a look of pure anger.

"Glory Bee, what is going on?! And why are there people in my house who don't belong here?! And where . . ." Birdie's voice rose to a shrill, "is my pitcher of water?!" Without waiting for an answer, Birdie slammed the door in Glory Bee's face.

As fast as her exhausted, bulky frame would allow, Glory Bee hustled down the stairs. In the kitchen, she filled a porcelain pitcher with water and laid a towel over her arm. Trudging back up the steps, when she reached Mrs. Peck's door, she set the pitcher on the floor, covered it with the towel, and knocked twice.

Holding her face close to the door, Glory Bee called out, "Here ya go, Miz Peck. I'm sorry it took so long."

Before Glory Bee could hustle back to the stairs, Birdie pulled the door wide open. Staring into Glory Bee's face, she mumbled, "It's about time."

Glory Bee picked up the pitcher and towel and handed them to Mrs. Peck.

Birdie's double chin, as well as her voice, quivered as she took hold of the pitcher. "When I've dressed, I want an explanation as to why I've had to wait for this." She looked down at the pitcher then up to Glory Bee's face again. "And I want an explanation as to why that fisherman and that child were upstairs in my house . . . or in my house at all!" She backed into the bedroom. "Now close the door."

Glory Bee mumbled, "Yes'm," and reached for the doorknob. Quietly pulling the door closed, she lifted her head and whispered. "Lawd, I'm prayin' fer the strength I'm gonna' need befo' this day is out.

She glanced at the other closed door. "And Lawd, I'm prayin' fer that woman in that bedroom that Miz Peck show her mercy and don't throw her out in the street.

Glory Bee thought for a moment then added, "An' Lawd, I'm prayin' that whatever misfortune that woman experienced that brought her ta this here island that we're able ta help her with it. I thank ya, Lawd."

With that, Glory Bee headed downstairs. In the kitchen, she filled another porcelain pitcher with water. She collected an assortment of towels and soap bars then gulped down a glass of water and mopped the perspiration from her face.

Heading back to the staircase, Glory Bee raised another prayer:

"And Lawd, I'm prayin' these ol' legs keep on carryin' me up and down these stairs 'cause it's lookin' like I'll be doin' a whole lot more of it now."

Chapter Four

She woke to bright light penetrating her closed scratchy eyes and the sound of someone humming . . . maybe a lull-a-bye. Nausea gripped her as firm hands had gently turned her onto her side and applied cool, wet cloths to her burned skin.

How long ago was that? An hour, a day, a week? Whatever I'm lying on is soft and still. If only my body would stop this incessant rolling and pitching.

Her skin felt hot, yet she shivered. Desperate for sleep, she managed to pull the coverlet over her shoulder and slept. She woke to someone turning her onto her back.

Whoever it was spoke to her, a kind, soothing voice. "It'll be a'right now. Jus' let me wash this crusty salt off o' ya."

Water sloshed and a glass was held to her lips.

"Try a little now. Ya got ta try an' drink so ya git rid o' that seawater. I got a bucket right here if ya git sick." Strong hands lifted her head slightly. "Docta' Bartlett be comin' in from Otter Creek tomorra'. I'll be doin' the best I can fer ya' fer now."

Cool, fresh water drizzled into her mouth. She swallowed, relieving her parched throat. She coughed then ran her tongue over her dry, cracked lips. The lingering taste of salty seawater turned her stomach. She wanted another drink and opened her mouth.

"Can't have too much. One more fer now," the soft voice cautioned.

More water drizzled into her mouth, seeping around her teeth and under her tongue, and she longed for another drink. The strength to ask for more water exhausted her . . . but not enough to fight troubling images that began to surface, images of strange men, of running, of boats, and thrashing seas.

Somehow she slept again. She woke to angry voices from below, women's voices.

"This is my house!" one woman stormed.

Only scant words in the familiar soothing voice reached her ears. "Where" and "room" and "rest." She had to assume they were speaking of her.

She grimaced at the smell of food, a pungent, unfamiliar odor, and slowly opened her swollen eyelids. She squinted at a partially raised window, its white curtains floating back and forth in a gentle breeze. She guessed from the subdued light that it was late in the day, perhaps early evening.

Thirst overcame her and she struggled to swallow. She reached for a glass half filled with water on a bedside table. Managing to raise herself enough to avoid spilling it, she filled her mouth and swallowed. Returning the glass to the table, she fell back onto the pillow.

As she blinked away the bleariness and grit in her eyes, she took in her surroundings. The sparsely furnished room was cozy in its simplicity. A straight wood chair and a large trunk against the far wall looked old and well used. Next to the bedroom door, a bureau's mirror reflected light from the window. Unadorned yellowed walls, while in need of painting, captured artful shadows from tree branches outside the window. She managed a slight smile as she considered how lovely the shadowy wall scene would look in a painting. Despite its plainness, so different from the cluttered grandeur of her expansive bedroom in New Orleans, the room and everything in it appeared well cared for.

The voices below had quieted to a murmur. As exhaustion overtook her again, she wondered where on earth she was.

Whose house is this? Why is that woman apparently so angry?

She turned her head toward the window, her eyes following the slow movement of white clouds beyond the tree branches.

Most of all, why . . . and how am I still alive?

It had not been her intention to live when she walked into the Gulf of Mexico, deliberately swimming far from the coast of Grand Isle, Louisiana.

Why couldn't those fishermen have just let me be?

Those thoughts and more were too much for now. Where her unfathomable, unexpected water journey that intervened in her determination to end her life had brought her, she would soon learn . . . but not before she fell into a deep sleep again.

***

Charles Bartlett, M.D., dropped onto a chair at the worn wood table in Sylvester Truegood's Pine Cove dockside café. He was grateful to have the twenty-mile buggy ride from his Otter Creek office that began early that morning behind him. Drenched with perspiration, he removed his black, broad-brimmed hat and set it on another chair. After running his hands through his thinning gray hair, he rolled up the sleeves of his white shirt, wet and wrinkled from the moist summer heat.

"Good ride in ta town, Doc?" Sylvester called from behind the counter, mopping his brow and balding scalp with his hairy bare arm.

"Good enough, Sylvester. Sure could use a glass of water." Dr. Bartlett leaned back in his chair and stretched his legs, at sixty-one, grateful his only ailment was a pair of arthritic knees. "Is that swamp cabbage stew you got cooking back there?"

Glancing over his shoulder at the kettle steaming behind him, Sylvester bobbed his head. He ran his hands down the front of his apron stained with countless spatters from countless meals cooked up over the years.

"Yessir. Wanna' a bowl with some biscuits?"

"That sounds right delicious, Sylvester." Dr. Bartlett leaned forward, rested his elbows on the table, and looked around the empty café. "Doesn't seem too busy today. What's Elmer up to? Staying out of trouble, I hope."

His hands laden, Sylvester came out from behind the counter. He set a glass of water and a bowl of stew topped with a plate of biscuits on the table in front of Dr. Bartlett.

"Aw, Doc. Had ta cuff the boy's ears this mornin'. Big as he is at fifteen with a mind of a five-year-old and a head hard as a rock under that mop o' hair, he don't know 'nuff ta keep his hands ta hisself."

Sylvester pulled out a chair and sat down at the table. "His Mama, God rest her soul, would o' had more time an' patience with Elmer. I got all I can do ta keep this café operatin' and puttin' food on the table."

Dr. Bartlett nodded as he dunked a biscuit into his bowl of stew. "Wish there was something we could do for the boy, Sylvester. Shame his birth killed his Mama and worse leaving the boy slow witted." Swallowing his spoonful of stew, he asked, "What did Elmer do this time?"

Sylvester shook his head. "Oh, that woman wha' lives at the hotel, that Jean Murphy? She eggs him on, yellin' at Elmer out o' her window, tellin' him one o' the girls wha' lives down yonder at Hungry Bend wants ta give him a kiss. So off he goes, headin' down to Hungry Bend. O'course, there ain't no girl even in Hungry Bend wantin' to give Elmer so much as a second look, but he don't know that. He sees that little Penelope Worth wha' lives down there and grabs a'hold o' her and plants a smooch on her. Nathan come up from the dock ta tell me Penelope come runnin' ta him sayin' Elmer was after her, wantin' ta kiss her."

Sylvester shook his head and scowled. "Elmer's a big boy, Doc. Penelope can't weigh more 'n forty pounds soakin' wet. Imagine she was pretty scared."

Dr. Bartlett wiped up the remaining stew in his bowl with a biscuit. Reaching into his pocket for money to pay for his meal, he pondered what could be done with Jean Murphy. He tossed a dollar bill on the table.

"I'll have a talk with Jean once I get my room at the hotel. Poor woman hasn't been right since her little girl died two years ago. On top of that, losing her husband. Tim Murphy never should have brought her here in the first place.

He pulled a handkerchief from his pants pocket and blew his nose. "Then goes back to New York and gets himself killed by a gang of thugs . . . all for a couple hundred bucks Tim claimed they owed him. Stubborn Irishman should have known how that would turn out.

Dr. Bartlett pushed himself away from the table. "Not enough the heartbreak of leaving their family in Ireland. Now having to lower herself just to . . . well, enough about that. I'll talk to her about Elmer."

"Thanks, Doc. Yeah, worries me somethin' awful thinkin' o' what might become o' my boy.

Sylvester slipped the bill into his apron pocket. "Say, before I ferget. Nathan tol' me Penelope found some woman washed up on the beach yesta'day. Nathan carried her up ta Birdie Peck's house. Glory Bee's hopin' you can go on up and take a look at her, see if she's gonna' be alright."

Dr. Bartlett reached for his hat and looked up at Sylvester. "Washed up on the beach, you say?"

'Yessir, half drowned so I hear but alive. Nekked as a jaybird, too. Ain't anybody so far knows who she is. Now how do you s'pose somethin' like that could happen? Right out o' nowhere, somebody comes ridin' in on a wave and lands on a Pine Cove Key beach?"

Dr. Bartlett stood, pushed his chair under the table, and placed his hat on his head. "Sylvester, you got me, but I'll head on up to

Birdie's and see what I can find out. Need to check on her anyways. That woman's going to have a heart attack one of these days if she doesn't take better care of herself. Imagine she isn't taking too kindly to a stranger in her house either. I bet Glory Bee's got her hands full about now."

Dr. Bartlett headed toward the door then called over his shoulder. "I'll be seeing you, Sylvester. Try and keep an eye on that boy now."

Chapter Five

"Glory Bee, please!" Clutching a fistful of wild violets, Penelope stomped her foot on Birdie Peck's back porch. Having pleaded with no results, she raised her voice higher. "I'm the one who found her! I wanna' see her and give her these flowers!" Penelope pressed her lips together and scowled.

The rocking chair creaked as Glory Bee leaned forward. Looking into the child's eyes, she held up one finger close to Penelope's nose.

"Penelope, I'm sayin' it one las' time. You ain't goin' up ta see that woman 'til we know if she'll be alright. Now, Docta' B, he'll be comin' sometime t'day an' he'll be checkin' on her. 'Til then, the only person goin' in that bedroom is me.

Glory Bee pushed herself up from the rocking chair. "An' I'm goin' up there right now 'cause she more'n likely needs tendin' to.

Swatting away flies as she opened the screen door, Glory Bee turned back to Penelope. "Docta' B always uses this back door, so you can wait right here fer him if ya want to."

Penelope stared after Glory Bee as she disappeared into the kitchen. Mumbling "it ain't fair," she plopped down onto the porch step, crossed her arms on her knees, and sighed. Waggling the violets back and forth in her hand, she wondered how long they would live in the midday heat without water.

Spotting a small Mason jar next to the backyard pump, she

filled it with water and dropped the violets into the jar. As she sat back down on the steps, she heard the clop-clop of horse's hooves and a man's voice shouting, "Whoa, Bessie!" Bolting off the porch, Penelope ran around to the front of the house.

Dr. Bartlett stepped out of his carriage and reached behind the seat for his medical bag, the black leather cracked and worn from years of opening and closing. Tipping back his hat, he squinted up at the scorching sun. He set the bag on the front carriage seat, adjusted his suspenders, and rolled down his shirtsleeves. As he reached for the bag again, he heard a child's shout from behind.

"Dr. Bartlett, Dr. Bartlett! Ya' gotta' come quick! I found a lady on the beach yesterday!" A plume of sand and gravel erupted around Penelope's bare feet as she nearly collided with the doctor. She pointed to the second floor of Birdie's house. "She's up there!"

Dr. Bartlett smiled at the child's wide-eyed face. "Heard a little about this at the café, Penelope. How'd you happen to find her?"

Penelope spewed out the details of the discovery and rescue of the strange lady she found washed up on the shore. Pulling on the doctor's free hand, chattering breathlessly, she propelled him to the rear of the house.

As they reached the back porch, Glory Bee emerged from the kitchen and nodded at the doctor. "How'do, Docta' B."

Bobbing his head, Dr. Bartlett removed his hat and ran his forearm across his moist forehead. "Good day to you, Glory Bee."

Letting go of Penelope's hand, the doctor set his medical bag on the step. "Penelope here tells me Birdie has a houseguest." Dr. Bartlett climbed the porch steps with Penelope not far behind. "How's she doing?" Raising his eyebrows, he added, "Meaning the houseguest, of course. I'll get to Birdie later."

"I sure am glad ta see ya, Docta' B. You know I ain't no docta' but I'm doin' what I can fer this woman, givin' her water, gettin' her ta eat a bite, swabbin' her sunburnt skin with a wet cloth." She raised her shoulders. "Don't know nothin' else ta do."

"That's good, Glory Bee. You did very good. Has she spoken? Do we know anything about her?" asked the doctor.

Before Glory Bee could reply, Penelope tugged on Dr. Bartlett's shirtsleeve and motioned for him to bend down. She whispered in his ear. "I know who she is."

He whispered back, "Is that so? And who do you think she is, Penelope?"

"It's my Mama. I jus' know it," she whispered. Dr. Bartlett did his best to avoid looking stunned. He forced a thoughtful look on his face and whispered back, "Penelope, I believe you think that might be true. And if it is true, we'll sure find out." He straightened and turned to Glory Bee, his eyebrows raised.

When their eyes met, Glory Bee looked skyward. Even though she had told Penelope more than once and as gently as she could that Adelaide Worth likely would never come home, at that moment, her heart would not let her shatter the child's hope.

Shooing away dozens of flies clinging to the screen, Glory Bee opened the door. "Docta' B, you come on in an' go on upstairs. She's in the front bedroom."

Penelope took hold of Dr. Bartlett's shirtsleeve again. Looking up into his eyes, she pleaded, "Please, Dr. Bartlett. Can I come, too?" She reached down and picked up the Mason jar of flowers, now showing signs of wilting in the hot sun. "I brung her these violets."

The doctor looked down at Penelope's hopeful face then glanced up at Glory Bee, who gave her head a slight shake. He placed his hands on Penelope's small shoulders.

"Penelope, I think it best you wait here until I can see if she's ready for visitors. From what you told me, she's lucky you found her and even luckier to be alive. I want to be sure she's well rested and recovered before we tire her out too much."

Penelope held up the jar of violets. "But Dr. Bartlett, I picked these ta help her feel better. Please?"

Dr. Bartlett's sound judgment had been tested over the years, especially with children. So much suffering since the hurricane, along with sickness, deaths, poverty, pulling at him from so many directions, it was difficult to be rational at times. His heartstrings tugged as he considered letting Penelope see the woman she believed to be her long-lost mother. But the reality of the woman's near drowning, that she could be very sick from the seawater and exposure, caused him to shake his head.

"Not this time, Penelope." He smiled at her. "Now what I can do is take your flowers to her. How would that be?" Picking up his medical bag, he held out his other hand for the jar of violets.

Penelope's eyes lost their hopeful look. She mumbled "okay" and slowly handed the flowers to Dr. Bartlett.

Clutching the jar, he turned and followed Glory Bee into the kitchen. After closing the door, he turned back and spoke to Penelope through the screen. "You'll get to see her when she's feeling up to it. I promise."

As Dr. Bartlett followed Glory Bee up the stairs, he quietly expressed his concerns for Penelope. "She can't think this woman is her mother," he whispered.

"I know it, Docta' B, but ain't nothin' I tell her is gonna change her mind."

At the top of the stairs, Dr. Bartlett glanced at Birdie's bedroom door. "Has Birdie been in to see this woman?"

"Not so far as I know. She's mad as a hornet about this woman bein' here and ain't come out o' her bedroom since yesterday, leastways durin' the day when I'm here. I can tell she goes to the kitchen after I go home just by how much food's missin' from the larder.

Glory Bee whispered, "I'll tell ya one thing, Docta' B. I've had 'bout enough o' this attitude, especially when somebody's near dead. Miz Peck can't show no more sympathy than fer a fly. She can jus' come down the stairs and git her own breakfast if she keeps actin' like this."

At the guest room, Glory Bee placed her ear to the door but heard no sound. She tapped lightly then opened the door. The woman lay on her back as still as a corpse. Both Glory Bee and Dr. Bartlett at first suspected the worse.

Dr. Bartlett placed the jar of violets on the bedside stand. Setting his bag on the floor, he took the woman's hand that rested on the bed sheet. He rubbed her wrist and felt for her pulse. Smiling, he said, "We'll be fine, Glory Bee. You go on and take care of your chores. I'll let you know if I need anything."

As Glory Bee left the room, the door to Birdie's bedroom swung open. "Is that Dr. Bartlett in there?" she asked, bobbing her head toward the guest room. The usual scowl line between her eyebrows deepened.

Glory Bee tilted back her head, her cold eyes looking down at Mrs. Peck. Rare as confrontations were between the two, Glory Bee was not deterred from standing her ground. Crossing her arms across her bosom, she spoke in a firm voice.

"Yes'm, he's examinin' this woman now an' he'll be seein' you when he's done." With a bob of her head, she left Birdie staring after her as she headed back down the stairs.

Birdie pondered whether or not to resume her self-imposed imprisonment in her sweltering bedroom.

This is my house. I have a right to know who's in it.

Tiptoeing toward the guest room, she peered inside.

At that moment, the woman in the bed began coughing and choking as Dr. Bartlett held her in a half sitting position. "That's good. Again now," he urged. "Need to get those lungs cleared. See if you can spew into this pan."

After a few more tries, Dr. Bartlett told her to rest and laid her back on the pillow. "I'll check in on you again before I leave town. Do your best to keep up that coughing, hear?"

Birdie was waiting for him as he left the room and closed the door. "Hello, Dr. Bartlett," she said with an imperious tone. "How is your . . . your patient?"

"Hello, Birdie," Dr. Bartlett said as he stepped toward the stairs. "I think my *patient* as you put it will be fine despite the likelihood of pneumonia if she isn't cared for. If you have any aloe plants around, you might consider applying some on her sunburns."

He turned to her and looked her in the eyes. "Think you can do that, Birdie?" With eyebrows raised, he continued staring at her.

"Oh. Well. I guess I . . . Why can't Glory Bee do that?" she asked, her voice rising with each word. "I mean, after all . . ."

"'After all' what, Birdie?" Part way down the stairs, he turned around. "Glory Bee could use some help now that her workload has been added to." He scowled and bobbed his head toward the guest room door. "That woman is going to need care for at least a few days. Probably longer. And you and I have had more than one conversation about your own health. I think this is a grand opportunity for you to take these stairs more than once a day."

He continued down the stairs, calling over his shoulder. "And I don't mean just to the larder. That's all I need to say to you today. I'll be back to check on your guest."

In a huff, Mrs. Peck returned to her bedroom and slammed the door.

* * *

The voice inside her head said *Breathe!* But she could not breathe! Pounding waves smashed into her pushing her down, down, down. Her arms and legs flailed and her hands clawed, struggling against the weight of the storm-driven water.

Surfacing in the distance, the overturned remains of a sailboat rose atop a mountain of water. A shredded sail clung to its splintered, floundering mast as the battered hull plunged and disappeared into a deep, dark trough. Pieces of debris floated then disappeared from sight. Slate-colored clouds billowed and rolled overhead, pelting down raindrops sharp as nails against her face. Day or night she could not tell. She only knew she would die.

Dying was what she had planned when she walked into the Gulf of Mexico off Grand Isle, Louisiana. Initially reveling in the warm silky current of the outgoing tide flowing against her bare skin, she was overcome with delicious feelings of peace and freedom.

I can't . . . I won't live like this any longer . . . like those bridled race horses at the track straining with each crack of the whip. How I longed for them to run free.

As the current carried her further into open water, leaving behind her stifled albeit privileged existence, she recalled the buggy ride with her lover, Alcée Arobin.

So exhilarating! But that poor tethered, broken horse that pulled us beyond the city . . . surely it, too, longed to be released to run wild. How insidious are women's roles . . . like frogs dropped into a kettle of cold water before lighting the flame and slowly cooking the poor unsuspecting creatures. I knew I would die . . . would rather die than be forced to live a life feeling hollow as a cavern.

The waves were growing stronger. Images of her young sons, Etienne and Raoul, of her husband, Léonce, their lavish home on Esplanade Street in New Orleans, faces of her sisters, friends, all and more raced through her mind. They would find her clothing shed on the beach and know. Her family and friends would mourn for a while. Eventually, maybe they would be relieved, eager to forget her embarrassing indiscretions.

Her small, young sons' faces swam before her eyes.

They will miss me. Or will they? They never sought me when they were hurt or longed for comfort. They ran to their father . . . or more often their nanny. I tried to be a good mother. At least I thought I had. I should have tried harder . . . like Adele. My dear friend . . . always thinking of the children.

The eccentric pianist, Mademoiselle Reisz, outspoken and strange as she was, seemed to understand her turmoil.

She questioned the strength of my wings in defying a world in which mothers are expected to sacrifice their "selves" for their children. Her cautionary words rang clearly: 'The bird that would soar above the level plain of tradition and prejudice must have strong wings. It is a sad spectacle to see the weaklings bruised, exhausted, fluttering back to earth.'

Edna had conceded. *My wings weren't strong enough.*

"Dear God, have mercy!" she screamed as her body tossed and rolled. "I don't want to die!"

Someone or something held her wrists then shook her shoulders. "Hush now. Wake up. Yer alright."

She gasped for air, certain she had only seconds before the next plunge into the water. She tried to sit up, tried to move her arms against the force holding her down.

"Just a dream," the soft voice murmured. "I'm right here. You ain't gonna die so long as I'm takin' care of ya."

The grip on her shoulders lightened as her rigid body began to relax from the raw edges of terror. Opening her eyes, she looked up into the kind . . . and very dark . . . face.

"Where am I?" she asked in a voice rough as sandpaper. "Who are you?"

Glory Bee smiled as she let go and straightened the tousled bed sheet. "Well, yer in Missus Winifred Peck's guest room in her house in Pine Cove. Now if ya don't know where that is, Pine Cove Key is an island on the coast o' Florida.

Glory Bee poured water from a pitcher into the glass on the nightstand and raised the woman's head. "Docta' B says ya have to drink more."

She swallowed then coughed. "Thank you," she whispered.

"An' ya can call me Glory Bee. That's what ever'body in this town calls me 'cuz that's my name."

The woman blinked. "Florida?" Struggling to clear the remnants of her nightmare, more questions arose. "How long have I been here?"

"Only since yesterday. Penelope . . . that's a child wha' found ya washed up on the beach. Thought sure ya was dead. She come a'runnin fer me and Mister Nathan . . . he's a fisherman . . . ta come and fetch ya and we brung ya here."

Glory Bee poured the remainder of the water into the glass. "I expect Docta' B be comin' back tomorrow to see how yer doin', so I'm goin' to git more water and fix ya a little somethin' ta eat. I be back after a while. Rest now, hear?"

Glory Bee opened the bedroom door to leave. "Keep up that coughin' an' don't go fallin' back ta sleep 'til ya try and clear those lungs." With a bob of her head, she left the room and closed the door.

Penelope and Mr. Nathan, Glory Bee and Winifred Peck . . . and, of course, Dr. Bartlett. Pine Cove Key, Florida. Surely on the Gulf coast, but where?

Too much to comprehend, she closed her eyes. As a slight breeze rustled leaves in the tree outside her window, she marveled.

I'm alive.

* * *

"Who are you?!" screeched the shrill voice of someone close.

Opening her eyes to a woman's stern face mere inches from her own, she pressed her head into the pillow. "Wh . . . what?" she whispered.

Obviously irritated, the woman asked again, the pitch of her voice rising. "I said who are you?"

Groggy and struggling to find her voice, she stared back at the woman and considered the question.

Who am I?

It was a good question, one she often raised when strolling the city blocks near her home.

Who am I indeed?

Too spent and weakened to do more than stare back at the woman, she could only reply with a whisper, "My name is Edna. Edna Pontellier."

Chapter Six

Dust rising off Pine Cove's main street swirled around Bessie's hooves and up into Dr. Bartlett's nostrils causing him to sneeze.

Shouts of "Bless ya, Doc!" and "Howdy, Doc!" erupted from people going about their business and followed Dr. Bartlett to the front of the decades-old two-story hotel. Climbing down from the buggy, he collected his bag and patted Bessie's neck, muttering "good girl." He stomped the dust off his boots, rattling the weather-beaten boardwalk, before walking into the dark-paneled, dimly lit hotel foyer.

With no one tending the front desk, Dr. Bartlett wandered into the dining room. "Lloyd!" he called. "You around here somewhere? I need a room."

Poking his head into the kitchen, he asked Molly to pump a bucket of water for Bessie. Dr. Bartlett then headed back through the dining room.

Only a smattering of visitors came to Pine Cove Key in the summer, so hotel staff was scarce. The hotel's owner, Lloyd Blauers, struggled to maintain an appearance of elegance, but the rundown building could not overcome the pretense. Tableware strategically placed on starched white tablecloths covered holes and stains; draperies remained drawn at the windows to prevent sunlight from revealing loose wallpaper and peeling paint; carefully placed tables and chairs hid the worst of the worn wood flooring. Even tantalizing aromas drifting from the kitchen could not overcome a slight musty smell.

Dr. Bartlett wandered into the bar where he found Lloyd washing glasses. "Afternoon, Lloyd." He removed his hat and set his bag on a bar stool. "Need a room for the night."

"Afta'noon, Doc. Help yerself. All of 'em at the back 'r empty. Jus' pick one."

The doctor placed his hat back on his head and picked up his bag. "Alright. Jean still in the front room?"

Lloyd looked at Dr. Bartlett over the top of his wire-rimmed glasses and scowled. His bald head glowed from the glare of an overhead lamp.

"Yep. She won't be though if she carries on agin like she did yesta'day. I tol' her she can conduct her business s' long as she don't call attention ta herself. I know she's got ta make a livin' an' I'm okay with the couple o' reg'lars comin' every now and then. Helps ta bump up bar sales. But hangin' out o' the window yellin' and carryin' on . . . well, anyway. Maybe you can have a talk with her, Doc. Make her understand. Don't need her men folk wanderin' the length o' the hallway up there, but if she pulls that stunt again, I won't have a choice but ta move her to a back room." He hesitated. "Or out."

Dr. Bartlett called over his shoulder on his way to the stairway, "I'll tell her, Lloyd."

In a room at the far end of the upstairs hallway, after opening a window and removing his shoes, shirt, and trousers, Dr. Bartlett stretched out on the bed. As the Gulf-driven breeze funneling through the alleyway and into the room cooled his hot, travel-weary body, his thoughts wandered to Jean Murphy. He did not condone her lifestyle, but like countless other destitute, unskilled, and abandoned women he treated through his medical practice, her choices for making a living were few. The best he could do for Jean was to be sure she was taking all of his prescribed precautions to prevent pregnancy and disease.

As his eyelids became heavy, a knock on the door jolted Dr. Bartlett out of his nap. "Yes?" he called, struggling to restrain annoyance in his voice. "Who is it?"

"It's Molly, Dr. Bartlett. Maid's off t'day, so Lloyd sent me up with fresh towels and a pitcher o' drinkin' water fer ya."

"Thank you, Molly. Leave them by the door please," he replied. "Oh, and Molly?"

"Yessir?"

"Give the door a knock in an hour so I don't oversleep." With that, Dr. Bartlett drifted into a deep slumber.

* * *

In her room at the front of the hotel, Jean Murphy sat before her dressing table mirror brushing snarls out of her long russet-red hair. Her bed's rumpled, tangled blankets and sheets from last night's engagement reflected in the mirror. Humming *I Dream of Jeanie with the Light Brown Hair*, she set the brush on the dressing table, opened a drawer, and pulled out a wooden trinket box. Inside contained the payment from her last customer.

With a sigh, Jean mumbled, "Bloody stingy dolt." Removing some coins from the box, she closed the lid.

Before putting the box away, Jean removed a letter from the drawer, its folds so creased as to be nearly falling apart. Dated July 18, 1903, the letter from Bellevue Hospital in New York City began, "We are sorry to inform you . . ." It concluded with a request for her to come to New York to handle her husband's medical costs and burial.

Tim Murphy had departed Pine Cove for New York on July 2, 1903, leaving Jean with enough money to cover room and meals at the hotel for two weeks. Kissing his wife and three-year-old daughter, Kathleen, good-bye, he had promised, "Sure ta be back a'fore then."

As if the shock of Tim's death and her nearly depleted funds had not been enough, Jean was struck with the reality of her sudden destitute circumstances. Travel ... to New York or home to Ireland, or to send money to the hospital ... was out of the question. In the end, Jean succumbed to total defeat. She would have to live with the likelihood Tim would be buried in a pauper's grave somewhere.

Less than two weeks after learning of her husband's death, Jean's anguish plummeted further when Kathleen fell seriously ill. Despite Dr. Bartlett's best efforts, even the town barber's bloodletting, the little girl suffered through raging temperatures, in and out of consciousness, often delirious. Barely a month after learning of her husband's death, Jean helplessly held her beautiful little girl as pneumonia took her last breath.

Jean was sure she would go mad with grief and despair. The crushing loss of Kathleen was one thing. Ambivalence over Tim's death was quite another. Of course, she mourned and missed him. But his decision to go to New York to try and collect money owed him from a gang of hooligans was nothing short of suicide.

"Don' do it, Tim," Jean had begged. "The bloody bastards 'll kill ye first!"

Tears welled in Jean's eyes as she relived the nightmare of losing the two loved ones she held most dear ... still as raw as two years ago. Staring at the letter, she once again considered throwing it away. After a few moments, Jean refolded it and placed it back in the drawer.

Drying her tears with the sleeve of her worn, patched robe, Jean mumbled, "Canna' let meself fergit wha' ye drove me to, Tim Murphy. A feckin' *hoor*."

After changing into one of the few dresses hanging in her minuscule closet, Jean gave her hair another brush. Having missed breakfast, she headed to the kitchen for something to tide her over until dinnertime.

Molly greeted her with a broad grin, her round, puffy, beet-red face glistening with perspiration. "Afta'noon, Miss Jean."

"Tis, ain't it." Jean reached in her pocket and held up the quarter. "Wha'll this git me?"

Wiping a towel around an earthenware jug, Molly bobbed her head toward a kettle simmering on the stove.

"Git yer'self a bowl o' that fish stew. Made it with a big ol' red snapper from Nathan's catch yesta'day. Threw in tomatoes and onions and carrots." She hung the damp towel on a hook and handed Jean a bowl. "Mighty tasty if I say so ma'self."

Jean helped herself to a small dipper of stew and sat on a stool at the end of the work table. "Mmmm. Good." She took a second spoonful. "Yer a fine cook, Molly."

Gulls outside the open back door squawked and danced as they pecked and fought over a few scraps of food.

"Thanks, Miss Jean," Molly said and added, "Doc Bartlett's here."

Jean quickly finished the helping of stew. She reached in her pocket for her quarter and laid it on the table. "Figered so." Sliding off the stool, she set her empty bowl in the sink and turned to leave. "May good be at ye, Molly."

As Jean reached the doorway, Molly called after her: "Yer a good girl, Jean Murphy. Don't let nobody tell ya any diff'ernt."

Glancing over her shoulder, Jean forced a smile. "Go raibh maith agat," she said. "Thank ye, Molly." She headed for the stairway.

***

"Jean, you did not kill Kathleen." Dr. Bartlett ran his gnarled fingers through his hair and shook his head. "Look at me." He clutched Jean's hands and said again. "Jean. Look at me. Kathleen's little body could not stand up against that fever. Like I've told you a hundred times, it was the pneumonia that killed her. Surely you must know that."

Jean raised her head, struggling to look at Dr. Bartlett through the flood of tears. "Aye. Ye keep sayin' that. But the bloodlettin'," she wailed. "Ever'body said it cures *ever'thin'*." Every "r" in her words stretched and groaned with heartbreak.

Dr. Bartlett let go of Jean's hands. He stood and walked around the small bedroom. At the front window, he raised the sash a bit to let more air into the cramped, warm room.

Turning to look at Jean slumped in her chair, Dr. Bartlett marveled at this poor, abandoned young widow's endurance in making the best of her tragic circumstances. Thin as a rail, a stiff wind could carry her away, yet something in her, some force of will, drove her to face each day.

Jean had little to call her own. All of the room's furniture . . . the straight chair he had been sitting on, the wrought iron bed, a three-drawer bureau, a stuffed rose print chair, and the dressing table . . . belonged to the hotel. Jean's personal belongings could have fit into Dr. Bartlett's medical bag. Her few dresses, nearly as worn and faded as the draperies matching the chair, shared the narrow closet with a robe, a threadbare coat, and other menial sundries.

In an effort to decorate, Jean had strung and draped seashells around the dressing table mirror and over the drapery valances. Incongruous to the drab, rundown condition of the room, a framed print of Fragonard's *A Young Girl Reading* hung on the wall over the bed. Peeling blue wallpaper, its pattern so faded as to be no longer recognizable, did little to complement the girl in the yellow dress.

Dr. Bartlett thought back to the number of times over the past two years he had tried to convince Jean of her innocence in her young daughter's death. Over and over, and over again, he explained how Kathleen died despite the relentless efforts to save her. Returning to the chair, he sat down and took her hands in his again.

"Jean, I'll say this one last time. You did not kill Kathleen." Dr. Bartlett's voice grew vehement. "No more than you killed Tim up there in New York. And neither did Claude. As I've said many times, a barber's got no business bloodletting anybody leastways a small child, and if I'd been here, I'd have put a stop to it."

He continued with compassion. "I know you were desperate and you both meant well, but either way, it wouldn't have mattered. The child ... almost any child ... cannot survive pneumonia." Dr. Bartlett let go of Jean's hands and patted her knee. "Understand? And I've warned Claude. No more bloodletting!"

Jean wiped her swollen eyes with a handkerchief that had grown soggy from sobbing. She bobbed her head. "Aye. Jus' had ta do somethin' sick as she was."

"Yes, she was. Very sick and we're all heartbroken, but you've got to stop blaming yourself."

Jean nodded and blew her nose. "I will yeah."

Patting her knee again, Dr. Bartlett stood up. "Jean, I'm sorry, but I've got to go. A near drowned woman up at Birdie Peck's needs attention."

Jean sniffled and wiped her nose again. "Go way out'a that!" she said in a nasally voice. "How'd she drown?"

"Well, she didn't drown, but she was near death's door when Penelope found her washed up on the beach yesterday.

Dr. Bartlett's voice grew stern. "Jean, listen. You can't be making a spectacle of yourself yelling out your bedroom window. Lloyd doesn't want to move you to a back bedroom and have your ... your visitors roaming the hallway. But he will move you ... or worse ... if you do it again." He raised his eyebrows at her. "Understand?"

Jean lowered her green eyes glistening with tears. "Aye. Got knackered at the bar. Weren't thinkin' ... an' so sad and angry. I won't do it again."

Smiling, Dr. Bartlett cocked his head. "Had a snort or two, eh?"

"Oh, aye, a nip 'er two from a bloke. Calms me nerves, ye know?" Tears brimmed in her eyes. "Couple o' nips help me fergit missin' me Tim."

"I understand. Just watch the alcohol with some of the medicine you're taking. Now, are you good with your tonic and the calomel I brought you a few weeks ago? Don't be overdoing that calomel now, hear? That's mercury and too much can hurt you."

"Aye. Sure plenty an' I will yeah." They both stood and walked to the bedroom door. "Sure hopin' tha' woman's gonna be okay."

"That's mighty nice of you, Jean. Now, take care of yourself and I'll see you next week." With a bob of his head, Dr. Bartlett left a sad but resigned Jean Murphy to prepare herself for her next dolt.

* * *

"Your pulse is good, Edna, and your lungs appear to be clearing. Keep up that coughing and drink as much water as you can. It'll help clear out any bacteria in your system." Dr. Bartlett dropped his stethoscope into his bag and closed it. "Keep up with the aloe on your burns, too."

Edna tied the neckline of her gown and pulled up the sheet. The scratchiness in her throat had eased somewhat, but she struggled to say more than a few words at a time without coughing.

"I will. Glory Bee is so kind." She coughed again. "The aloe is very soothing and . . ." Swallowing, she tried again. "She's very gentle rubbing it on my back."

Dr. Bartlett handed her the glass of water from the bedside stand. "Don't strain. This will take time, but I think you'll be fine.

Leaning back in the straight wood chair, he smiled. "You're very lucky, you know. Another hour and the tide would have pulled you right back out into the water. Penelope saved your life."

"Penelope." Edna smiled. "You must tell her thank you." She stifled another cough. "How old is she?"

"She's nine. And she's begging to come up to see you. I've told her you must have a bit more time to recover, so give it a few more days. I won't get back to Pine Cove before next week, so I'll leave strict orders with Glory Bee that visitors are off limits until you feel ready."

Edna nodded her head. She liked Dr. Bartlett. He reminded her in some ways of her family's doctor in New Orleans, Dr. Mandelet. Both doctors' quiet, unobtrusive manner appealed to her. Dr. Mandelet was quite elderly . . . from appearances much older than Dr. Bartlett and very set in his old ways, especially when it came to women's health.

Something about Dr. Bartlett that she could never reconcile with Dr. Mandelet caused Edna to consider his possible percipience toward women's well-being. Could she confide in Dr. Bartlett in ways she never felt she could with Dr. Mandelet? Would he understand unlike Dr. Mandelet, who would frequently discredit her concerns and ailments?

Dr. Bartlett cleared his throat. "One more thing. Eat sparingly for a few days. Mixing too much food with any seawater still in your system could make you dyspeptic. Hard-boiled eggs. Hot tea. Nothing greasy." He chuckled. "'Fried' is Glory Bee's middle name. I'll speak to her about that.

He picked up his bag and set it on his lap. "Now, of course you've managed to get up to relieve yourself, but be careful. You're very weak. Like I said, you need time to recover and a fit of dizziness could cause a fall."

Edna nodded. "I understand." She hesitated as Dr. Bartlett stood and headed for the door. "Doctor, speaking of dyspepsia."

Turning back around, he scowled at her. "Yes?"

"Well, if I did happen to feel dyspeptic, what would you have me do?"

Dr. Bartlett came back to Edna's bed side. "As I said, eat sparingly and slowly. Drink mainly water and some tea. If the discomfort persists, have Glory Bee give you a little plain dry bread. That may settle your stomach. None of her greasy biscuits.

At the door, he turned back to her. "Your system needs time to recover, Edna. Get some rest, and I'll see you next Wednesday." Tipping his hat, Dr. Bartlett left, shutting the door behind him.

Closing her eyes, Edna rested her hands on her stomach. Glory Bee would be coming soon to see if she needed anything.

Next week. Maybe next week I'll tell Dr. Bartlett what else is going on with my nausea. This isn't going away, so what's the point in waiting?

Curtains at the window ebbed and flowed in the afternoon sea breeze. In the distance, a horse whinnied, a dog barked, and a child's voice yelled, "Bell!" Tranquil sounds of life so unlike the clang and clatter of New Orleans lulled Edna's disquieting concerns.

Chapter Seven

Women's shrill voices shook Edna out of a sound sleep. An orangey glow and shadows on the bedroom walls indicated the sun would soon set.

Tossing aside her covers, Edna raised herself up and hung her legs over the edge of the bed. She relieved her parched throat with a sip of water from the glass on the night stand.

Edna noted a newly arrived assortment of towels, a wash bowl, and pitcher on the bureau. On weak and quaking legs, she slowly stood up. Taking a moment to steady herself, Edna stepped to the bureau and splashed her face and arms, relishing the cool effects on her sunburned skin.

More voices along with the clatter of silverware and dishes added to the clamor downstairs. The squeak of a door opening and closing indicated the arrival of more people.

The voices seemed to have collected into one area. Tiptoeing to her bedroom door, Edna opened it a crack. The rising chatter undoubtedly came from a room below her bedroom. She ventured a few steps into the hallway and peered down a flight of stairs, which ended at a front door and onto a porch. At that moment, footsteps onto the porch alerted her to someone arriving. She tiptoed back to her bedroom, cracking open the door enough to hear.

"Hallo!" a man's voice called as he opened the front door. "Sorry I'm late!"

The jolly Reverend Marcus Albright enjoyed caring for his flock of mainly female followers at Pine Cove's Congregational Church. Having transferred a few years prior from a much larger church and congregation in Gainesville, Florida, the widowed, but by no means decrepit, pastor found his functions in Pine Cove much less stressful and time-consuming. Aside from the weekly sermons, his activities pertained to rare funerals, occasional domestic disputes necessitating minor intervention, and social functions, his favorite being Birdie Peck's weekly Bible study.

"Reverend Albright! You're just in time!"

Edna cringed upon hearing the familiar ear-piercing voice.

Ah! The indomitable owner of the house . . . the woman who confronted me and demanded to know who I am . . . and who wants me out of her house.

"Birdie, you're a forgiving soul to be sure. Hello, ladies. Looks like a fine group this evening."

Several women's voices erupted in "hello" and "good to see you, too, Reverend."

"And just look at that cake! My goodness." Following a pause, Reverend Albright added, "And that piece looks to have my name on it. Thank you, Birdie." Following another pause, he crowed, "Delicious! My compliments to Glory Bee I trust."

"Of course," Birdie said in an animated voice. "I'll let her know you approve. Now, come in and sit down. And bring your cake with you. I've saved the most comfortable parlor chair for you as always. Over there in the corner. The maroon velvet . . . the one with the brightest light behind you."

Reverend Albright lowered his voice a bit but loud enough for Edna to hear. "Birdie, before I do. I say, it's all over town about some woman Penelope found on the beach. And she's staying here?"

Birdie's voice rose but without its previous spirit. "Indeed she is, Reverend. Much against my wishes, but as Glory Bee persists

Islands of Women

in reminding me, the woman needed rescuing." Adding with a note of finality, "So, there you have it." The consternation in Birdie's voice was palpable.

"But what a generous gesture, Birdie. Do you know who she is? Where she came from? How astonishing that little Penelope stumbled onto her at just the right time. Quite a miracle, wouldn't you say?"

Edna stepped out of her room and hovered near the top of the stairs.

How odd to be a topic of discussion within my hearing but unable to speak on my own behalf . . . as if I were dead.

"I've no idea where she came from or anything about her," Birdie replied. She added with indifference, "All I know is she says her name is Edna. Edna Pontellier."

"Pontellier. Sounds French. Can't think of any French families in these parts. Well, poor thing. And how is she? Will she be alright?" Reverend Albright asked.

With everyone having moved into the parlor, Edna, feeling a bit woozy, sat down on the top step.

Will I be alright? What a good question.

Her voice filled with indignation, Birdie replied, "Well, you'll have to ask Dr. Bartlett about that . . . and Glory Bee, who spends more time looking after this woman than she does me.

In an attempt to divert the conversation, Birdie resumed her animated chirping. "Now, what do you say we get on with our Bible study. Lydia . . . you know Lydia, don't you, Reverend? Teaches Sunday school every now and then? Well, she's prepared a nice presentation for us, haven't you, Lydia?"

With gusto, Lydia replied, "Indeed I have. See here? I've printed out the verse for everyone. It's from Isaiah, Chapter 61, Verse 1. 'The spirit of the Lord God hath anointed me to preach good tidings unto the meek; he hath sent me to bind up the brokenhearted to proclaim liberty to the captives, and the opening of the prison to them that are bound.'"

Several words captured Edna's attention.

'Proclaim liberty to the captives'? Opening of the prison to them that are bound'? Lord, when? If not on the beach on Grand Isle and if not in the sea then when? The freest I've ever felt in my life was standing naked on the shore caring not for who might see me. I could wait no longer ... not for Robert, not for Alcee' ... certainly not for Léonce to recognize my *need to live as he ... as well as most men ... lives ... free to be something of value ... more than a frivolous decoration for his friends to admire.*

A rather stern retort from Reverend Albright interrupted Edna's reverie.

"Yes, Birdie, of course I know Lydia. And we'll get to that lovely verse. I do feel compelled, however, to learn more about this woman. Was there anything unusual about her when Penelope found her?"

"Well, I should say so!" Birdie chirped. "Stark naked! Not a stitch of clothes on her!" She added with malice, "Nor any to be found either. Now, what does that tell you? No good is what I say. Up to no good and, well, like any floozy, how she ended up in the sea is anyone's guess. Probably got thrown overboard by some ... some untoward or other."

A cacophony of voices chimed in, whether to support or disagree with Birdie, Edna could not tell. She only knew she wanted to hear no more. Needing to get back to her bedroom, she gripped the stair railing to pull herself up. Dizziness compounded by weakness overtook her, and with a yelp, her ankles gave way. Clutching the stairway spindles as tightly as her strength allowed, she managed to stop herself from tumbling down the stairs. Much to her dismay, however, her efforts brought the entire sitting room of guests to the hallway.

Without hesitation, Reverend Albright dashed up the stairs, caught Edna under her arms, and pulled her to her feet. "Tell me where to put you," he whispered.

Edna tipped her head toward her bedroom. "There," she whispered back.

Once Reverend Albright helped Edna safely back to her bed, he dragged the straight chair from the far wall and took her hand. "Now, my dear, are you in any pain?"

Edna gazed into the Pastor's dark marble-brown eyes. A scowl deepened between his bushy graying eyebrows revealing only traces of his remaining brown hair. Clutching his hand, she shook her head. "No. I'll be fine. Thank you.

She squeezed his hand a bit tighter. "Why does she dislike me so? I didn't ask to come here and have done nothing but occupy this room. Glory Bee has been wonderful, but Mrs. Peck obviously does not want me here." A tear trickled down Edna's cheek. "I have nowhere else to go."

Reverend Albright patted Edna's hand. "Don't you worry about that right now. From what I hear, you've got a lot of recovering to do, so I expect you'll be here awhile. I'll have a talk with Birdie, but meanwhile . . . well, try to understand. I've learned since coming here that island people tend to be quite protective of one another. All's they've got is themselves.

Reverend Albright lowered his gaze to the floor before looking back at Edna. "Birdie's life was turned upside down when the hurricane hit this island . . . as were many others' I might add. And then Walter, her husband, lost his business and eventually died leaving her nearly penniless.

Shifting his gaze to the window, Reverend Albright seemed to contemplate what else to say. His voice became serious when he resumed.

"Just like most places, there's a lot of family history on this island, Edna. A lot of good history but some folks struggle with . . . well, certain history that contributed to a lot of hurt. Take Birdie and Glory Bee, for example. They've got their own history. Tied together like . . . well, . . .

Reverend Albright patted Edna's hand and abruptly stood up. "You look like you'll be okay now, and I've got to get back to that Bible study." Chuckling, he added, "And that piece of cake!

After setting the chair back by the wood trunk, Reverend Albright rushed to the bedroom door. "It's a pleasure to meet you, Edna. Get some rest now. You'll be up and about before long. Glory Bee will see to that." Smiling, he backed out of the room and closed the door.

With the setting sun darkening the room, Edna closed her eyes. Tired as she was, sleep eluded her. She pondered Reverend Albright's precipitous departure and his defense of Mrs. Peck's treatment of her.

I certainly understand misfortune. Goodness knows New Orleans isn't immune to it, and I heard enough about it from Léonce with his dealings at the bank. But what did the hurricane and the death of Mrs. Peck's husband have to do with me? And the hurtful family histories. Whose family and what kinds of hurt? Mrs. Peck and Glory Bee?

Unable to quiet her mind, Edna threw off her sheet and blanket. Standing slowly to steady herself, she walked to the window and looked out to the dim glowing lights appearing in windows of various houses below Mrs. Peck's. Hoping for a better breeze, she raised the window's sash as far as it would go. Sweet ocean air flowed through her gauzy linen nightdress cooling her damp skin. A dog bark echoed in the distance. No one seemed to be about for as far as she could see.

After lighting her bedside lamp, Edna sat down on the straight chair vacated by Reverend Albright, the wood's firm support lending itself to memories of her mother's warnings about proper posture.

How many miles did I walk around the dining room table balancing a book on my head?

Sadness filled Edna's heart remembering her deceased mother, father, and grandparents. Others... her sons, her sisters, acquaintances... an endless stream of faces flashed before her.

Recalling family travels, Edna ran her hand over the trunk's grooved lid, its finish worn to dullness. Discovering the hasp opened freely, she raised the heavy, creaking lid as high as it would go. Tarnished hardware locked it in place. The pungent aroma of cedar filled the air.

At first glance, in the dim light, Edna thought she might be looking at white bed linens. Bending to get a closer look, she realized the items were, in fact, carefully folded, delicate linen clothing.

Picking up one of the pieces, she unfolded it to discover it to be an infant's dressing gown monogrammed with the letters *PPP* in yellow across the front. More items of clothing showed little or no wear and nearly filled the trunk. Many were stitched with the same three-letter monogram. The sharp creases of all she removed indicated the items had not seen the light of day in quite a long time.

Edna carefully refolded the pieces she had removed and placed them back in the trunk exactly as she found them. She closed the lid and sat back down. Muddled as her mind was from sheer weariness, she considered who the clothing might belong to.

Whose initials were they? A grandchild of Mrs. Peck's? Hard to imagine her coddling a child. And why did they show so little, if any, wear? Maybe she collected clothing for children on the island. Or maybe she took up stitching clothing to earn income? But then why were the items still in the trunk? Did the letter "P" even refer to "Peck"?

A dreadful thought struck Edna, and she brought a hand to her mouth.

Perhaps whoever the child was had died.

A rumble of thunder jolted Edna from her pondering. She lowered the window's sash against the possibility of rain. Turning off her lamp, she crawled into bed and rested her hands on her abdomen.

A whole week before Dr. Bartlett returns. I'll ask Glory Bee for a bit of dried bread tomorrow morning. And a cup of hot tea. Maybe I'll get to meet Penelope tomorrow. I need to thank her.

Turning onto her side, Edna did her best to ignore the squeak of the front door with each departing guest scrambling to beat the rain. As the wind whined with the coming storm, Edna soon fell asleep.

Chapter Eight

Edna's eyes squinted against the first rays of sunlight rising above the window sill. She rose from her bed, testing her balance on wobbly legs. After relieving herself, she poured water from the pitcher and splashed her face. Startled by her reflection in the mirror above the dresser, she gasped releasing yet another coughing episode. She closed her eyes and held her hands to her chest, willing it to relax the urge to cough again.

Once normal breathing resumed, Edna studied the splotches of red sunburn on her face now beginning to flake and peel. Turning her head side to side, she feared her flawless complexion would never return. She ran her fingers through her hair stiff and caked with sand and salt. She coiled the shoulder-length dark brown tresses high on her head, but the heavy coiffure fell back to her shoulders. She shrugged and sighed.

Oh, for a few pins for a chignon . . . and a bath.

A noise behind her, something hitting glass . . . a pinging sound . . . drew Edna to the window. As she raised the sash, fresh gusts rushed into the room rippling her night dress. Inhaling the refreshing air, she lifted her hair off her neck, relishing the cooling draft against her moist skin. Sunlight peeked through rustling leaves overhead as branches and boughs swayed in the early morning sea breeze.

A youthful voice from below called out, "Hello? Hope I didn't wake ya up!"

At the base of the tree, a young girl with hair the color of corn silk sat lotus-like on the ground. Next to her a dog panted and wagged its tail.

A sheepish smile spread across the girl's small face. "Act'ally I do hope I waked you up 'cuz I been sittin' here awhile waitin' ta see if you'd come ta the window. If I git caught, I'll have ta skedaddle. I'm Penelope." She added in a matter-of-fact tone, "I found you on the beach."

Delighted with the girl's forthrightness, Edna smiled back. "Well, hello, Penelope. And, no, you didn't wake me. I'm so glad to meet you. I owe you a huge thank you.

Taking in the child's patched and frayed blue dress, she pondered more to say. "What's your dog's name?"

"Bell. Cuz her tail wags all the time." She patted the dog's head. Bell woofed and nuzzled her nose under Penelope's arm. "Can you come down?"

Edna smiled and shook her head. "Not yet I'm afraid. Dr. Bartlett . . . I guess you probably know Dr. Bartlett? He says I should rest for a few more days before I have visitors or venture out.

Edna looked down at her gown then back to Penelope. "Besides, I don't have anything to wear other than this night dress." Smiling, she added, "I don't believe that would do walking around town, would it?"

Penelope giggled. "No. Guess not." Her face turned serious. "Um, how'd you get in the ocean? Were you scared?"

Edna closed her eyes for a moment.

What will I say? What do I say to this child? Do I lie? I can tell her I fell off a boat. But how do I explain my nakedness? I need time to think.

Choosing to ignore Penelope's first question, Edna replied, "Yes, I was very scared. But I'm so glad you found me. I can't thank you enough." Feeling the need to sit and to escape more questions, Edna added, "I think I need to rest now.

The aroma of bacon drifted up from the kitchen. Although

unappetizing given her queasy stomach, she was grateful for the convenient pretext. "And Glory Bee will be coming up with my breakfast soon, so I should go. I'm so glad to finally meet you, Penelope." She began to walk away from the window then returned. "You'll come back, won't you? Let me know you're down there like you did this time, alright?"

Penelope beamed as she hopped to her feet. "Yes ma'am! I shore will!" She raised her hand in farewell. "Bye!"

Edna called after the departing child. "Bye, Penelope. I hope to see you soon!"

Penelope yelled, "Come on, Bell! Let's go check the crab traps!" Bell's bark faded into the distance.

Overcome with weakness, Edna gratefully returned to her bed. She stared across the room at the trunk.

Could the letters have been for Penelope?! No! I cannot imagine that monogram has anything to do with Penelope. If they did, surely Mrs. Peck wouldn't allow this waif of a girl to be dressed as she is.

Considering Mrs. Peck's attitude when confronting Edna in her bed, as well as her belligerent conversations with Reverend Albright and Glory Bee, Edna gave pause.

Or would she? I don't think Penelope was wearing any shoes. Dr. Bartlett said she's nine. Awfully small for nine. Seems like a happy child. Still, something about her, something . . . I don't know . . . maybe in her eyes. She seems older.

Following a light tap on the bedroom door, it opened and Glory Bee entered carrying a breakfast tray. "Mornin', Miss Edna."

"Good morning, Glory Bee. Such a lovely morning, isn't it?" Clearing her raspy throat, she struggled against a cough.

"Yes'm. It shore is." Glory Bee set the tray on the bureau. "Now, Docta' B tells me ta just bring ya dry bread an' tea fer a while. Don't look like much of a breakfast, so if ya feel like havin' somethin' more, jus' let me know, alright?"

"Yes, of course. Thank you. I think the bread and tea will be fine for now." Holding a hand against her stomach, Edna added, "The seawater seems to still be causing a bit of churning."

She looked away, her gaze landing on the trunk. Edna considered mentioning its contents to Glory Bee then thought better of it.

A bit soon to be prying into matters that don't concern me.

She turned toward the window. "I just had a visit from Penelope from the window. It was nice to finally meet her and to thank her."

"Oh, my yes, that child's been beggin' ta come up here." Glory Bee slowly shook her head. "She will wear you out, so don' be in no hurry." She turned to the bureau and lifted the pitcher. "Now before Miz Peck rouses herself, I'll go down ta refresh yer water. Anythin' else ya need?"

Edna thought briefly about the hair pins and a bath. As much as she longed for them, she felt it best to wait a few more days to regain more strength.

"You're too kind, and I'm so grateful for . . . well, for everything. Please don't worry about me. I'm fine . . . or at least I'm sure I will be fine."

Glory Bee stared at Edna for a moment, her lips puckering. "Kids sayin' a mermaid washed up on the beach. A hun'erd years from now, people be sayin' a real life mermaid washed up on the shore o' Pine Cove Key."

Cocking her head to the side and raising her eyebrows, Glory Bee continued to stare at Edna. "You a real life mermaid, Miss Edna? That how ya managed ta flounder 'round in the ocean like ya did?"

A mermaid?

Edna was taken aback by the seriousness of Glory Bee's tone. She stifled a smile. "Glory Bee, of course not. Why, there's no such things as mermaids. They're . . . they're fairy tales, seafaring lore." She faced Glory Bee's gaze. "Surely you don't believe in mermaids." Hesitating, she added, "Do you?"

Glory Bee took a deep breath. "It don' matter what I think. Thing is stories git told 'til whatever the true story is gets told." She turned toward the door. "I'll be back up with yer water di'rectly."

Shaken by Glory Bee's clear message, Edna stared at the closed door for several moments. Turning to her bed, she sat down and sipped from the glass of water on the night stand.

I need to explain myself. This isn't New Orleans where people can disappear among the throngs, where many people wouldn't give a whit about someone washing up on the shore. Who do I tell? Glory Bee? Certainly not Mrs. Peck. Reverend Albright? Dr. Bartlett when he comes next week? And how much do I tell? Choosing to end one's life is an unforgiveable mortal sin for many. I suspect that's how it would be looked upon here.

Edna lost any appetite she might have had before Glory Bee brought her breakfast. She closed her eyes, too weary to think clearly. She considered lying down, but the discomforting itch of peeling skin, especially on her arms and back, was making rest more troublesome.

Tempted to scratch, despite Dr. Bartlett's caution, Edna peered at her fingers. She caught her breath and struggled against another cough. "My wedding ring! It's gone!"

It was the first time she noticed the missing gold band surrounded by a cluster of diamonds. An initial reaction was to search the bed and the room.

The drawers. Maybe Glory Bee removed it and placed it in a drawer.

A search of the dresser's contents revealed only bed linens and blankets in all but one drawer. The bottom one contained a tin filled with pencils.

Muttering, Edna returned to the bed. "I can't ask her. She'll think I'm accusing her." A thought struck her. "The sea! Of course! I lost it in the sea. My fingers would have shrunk and the force of the water would have pulled it off."

What does it matter? One less thing to have to explain. For now.

As the room grew brighter with the rising sun, Edna finished her breakfast and set the tray on the dresser. With nothing left to do, she wandered back to the window, drawn to think seriously about her circumstances.

Maybe the mermaid story isn't such a bad idea . . . at least for a while. Eventually, I have to think of what I'll tell everyone and what I'll do once I'm recovered . . . how to get back to New Orleans . . . if there is even a way to get there. If I even want to . . . or should. I don't want to think about that right now. But I must. This isn't just about me anymore.

The enormity of the situation made Edna's head hurt. She rested her forehead against the pane's cool surface.

A red streak darted through the tree's branches followed by the rat-tat-tat of a busy, determined woodpecker clinging to the trunk. Below, to the right of the tree, deep pink oleander blooms swayed on their branches. Off to the left, beyond the yard, a woman holding a little girl's hand walked along the incline of the dirt street. Somewhere in the distance a horse whinnied.

The familiar odor of sawn wood reached Edna's nostrils. She was instantly thrust into the chaos of renovation in her house in New Orleans.

That constant banging, sawing, and the dust . . . there was no end to it and no escape . . . except I did escape, and look where I am now.

Physically and emotionally spent, Edna returned to her bed. As she sipped from the glass of water, she again took note of a glass jar holding a bouquet of violets. She recalled Dr. Bartlett saying they were from Penelope. Edna loved violets.

Looks like Penelope likes them, too. I must remember to thank her for them.

Settling into the comfort of the bed, Edna thought about the tin of pencils in the bureau drawer.

If I had some paper . . . and some hair pins. I do long for a bath.

Closing her eyes, as sleep lulled her senses, she envisioned her body immersed into a tub of steaming, soapy water fragranced with her favorite lemon oil. She then imagined someone wrapping her in a sumptuous Turkish towel as she emerged from her bath. Warmth enveloped her, and she drifted toward sleep.

Chapter Nine

Somewhere between that murky lucid state and deep sleep, when dreamy images sometimes slip into recall, the tub of soapy bath water metamorphosed into a boat. The Turkish towel Edna had imagined she was wrapped in following her luxurious imaginary bath transformed into a coarse blanket. She was in the boat's cabin below deck. In the cockpit overhead, voices ... men's voices ... were speaking of their plans for her after a meal at a nearby tavern.

"What if she escapes?" one coarse voice barked.

"She ain't goin' nowhere with no clothes on," another growled then snickered. "She's a right perty little thing. Mebbe have ..."

His crude remarks were lost in the sounds of back-slapping and laughter. One of them mentioned her ring and what it could be worth. "Git rid o' this tub. Them diamonds'd cover the cost of a boat fit fer real fishin'."

"Let's go git it," one of them snarled.

"Naw. I'm hungry. Besides she's out cold an' even if she comes to, she ain't goin' nowhere in the buff. I'm ready ta tie one on. No sense riskin' losin' that ring in a brawl neither. We'll yank it off that finger when we git back."

Despite her weakened state, Edna's adrenalin surged.

I have to get out of here!

The rocking of the boat and the men's retreating footsteps on the wood dock alerted Edna they had left. Wrapping the blanket snugly around her body, she crept up the ladder and peered into a dark, moonless night. With no one about, she climbed out of the flimsy, rocking craft and onto the dock. The only choice of escape, or at least to hide until help in some way surfaced, was another boat.

Hearing voices approaching, Edna scurried toward the end of the dock as quickly as her weakened strength and the awkward blanket would allow. Reaching a sailboat rigged for fishing, she traversed the gang plank, praying no one else was on board. Working her way forward, she reached a berth piled with rain slickers and climbed in. She pulled the companionway door nearly closed allowing for some air flow and a sight line in case anyone came near.

The boat's empty cockpit loomed overhead. Feeling safe at least for the moment, her raging, mobilizing adrenalin and her pounding heart succumbed to exhaustion. Breathing deeply, she settled into the bulky layers of rainwear and closed her eyes. Her last thought before falling asleep was what she would do come daybreak.

Edna awoke to the boat's movement and waves slapping its sides. Crawling toward the opening of the berth, her first sight was of bulging sails in winds growing stronger by the moment. It became apparent the boat was far out to sea, and no one appeared to be in the cockpit.

Was anyone else even on board? Had the boat somehow torn loose from the dock? Where was the captain . . . or anybody?

Edna felt she was being carried away on a ghost ship.

The sky darkened and billowing slate-gray clouds soon gave way to torrential rain. In the storm's escalating fury, the boat listed further and further in mounting waves. Edna's screams as the storm slammed her against the boat's interior were lost in the howl of the wind. Thunder boomed and streaks of lightning cracked overhead while rigging rattled and clanged. Water poured into the berth, soaking her blanket. Another sound ... a groan ... then the cracking of wood suddenly gave way to the mast breaking in two, toppling the sails into the foaming, black water.

As the boat began to break apart in the pounding mountainous waves, Edna grabbed hold of the companionway door, wrapped her arms around it, and braced for her inevitable plunge into the sea. Though she hung on to her flimsy wooden raft for dear life, she never thought for a moment she would survive.

A thunderous boom and sharp flashes of light jarred Edna out of her nightmare. Her eyes popped open. Shaking, she sat up in her bed. The bedroom curtains whipped in a strong wind blowing through the open window. Rain pelted the sill and onto the floor. Tree branches thrashed and bent, sending broken boughs to the ground. Day had turned into night.

Struggling to shake herself from the nightmare and stunned by the intensity of the storm, Edna tossed her covers aside and swung her legs off the bed.

The bedroom door flew open. Glory Bee hastened to the window and lowered the sash. Grabbing a towel from the dresser, she dropped it on the floor and swirled it with her foot to mop up rainwater.

"Lawd a mercy! That one popped up out o' nowheres!" She peered at Edna's face. "Ya alright, Miss Edna? Yer lookin' like ya seen a ghost!"

Still shaking from reliving the horror of near death and the ferocity of the storm raging outside, Edna looked up into Glory Bee's worried face.

I have to tell someone what happened ... that I should have died ... twice! And if Glory Bee doesn't understand, well, at least maybe I won't relive it each time I go to sleep!

With shaking hands, she picked up the water glass and took a long drink. Stifling a cough, she took a deep breath and set the glass back on the table.

"Glory Bee, would you happen to have a few minutes? I . . . I'd like to talk to you."

After checking on Mrs. Peck, Glory Bee returned to Edna's room and pulled the chair close to the bed. An hour later, she leaned back in the chair and let go of Edna's hands. The storm having subsided and sunlight now brightening the bedroom, Glory Bee stood and opened the window. A rush of fresh, rain-cleansed air filled the room. She returned to the chair and sat down.

Edna was grateful Glory Bee had remained silent the entire time she shared her story. If interrupted, she might not have had the courage, or the will, to continue. She revealed details of her marriage and her family; of her despair that the man she truly loved, Robert Lebrun, had abandoned her; of her heedless enamor for the rake, Alcée Arobin, father of the child she was carrying.

In a stoic voice, she told of traveling alone from New Orleans to the shore of Grand Isle, Louisiana. "I barely recall the lengthy journey, or the shedding of my clothes on the shore, or walking into the water."

Edna told of the fishermen who pulled her out of the Gulf, of their intent to harm her, of her flight to another boat, the one that foundered, and how she miraculously survived in the raging sea. When she finished, she hung her head and stared at the floor.

Glory Bee reached for the water glass and handed it to Edna. "Here. Drink. Yer voice startin' ta sound like one o' them blue jays screechin' up in that tree." She leaned forward and chuckled then whispered, "Or like Miz Peck."

Edna smiled as she gratefully took the glass and swallowed the remainder of its contents. "Thank you." She looked up at Glory Bee. "For listening."

Tears overflowed and ran down her cheeks. The relief was

overwhelming. Whether Glory Bee judged her or not no longer mattered. The burden, the weight of all she had been holding in, was lifted, as if she had been holding her breath for a very long time. Although physically and emotionally spent from unloading her story, Edna suddenly felt refreshed and as light as dew on a rose . . . that if she had wings, she could fly.

Glory Bee held out her hand for the glass and rose from the chair. She poured water from the pitcher, handed the glass back to Edna, and sat down again. She took a deep breath.

"Firs' thing I'm gonna say is nobody gonna hear any o' this from me. Yer gonna decide who else needs ta know or not know. That's yer business." She looked up at the ceiling then back to Edna. "Lawd knows ya been through a whole lot an' He's the only one has the right ta judge ya for it." A reflective expression appeared on Glory Bee's face. "Or anybody.

She lowered her head and looked at Edna squarely. "Second thing I'm gonna say is we all be human. We all make mistakes." She shook her head and mumbled. "Lawd knows I made enough o' my own.

Regaining her focus, Glory Bee continued. "Las' thing I'm gonna say is about bein' a Mama. Changes yer life. Feels sometimes like it steals yer life. Ya ain't you no more. It's all about those young'uns, pullin' on yer skirt, wantin' this and wantin' that. Before long, what was you disappears into the woodwork. Feels like yer dreams went up in smoke." She tilted her head and raised her eyebrows. "That sound 'bout right?"

Edna looked at the floor. "I so often didn't want to be with my children. Frankly, I don't think they wanted to be with me." She scowled. "But my friends . . . those with children. They seemed to thrive on their motherly instincts . . . on their children's demands. What's wrong with me? Why don't I have that same instinct, like them, to want to be with my children?" Tears overflowed onto her night dress. "I didn't deserve them."

"Now you hush 'bout that. If the good Lawd didn't see fit fer ya ta have'em, ya wouldn't o' had 'em. Thing now is ya jus' gotta make peace with yerself that ya ain't a bad person. Those young boys gonna be fine. Time'll come ya might figure out a way ta . . . well, if nothin' else, let'em know ya didn't drown . . . or ya might even want ta get back to 'em.

With a groan, Glory Bee raised herself from the chair, replaced it next to the trunk, and returned to Edna. "Now, drink some more and crawl back into that bed and git some rest. Beautiful day out there, Miss Edna. Let's git ya well an' on yer feet so's ya can git out there an' see what these islands is all about.

At the bedroom door, Glory Bee turned to Edna. "Funny thing 'bout livin' on a island. It can be an escape from . . . well, a whole lot o' things in life, an' it can feel real lonely. Thing ta remember is each of us is livin' on our own kind o' island with our own problems. All up ta you how ya decide ta look at it.

She opened the door and turned to Edna again. "So don't go thinkin' yer all alone in wrestlin' with guilt or shame or whatever else yer feelin', cuz ya got lots o' company." Before closing the door, she poked her head back into the room. "An' they be right here on this island."

Staring at the closed door, Edna sipped more water then set the glass on the bedside table. She crawled between the sheets and burrowed into the soft mattress. Every square inch of her body gave way to blissful solace. She felt a renewed clarity of mind she could only credit to her unburdened soul. The practice of prayer, which she abandoned years ago, discrediting its efficacy in her life, now seemed imperative.

How do I begin? Ask for forgiveness? I tried to take my own life.

She placed her hands on her abdomen.

And yours. But through God's grace, I escaped with my life . . . our lives . . . not once but twice. Dear God, forgive me! I will not take your mercy for granted.

Turning onto her side facing the window, she spoke to the sun peeping through the tree branches.

And thank you, Lord . . . for allowing me . . . us to live . . . for your redemption.

With sleep overtaking her, she mumbled "Amen." Very quickly, however, the weight of her reality roused her.

But Lord, how? If this were just me, but . . . Is it fair to bring a child into a life filled with so many unknowns?

She sighed deeply and closed her eyes. Before drifting off, she recalled Glory Bee's mention that Edna was not alone in her guilt and shame. She thought about Reverend Albright's subtle reference to the history Mrs. Peck and Glory Bee shared and little Penelope sitting barefoot at the base of the tree clad in her worn and faded blue dress. Edna opened her eyes and glanced across the room at the trunk.

With eyelids growing heavier, she yawned while the pungent odor of sawn wood drifted into the room.

***

"Atsena Otie." Glory Bee removed the bottom sheet from Edna's bed and tossed it on the floor with the other bed linens. She then pulled fresh linens from a bureau drawer.

Edna, who was sitting in the chair next to the trunk, scowled. "Excuse me?"

"What yer smellin' is cedar bein' sawed. Pro'bly somebody fixin' a porch or a roof." Glory Bee bobbed her head toward the window. "That land ya see over yonder through the tree? That's Atsena Otie. It ain't the mainland like you were askin'. It's another island. Used ta be a cedar sawmill an' a factory makin' pencils over there. Hurricane wiped it clean off the map."

Edna glanced at the bureau's bottom drawer with the tin of pencils. "It must have been devastating."

"Sure was. Killed a whole lot o' people. Destroyed the railroad.

Pine Cove Key weren't the same after that storm. Prob'ly won't ever be again."

Glory Bee snapped open a fresh sheet. Once it floated to the bed, she bent over and tucked it firmly around the edges of the mattress. She stood and groaned, pressing her hands against her back.

"One o' these days, this ol' back is gonna seize up like a' old rusted pump handle." She finished making the bed and turned to Edna. "Now, git back in bed and rest. Sheets nice 'n clean. I'm goin' down and start supper. Anythin' I kin git ya before I go?"

Edna stood and walked slowly toward the bed. Feeling a bit awkward given her confession earlier and conflicted over her present circumstances ... an uninvited guest in dire need ..., she pondered how to begin. After staring at the floor for a moment, she faced Glory Bee.

"Thank you again for listening and for your understanding." She took a deep breath. "I realize I've intruded ... even though unintentionally ... into Mrs. Peck's home and, of course, your responsibilities for her. And now you have me to tend to."

"Awww, Miss Edna. It ain't no trouble ..."

"Please, let me finish. I'll be stronger soon. And when I am, I want to help you. I mean it. I confess it's been a while, but I can make beds. I can clean." Edna smiled. "I'm not much of a cook, but I can learn.

Though lightheaded and looking forward to crawling back into bed, she took hold of Glory Bee's hand. "Glory Bee, listen. I have nowhere to go or any means to get there if I did. Surely you realize that. So, if you ... and maybe Mrs. Peck ... will have me, once I'm able, I want to relieve you of some of your chores." She stared into Glory Bee's eyes. "Please. It's the least I can do."

Glory Bee puckered her lips and took a deep breath.

I sure ain't gettin' any younger. Fifty-six startin' ta feel like 86.

She patted Edna's hand. "You been here jus' a couple o' days,

Miss Edna. No sense puttin' the cart before the horse. Let's git ya feelin' like ya can even git down those stairs. Then we'll talk about what ya might be doin' around here."

Beyond Edna's bedroom, a door opened. "Glory Bee!" Mrs. Peck's shrill voice reverberated throughout the upstairs.

"I'll be goin' now." Glory Bee picked up an armload of bed linens off the floor. She whispered, "I'll be back up with yer supper after 'while."

Edna crawled into bed and closed her eyes, irritated that merely sitting up in the chair while Glory Bee changed her bed linens caused such exhaustion. The pressure of a cough erupted in her throat. She sat up and sipped from the glass of water then fell back onto her pillow.

From somewhere outside, the repetitious squeak and intermittent gush of water from a pump recalled her summers visiting her grandparents' farm in upper Louisiana. How she loved the openness of the land, the quiet broken only by the clucking of chickens, the crow of a rooster early in the mornings, and the neighing of her grandfather's horses. She gathered eggs for her grandmother and groomed the horses for her grandfather. She made her own bed every morning and helped her grandmother hang laundry on a clothesline. How she loved the smell of clean sheets on her bed fresh off the clothesline. All of that changed when she married.

Léonce would scold, "Edna, we have maids to do these household chores."

"But I can make my own bed."

"We pay maids to make the beds, Edna. Now, plan what you'll wear to tea with the other bankers' wives come Thursday. And shop for new hats . . . styles to match your new French gowns."

Edna gradually grew weary of the days, weeks, months, then years filled with teas, teas, and more teas. Her drained sense of purpose drove her to seek other outlets and gradually other people. Life for Edna had lost meaning, so even her favorite pastime, her love of painting on canvas, no longer interested her.

Gazing out the window, Edna stifled another cough. She pulled the top edge of the bed sheet to her nose and inhaled the fresh outdoor scent. Closing her eyes, she reflected on Glory Bee's comments regarding life on an island . . . a refreshing escape from the life I was living, or a lonely, isolated existence.

So here I am. And here I'll be. I have a choice, and I have to make the best of whichever one it is.

As drowsiness settled in, Edna smiled. "Of one thing I'm sure. I don't think I'll be invited to tea anytime soon."

Chapter Ten

Edna smiled at her reflection in the bureau mirror. "Glory Bee, thank you! These pins work perfectly. It feels so good to get my hair up and off my neck!"

"You sure is welcome. And I'm glad ta see that red flaky mess on yer face finally lookin' better."

Edna turned her head side to side. "It does seem to be getting better, doesn't it? I've been spreading aloe from the plant you brought me. I think it's helping." She pushed up the sleeves of her dressing gown. "My arms, too. The itching isn't so bad now."

Glory Bee scooped up Edna's empty breakfast tray from the bureau. "Been five days now. Glad ta see yer feelin' up ta eatin' more'n tea and dry bread, too. Me'n Tom's chickens'r layin' a lot o' eggs ev'ry day, so ya can have as many o' those whenever ya want. Hard boiled, fried. Don't matter."

Edna smiled. "I'm sure my appetite will pick up. The hard-boiled egg tasted wonderful. One for breakfast is perfect for now . . . if it isn't any trouble. Oh, and those tomato slices with the bread for my supper were delicious."

"Ain't no trouble. Miz Peck has at least one egg ev'ry day so I keep 'em handy. Good crop a 'maters this year. All ya want."

As Glory Bee turned toward the door, thunder rumbled in the distance. "Here we go a'gin. If this rain don't let up, we're never gonna git ya out o' this house. Ya need some color! Except for those splotches, yer pale as the inside of a egg shell."

Edna stared at her reflection in the mirror. "I've always carried a parasol to protect my complexion. Once I'm able to go outside, maybe I can borrow one, or perhaps a hat." She leaned closer to the mirror. Turning her head side to side, she peered at her face. "And I'll need cold cream to moisturize."

Looking down at her hands, Edna scowled. "My hands do tend to freckle if I don't wear gloves.

Raising her head, her eyes lost their focus replaced by a dreamy, vacant expression. "When vacationing on the Riviera, I neglected to bring along my assortment of gloves. My lady's maid discovered a few pairs at a boutique so damage was avoided . . ."

Edna's voice trailed off as visions of indulgent servants marched before her. A promenade of stylish attire complemented every occasion . . . elegant pearl- and lace-trimmed silk and bustled brocades, racks of matching feathered hats and parasols, limitless grand engagements mingling and consorting with foreign dignitaries and New Orleans' wealthiest.

Amid the vivid reeling visions, fragments of Robert's face and words of love emerged then evaporated replaced with the expressionless face of Alcée Arobin.

Gone. They, my family, everything in my life as I knew it . . . all gone.

A noise . . . maybe a dog's bark or the slam of a door . . . wrenched Edna from her reverie leaving her slightly breathless. In her weakened state, she gripped the edge of the bureau. Flushed with embarrassment, she inhaled deeply and cleared her throat.

"Glory Bee, I . . ." She struggled for words to relieve the weight of palpable silence hovering over the room.

Glory Bee chuckled. "Well, whatever ya was thinkin' about, ya shore got color now!"

Edna attempted a smile. She pressed her hands against her warm face. "It appears I do."

Opening the bedroom door, Glory Bee cautioned. "Now don't be strainin' yerself, hear? We're gonna do just fine. As my

Gran'pappy used ta say, 'You is what you is an' I is what I is. That's the way the good Lawd made us.'" She soberly added, "Jus' wish ever'body felt that way.

Seeming to reign in further comments on the subject, Glory Bee backed out the door. "Now, I can't promise ya no parasol or gloves, but there might be a floppy straw hat 'round here somewheres. As fer yer cold cream, well, I can mix some lard with some o' that aloe ya got there. Lots more growin' in the back yard. Let me know if ya think that'll work for ya.

Lightning flashed and more thunder rumbled closer. "Don't look like ya be goin' anywhere anyway 'til this rain lets up, so may as well git some more rest. And anyhow, first thing is we got to git ya some clothes." She turned to leave. "I'll be back up later on with yer lunch. Anything else I can git ya before I go?"

Chagrined for her thoughtless remarks, Edna hesitated before quietly replying. "A hat would be lovely . . . when the time comes. And only if there's a spare one, of course." She swallowed. "I've never used lard and aloe, but, well, alright. Yes, I'd like to try it. After all, nothing ventured, nothing gained, right?" She quickly added, hoping she sounded convincing, "And I can help make it, so please don't trouble yourself.

Edna glanced at the bureau with a sheepish smile. "There is one other thing. I hope it was alright. I found a tin of pencils in the bottom drawer and I thought I might do some drawing. I wondered, would you, or maybe Mrs. Peck, have some paper to lend me?"

The peculiar look that crossed Glory Bee's face puzzled Edna and she hastened to add, "It's okay if you don't. I'll be fine. I just thought I'd . . ."

Glory Bee set the tray on the bureau. In a hushed voice, she said, "Come with me." At the door, she turned to Edna, who stood motionless. "Come on. Jus' goin' ta the back bedroom."

"But I'm not dressed. What if . . ."

"Ain't nobody in there. An' Miz Peck ain't dressed neither.

She'll be in her bedroom a while eatin' her breakfast. She won't open her door 'til I bring up her pitcher o' water. Now come on. Jus' be quiet."

Tiptoeing into the hallway, Edna followed Glory Bee to a bedroom at the back of the house. Once inside, Glory Bee quietly closed the door.

As with Edna's bedroom, this one was sparsely furnished with only a dark hardwood-framed double bed, matching nightstand, and bureau with mirror. Against the wall to the room's right, a writing desk captured natural light from the room's only window. If anyone had occupied the room, any and all traces of personal belongings had been removed.

As the storm approached, darkening clouds cast shadows on bare yellowed walls. Echoes of pictures once hung on the walls evoked a ghostly presence. Another door, partially open, revealed an empty closet.

Glory Bee yanked open one of the desk drawers swollen and sticky from heat and lack of use. She removed a tablet of paper, closed the drawer, and handed the tablet to Edna. "Might wanna keep this in yer room ... or at least don't be leavin' it layin' around anywheres."

Edna gazed down at the tablet, the feel of it so familiar ... so friendly. "Glory Bee," she whispered, "this is perfect. Are you sure it's alright for me to take this?"

Glory Bee whispered back, "Ain't nobody gonna miss it. Been in there fer a few years. Somebody may as well git some use out of it. Now come on. We need ta go."

Once back in Edna's bedroom, Glory Bee picked up the breakfast tray and turned to leave.

Edna continued staring at the tablet of paper, by now realizing it was a sketch book. "I didn't dream of something like this." She looked up and smiled. "Thank you again for everything. And I hope you know I didn't intend ... "

Glory Bee interrupted her. "Like I said, Miss Edna, we're gonna do jus' fine so stop worryin' yerself." With a bob of her head, she left the room.

Now alone, Edna embraced the sketchbook to her chest. She inhaled with pleasure as if reunited with a beloved acquaintance. Removing a pencil from the bottom drawer, she sat down on the edge of her bed and ran a hand over the tablet cover.

Whose was this? Could it possibly be Mrs. Peck's? And why the secrecy?

Turning back the front cover, Edna poised the pencil over the top sheet and stared at it for several moments. She then closed the cover. After returning the items to the bureau, she stretched out on her bed. Exhaustion continued to plague her, and she could think of nothing but closing her eyes and resting.

It's been a long time. Something will come to me.

She opened her eyes and stared at the trunk at the opposite end of the room.

That . . . or maybe the tree outside my window.

Rain pattered and drizzled down the glass. The warm room added to Edna's drowsiness and she slept. A rumble of thunder and a flash of lightning woke her with a jolt. Shaking herself fully awake, she rose and brought the sketch pad and pencil back to her bed. Opening the cover, she once again poised the pencil over the blank paper but this time for only a moment before beginning to draw.

Edna delighted in the reminiscent scratch of pencil on paper and the smell of the lead. She began with the eyes and moved to the nose and mouth. Slowly, a face took shape, a child's face. Without paint or chalk, Edna could only picture in her mind the translucent-like blue eyes and fair and wispy blond hair. She recalled enough from her first meeting with Penelope that the rendering came very close to that of the little girl who sat at the foot of the tree.

As Edna stared at the drawing, paintings by Mary Cassatt popped into her mind. While she greatly admired the artist's talent, Cassatt's recurrent mother-and-child themed paintings ... a child snuggled in bed with her mother, the bathing of a child while sitting on his mother's lap, a mother reading to her children ... often troubled Edna.

At an exhibit of Cassatt's works not long ago, Edna searched for something ... anything ... to connect with the doting mothers in the paintings. She wanted to meet Mary Cassatt, wanted to stand next to her in front of a mirror to see if obvious external characteristics indicated differences in their maternal instincts. Nothing ever surfaced for Edna, nothing to help her understand Cassatt's ability to illustrate such warmth and comfort between mothers and their children.

In contrast, another of Cassatt's paintings ... of a little blond girl wearing a blue pinafore and a straw hat ... was so unlike any of her other masterpieces as to be somewhat disturbing. The child in this painting stood alone with her arms crossed in front of her, her distant, melancholy look implying loss or loneliness ... or maybe the result of a scolding. Edna often pondered who the little girl might be. She felt sadness for the child unlike any feeling she ever felt for her lively, spirited, spoiled sons, who wiggled away from her apathetic, clumsy efforts to embrace them.

Gazing at her drawing, recalling her brief moments chatting with Penelope from her window, Edna sensed that same despondency in the girl as that of the child in Cassatt's painting.

Edna closed the tablet and put it and the pencil in the drawer. The rain having stopped, she opened the window, relishing the swift breeze carrying the scent of salty air off the Gulf. She looked down at the base of the tree, but no one was there.

I wonder where she lives and when she'll come back. It has been raining a lot.

Returning to her bed, Edna stretched out and rested her hands on her abdomen.

I've been here five days now. Stomach still feeling a bit queer. Probably normal given all the saltwater I swallowed.

She squeezed her eyes shut. She knew, of course, the queasy feeling likely had more to do with the life growing within her.

* * *

Since arriving at Birdie Peck's house, Edna gradually became attuned to the island's rhythmic spasms as well as those of the household. The early morning jingle of horses' bridles and wooden wheels bumping along distant streets blended with barking dogs and shouting children. Throughout the rest of the morning, women's voices competed with the clatter of dishes, the squeak and squawk of pump handles, and water splashing into buckets and kettles.

Except for the incessant gulls' calls, birds chirping in the tree outside her window, and other more unfamiliar distant noises, quiet fell all around during midday. Evening brought many of the same early morning sounds as people returned home from wherever they worked or otherwise spent their day.

On Sunday morning, Edna's sixth day in Pine Cove, she awoke to the squeak of a pump handle gushing out seemingly endless amounts of water. Glory Bee did not appear with her breakfast tray, but Edna did hear her tap on Mrs. Peck's bedroom door followed by her usual "Mornin', Miz Peck."

Puzzled, Edna got up from her bed and carried out her minimal morning ablutions. She fussed with her hair, still stiff with sand and sea salt. Outside her window, through the tree's leafy branches, blue sky appeared cloudless at last. She was about to pull out the sketch pad and pencil when, following a light tap, her bedroom door opened.

Glory Bee came into the room carrying a small bowl, which she set on the bureau.

"Alright, Miss Edna. Here's yer lard an' aloe fer yer skin. And I know ya been achin' fer a bath. If ya think ya kin make it down those stairs, I got a tub 'o water in the larder for ya to soak in. Lawd knows it ain't hot, but Florida well water this time o' year ain't that cold. Soap and a towel already fer ya, so come on."

Edna looked down at her night dress. "Glory Bee, thank you for the ... um ... for the moisturizer, but I can't go downstairs like this."

"Ain't nobody around and if they were, the larder door'll be closed. So come on an' I'll help ya down the stairs if ya need it." She held open the bedroom door. "Come on," she coaxed.

At the stairway, Edna gripped the banister. On quivering legs, she made her way to the bottom of the stairs and followed the housekeeper into the kitchen at the back of the house.

Glory Bee pointed to a pantry adjacent to the kitchen, its shelves laden with glass jars, assorted pots, pans, kettles, and bowls. On the floor in a far corner, a sack of flour collapsed on itself surrounded by a white dusting. A large, water-filled galvanized tub awaited Edna.

Once alone, Edna removed her night dress and slowly immersed herself into the water. Resting against the curve of the tub, she closed her eyes and sighed. After days in the hot, often airless bedroom, she relished the tepid water soothing her still slightly sunburned, dry skin. Acquiescing to the simplicity of a coarse cloth and lye soap, she scrubbed away dead skin and the remains of tiny pieces of shell, sticky sand, and salt from her body and her hair.

Smiling, Edna mumbled, "I'll probably look like a boiled lobster when I finish."

Casting off reminiscences of her imported coconut, lemon, and palm oil soaps and fragrances, Edna reflected on her vain, thoughtless utterances in Glory Bee's presence.

Uncomfortable flashbacks surfaced ... particularly of her imperious and overbearing treatment of house staff in her New Orleans home. Edna had never considered if her callous, impassive behavior toward Etienne and Raoul's quadroon nanny was hurtful or offensive. She never showed the woman any gratitude, never asked about her family and the struggles they may have encountered throughout their lives.

I never once said thank you. I blamed her for so many of my own misdeeds, for my own negligence in caring for my sons.

With dismay, Edna cringed. "I can't even recall her name."

Edna recognized with shame the hideous, blatant oppression reserved for those she invariably considered beneath her.

I never wanted for anything, never had to be responsible for anything . . . or anyone. How could I have been so insensitive . . . so cruel? What must Glory Bee think of me, of such vanity?

A knock presumably at the back screen door interrupted Edna's troubling thoughts. A child's voice and the squeak of the door opening followed then murmurs of conversation. A few moments later, the door squeaked closed.

Glory Bee tapped on the larder door. "It's jus' me, Miss Edna. Don't put that dressin' gown back on yet. I got some clothes here that might fit. Mind if I open the door?"

"Not at all," Edna replied.

Glory Bee opened the door, her arms laden with a pile of clothing topped with a pair of creased and scuffed black lace-up shoes.

"Give these dresses a try an' if they fit, leave yer night dress in the kitchen. I'll wash it and git it back to ya soon as it's dry." She placed the garments on a shelf. "Wrinkled and stained. Prob'ly worn through in some places, too. If they fit, I kin wash 'em an' put a hot iron to 'em."

"Thank you, Glory Bee. I'm truly grateful. And for the bath, too." Edna smiled. "I feel almost human again."

"I 'spect ya do. Now see what ya think o' those clothes. I'll be takin' Miz Peck's pitcher o' water up to her now and tidyin' up her bedroom. She's been stompin' across the floor up there, so she's gettin' beside herself. I'll be back after 'while."

Edna climbed out of the tub, dried off, and wrapped her soaked hair in a towel. Setting the shoes on the floor, she unfolded a pair of white bloomers and a frayed and yellowed camisole. Once attired in the under garments, after removing the towel from her head, she shook out a yellow gingham dress with a gaping tear at the shoulder. Refolding it, she made a mental note to ask Glory Bee for needle and thread.

She unfolded the other dress, a pink and white stripe. A faded rust-colored stain stretched from the bust line nearly to the hem. Puzzled over what could have caused such a large stain, Edna fidgeted with the skirt.

Maybe I can hide the stain in the gathers. It's a bit loose, but it certainly will do.

Edna pulled on one of the shoes. Though damp, her foot slipped into it easily as the size was a little larger than her normal shoe size. She pulled on the other shoe and laced them both.

Opening the larder door, Edna placed the night dress and the dress with the tear over the back of a kitchen chair. Her distorted reflection in a large kettle on the cast iron stove stopped her in her tracks. Inhaling sharply, she covered her mouth with one hand and gripped the back of the chair with the other.

"I can't go out in public looking like this," she muttered. "I look like a . . . like a street vendor at a market!" She held out the skirt and gawked at the stain. "Or worse!"

Pulling out the chair, Edna dropped onto the seat and tried to imagine what her family and friends would say if they saw her dressed like this.

They would point fingers and laugh! They would ridicule! They would think it was a joke!

Recollections of parties and gala affairs surfaced along with utterances from groups of women about another's unsuitable attire.

If they could see me now. I'd be an outcast!

An unfamiliar arousal began to fester in Edna's mind and

mostly in her heart. She became incensed . . . with those women and sadly with herself.

I was a part of it. I joked and ridiculed, too.

Edna looked around the kitchen with its peeling paint, its worn wood floor, shelves of chipped and cracked dishes. She ran a hand over the stain in the dress and stared at the worn, creased leather of the shoes. When she thought of the forces driving her life of privilege in New Orleans, the sobering irony of her situation quickly became clear. Suddenly the wrinkles, the stains, the less-than-perfect fit, the hand-me-down appearance no longer mattered, and she almost laughed.

I'm free . . . free of all of it! No one knows me here. If I wore this dress every day, which I might have to, who here would care?

Edna stood up and shoved the chair back in place. With a new lightness in her steps and far from ready to go back to her warm bedroom, she decided to let her hair dry while sitting on the back porch. Opening the door, she hissed "shoo" and waved away flies clinging to both sides of the screen.

Gathering the dress's skirt around her legs, she sat down on the porch steps. Delighting in her new sense of freedom, she closed her eyes and raised her face toward the sun, grateful beyond words to be outside.

At the sound of movement behind her, Edna turned to see Penelope sitting in a weathered wicker chair at the far end of the porch. Her dog sprawled alongside the chair fast asleep. Before Edna could speak, the child slid out of the chair and hopped off the edge of the porch. Bell raised her head, her ears perked.

Recovering from the unexpected encounter, Edna said, "Well, good morning, Penelope."

The slight girl clasped her hands in front of her and rocked side to side on grimy bare feet. Her frayed blue dress swayed around her legs while long, unkempt hair, in obvious need of a shampoo, blew around her face. Edna had to blink away Cassatt's painting of the little girl in the blue dress and straw hat looming before her. The likeness to Penelope was remarkable.

"Mornin', Miss Edna."

Penelope seemed intent on chewing her lower lip. She appeared shy . . . so different from her precocious demeanor sitting at the base of the tree a few days before.

Edna smiled. "I want to thank you for the violets. They're lovely. I still have them next to my bed."

Penelope continued to sway side to side. "Yer welcome. I can get s'more when those die." She stared at Edna's face. "You look perty."

"Why, thank you, Penelope."

"Yer welcome." Penelope added in a voice filled with hope and urgency. "Are you my Mama?"

Chapter Eleven

Her Mama? I'm sure I heard her right. Why would she think . . . ?

Raucous voices from the kitchen shook Edna out of her bewilderment.

"Just where's she s'pposed ta go?" demanded Glory Bee.

"That's not my concern." Mrs. Peck's voice grated like the backyard's rusty pump handle.

"Jus' like Jeremy, yer own son! An' Olivia . . . even little Priscilla. Yer own granddaughter! They ain't yer concern neither!" The vehemence in Glory Bee's voice heightened. "Just like them, ya drive ever'body away just 'cuz they an embarrassment in yer eyes."

Deafening silence lasted only moments before Mrs. Peck's retort. "That's enough, Glory Bee. Not another word. I want that woman out of my house." The front screen door slammed. "See to it."

Glory Bee called out, "Well, when ya git ta church, ya might think 'bout askin' Reverend Albright fer fergiveness again cuz Lawd knows yer gonna need it!"

Edna and Penelope could only stare at one another. The heated exchange between Glory Bee and Mrs. Peck intensified Edna's tremulous state. Swallowing hard, she struggled to calm herself.

Taking hold of Penelope's hand, Edna spoke barely above a whisper. "I think we need to have a talk, Penelope, but I'm not feeling too well right now. Can you come back tomorrow? Maybe we can have another chat from my bedroom window."

Penelope hesitated then nodded. "Okay." She let go of Edna's hand and turned to leave. Turning back, she asked, "Wanna see my boat?"

Edna was once again caught off guard. "You have a boat?"

Penelope rubbed the sole of one bare foot against the opposing ankle. "It's just a little one. But it'll fit both of us."

Amid Glory Bee's loud grumbles, dishes and silverware rattled and clinked in the kitchen. The pantry door opened then slammed shut.

"Yes, of course. I'd love to see your boat. Is it very far from here?"

Penelope pointed behind her. "Just down the hill in the cove."

Edna surveyed the barren, dusty yard and the glistening water beyond. "I'll need some time to get stronger, but I think I'll be able to make it down there in a few days. Would that be alright?"

Penelope's solemn face brightened. "Yes, ma'am."

"Alright then. I'll see you soon."

Penelope smiled and nodded. Turning, she trotted around the corner of the house leaving a small cloud of dust in her wake. Her shout faded as she called to her dog. "C'mon, Bell!"

At that moment, the screen door opened and Glory Bee emerged from the kitchen. She pulled the rocking chair closer and sat down. "I know ya heard all that commotion, Miss Edna. An' I'm sorry but sometimes I just got ta say my piece."

Edna turned and slumped against the porch railing, drained from the morning's activity. "Glory Bee, I'm so sorry. If only I had somewhere else to go."

"Now don't ya' go worryin' yerself thinkin' ya need ta hightail it somewheres else. Lawd knows where ya'd go. An' yer too weak yet anyways. Docta' B comin' on Wednesday and you . . . well, you and he got ta have a conversation about yer . . . yer condition.

Islands of Women

Let me worry 'bout Miz Peck. Knowin' her like I do, she tends ta get on her high horse ev'ry now an' then. I'll calm her down, let her know she ain't makin' no sense."

Edna's head swam with countless questions and revelations but mostly from mounting hunger.

"Glory Bee, I think I need something to eat. Maybe I'll just sit at the kitchen table if you don't mind." She gripped the railing and pulled herself up.

"Goodness me, yes, ya ain't had no breakfast. C'mon. I got eggs and biscuits on the stove. Git on in there and sit down."

Ignoring Dr. Bartlett's advice to avoid fried food, Edna nibbled on a biscuit and a freshly fried egg. Between bites, she sipped from a glass of water. Glory Bee gave her a cool, damp towel, which she rubbed over her neck and face. The shaking and lightheadedness slowly began to dissipate.

"Glory Bee, . . ." Intending to bring up her conversation with Penelope, Edna's thoughts shifted gear. "That is such a lovely name. I can remember my grandmother shouting 'glory be' whenever something exciting or alarming happened on my grandparents' farm." She smiled at the memory.

Glory Bee chuckled as she rinsed soap suds off her hands and arms under the sink pump's spout. "Well, that's sort o' how I got my name."

After drying her hands, Glory Bee pulled out a kitchen chair and sat down. "Whole time my Mama was birthin' me, she was yellin' 'glory be! glory be!' at the top o' her lungs. Come time ta name me, she was still yellin' 'glory be!' So that's what the woman who tended my Mama wrote down. She just added another 'e' to 'be.' That's how I come ta be 'Glory Bee.'"

The two women laughed then grew solemn, the weight of unspoken explanations pressing on them both.

Edna toyed with the remaining food on her plate with her fork. "Penelope asked if I'm her Mama." She pushed the plate away and looked up at Glory Bee. "Why on earth would she think such a thing? I was speechless, and then . . . well, then I heard you speaking of Mrs. Peck's family. None of this is any of my business, of course. There's just so much I don't understand, so I told Penelope we'd have a talk maybe tomorrow." Edna shrugged. "I just don't know what to say to her . . . what to make of it."

Taking a deep breath, Glory Bee leaned back in her chair and crossed her arms over her ample bosom. "Well, far as Penelope's concerned, she's like a lost puppy tryin' ta find its Mama. I tell her over an' over her Mama ain't comin' back, that she . . . name was Adelaide . . . that she died in some kind o' accident . . . at least accordin' to Penelope's father, Jasper Worth.

Glory Bee snorted. "No tellin' what happened ta that poor woman. Only thing we know is Adelaide was with him and Penelope when they headed up the Suwannee back a few years ago. Once he and Penelope got back ta Pine Cove, he swore up and down when they all were comin' back and stopped along the river, Adelaide went down ta the water by herself and disappeared.

Sadness flooded Glory Bee's face. "Penelope's been livin' hand ta mouth ever since and longin' fer her Mama. All the while that snake Jasper comin' an' goin' like nothin' happened."

Edna scowled. "My goodness. That poor child. So she thinks I'm her long-lost mother?"

"Oh, she knows you ain't, but when she saw ya washed up on the beach and then in her Mama's dress, well, I guess it's more about *wantin'* ta make ya her Mama than *believin'* ya are."

Edna looked down at the dress and back up to Glory Bee. "This was Adelaide's dress?"

"Yes'm. All them clothes I gave ya this mornin' was Adelaide's. Penelope's been keepin' 'em in a hidin' place at her house down yonder in Hungry Bend. She wanted ya ta have'em." Glory Bee smiled and shook her head. "Like I said, Penelope knows ya ain't her Mama, but maybe seein' ya in her Mama's clothes helps undo the hurt a little."

The susurration of palm fronds high above the house, combined with the summer heat, exhaustion, and her sated appetite, lulled Edna into a trance-like stupor. So much to take in since leaving her bed a short time ago, she suddenly longed to get back to her room, to lie down and close her eyes, and most of all, to ponder all she had learned that morning.

Glory Bee pushed her chair from the table and stood up. "Come on now. Yer lookin' like ya might topple out o' that chair any minute. Let's git ya back up ta yer room."

Although grateful to be in bed again, with so much to think about and so many questions, sleep eluded Edna.

I understand a little better about Penelope now. But where are Jeremy and Priscilla? And why, as Glory Bee said, did Mrs. Peck drive them away? And who's Olivia?

Edna glanced at the pink and white striped dress hanging on the closet door's hook.

Adelaide's clothes. Hidden away. But why?

Edna shuddered, recalling Glory Bee's reference to Jasper as a 'snake'.

Slipping into that dreamy, subliminal state before sleep, Edna recalled the contents of the trunk on the other side of the room, recalled holding up the infant clothing embroidered with the letters "PPP." *Penelope, Priscilla, Peck.* Too drained to think how the names might be connected, she drifted off to sleep.

***

Voices from downstairs rising in pitch startled Edna awake. Tossing away the sheet, she swung her legs off the bed. Breathless from the midday heat, she stood slowly and swabbed her perspiring face and arms with water. Feeling somewhat refreshed, she opened her bedroom door wide enough to hear yet another heated exchange between Mrs. Peck and Glory Bee.

"The hotel? You ain't serious. First of all, she ain't goin' nowhere 'til Docta B says she's fit to." Glory Bee's voice rose with each word. "Besides that, just how do ya think she's gonna pay fer a room at the hotel?"

Mrs. Peck replied with her piercing voice, "She can work that out with Lloyd. Maybe wash dishes or clean rooms. All I know is she isn't staying here, so when Dr. Bartlett gets here Wednesday, I expect him to give her a clean bill of health. Either you tell him or I will."

With apparent disbelief, Glory Bee's voice rose. "She can wash dishes an' clean right here! How long since that silver been polished? How long since them baseboards been cleaned? I sure can't git down on these knees ta do it! An' ya want ta send away somebody who needs a place ta stay who can help out with chores that need doin'? Ya done it once and yer gonna do it again? It ain't right, Miz Peck. An' it don't make no sense."

"I have my reasons, Glory Bee, and I don't need to explain them to you," Mrs. Peck grumbled.

A loud bang, presumably of a kettle slammed on the stove, caused Edna to jump.

Glory Bee's anger rose even higher. "Ya jus' can't stand it, can ya? Can't stand thinkin' we almost . . . !"

"Enough, Glory Bee! Enough! I'm going upstairs!" Chair legs scraped across the kitchen floor.

Glory Bee shouted after Mrs. Peck's apparent departure from the kitchen. "Ain't like the whole town don't know!"

Edna gently closed the bedroom door, baffled that a housekeeper would speak to her employer this way and alarmed to think she was the cause of so much distress between them. She needed to go . . . but where?

Maybe the hotel, wherever it is?

Shaken and confused, feeling helpless and hollow as an echo, Edna dropped down on the edge of her bed. Choking back tears, she rested her elbows on her knees and buried her face in her hands.

Following a heavy tread of footsteps up the stairs, Mrs. Peck's bedroom door opened and slammed shut. Shortly after, at the sound of a light tap on her bedroom door, Edna took a deep breath and said, "Come in."

With her head lowered, Glory Bee entered carrying a freshly laundered and folded night dress, which she placed on the bureau. She turned to leave.

Edna stood up and walked toward Glory Bee. "Don't go . . . please."

Glory Bee faced the door, her hand gripping the knob. "I'll be mendin' that other dress and git it to ya."

"Glory Bee, look at me. Please. I don't want you to bother with that now. I know I'm causing a lot of trouble . . ." Edna sighed. "Please turn around and look at me. I don't want to talk to your back."

Glory Bee hesitated before turning to face Edna. With slumped shoulders and swollen eyes, she pulled a handkerchief from her apron pocket and wiped her nose.

"Oh, Glory Bee!" Unaccustomed to heightened compassion for anyone, Edna pondered how to comfort the distraught woman. Her impulse for a consoling embrace would be unseemly. Spotting the chair on the far side of the room, Edna pushed it close to her bed and pointed to its seat. "Sit down. Please."

Sniffling, Glory Bee sat down. Her frown and the crease between her eyes deepened as she stared at the window, the curtains hanging limp in the heat and humidity.

Edna sat down on the bed. Clasping her hands on her lap, she cleared her throat, which had tightened with emotion.

"Glory Bee, I can't stay here knowing the trouble it's causing. You and Mrs. Peck spoke of a hotel. I don't understand why Mrs. Peck doesn't want me here. The fact is she doesn't, so when Dr. Bartlett comes on Wednesday, I'll speak to him . . ."

Glory Bee's sudden outburst cut her off. "Ya can speak ta him alright, but ya ain't leavin' 'til he says yer well enough ta leave!

Exhaling a deep breath, Glory Bee paused before continuing, her voice now solemn. "Miss Edna, Miz Peck's a sick woman... sick in her body and sick in her soul. Her heart's hard as a rock from... well... it ain't 'cuz o' you." She pressed her lips together and closed her eyes for a moment. Her face revealed deep sadness when she opened them. "You explained all o' what brought ya here. Maybe time I explained things what make Miz Peck act like she does."

Edna suspected Mrs. Peck was not well physically, but what circumstances could possibly cause her to be so angry and so heartless? And how grievous could it be to cause this kind woman such distress?

She recalled Reverend Albright speaking to her the night of Mrs. Peck's Bible study. "There's a lot of history on this island, Edna. Family histories some folks struggle to deal with. Some have contributed to a lot of hurt among some folks. Birdie and Glory Bee... Tied together like..." He did not finish the sentence. Edna wondered then and wondered now.

Like what?

Glory Bee sat quietly toying with the fringe of her apron apparently pondering how to begin. At last, she looked up at Edna.

"That pad o' paper I got out o' the desk in the other room? That belonged ta Miz Peck's son, Jeremy." Glory Bee smiled. "Handsome boy... young man I should say. Oh, how he could draw and paint. Wanted ta have a' art studio here in Pine Cove.

Looking toward the window, she continued running her fingers along the edge of her apron. "An' oh, how his Mama doted on that boy. Boasted he'd be a famous artist. Had all kind o' ideas ta take his paintin's to a big city... Atlanta or maybe New York." She snorted and shook her head. "An' take his Mama with him, o' course. Miz Peck always had high hopes o' gettin' off o' this island."

Edna thought back to the ghostly images on the walls in the back bedroom.

Perhaps Jeremy's paintings? If so, where are they?

Glory Bee rested her clasped hands on her lap. "Things changed when Jeremy fell in love with a young woman name o' Olivia. Miz Peck was havin' nothin' ta do with him and Olivia courtin', but there wasn't nothin' gonna stop'em seein' one another.

Glory Bee looked at Edna and inhaled deeply. "And then Olivia got pregnant. She had a baby girl an' she an' Jeremy named her Priscilla." Shaking her head, she rolled her eyes skyward. "Lawd a mercy, when Miz Peck found out they'd run off and got married, I swear these here walls shook from all the yellin' and the shoutin'.

Tears welled in Glory Bee's eyes and trickled down her cheeks. "Thing is . . ." She took another deep breath and pulled her handkerchief out of her apron pocket. "Thing is, Miss Edna, Olivia is my daughter. And Priscilla ain't just Miz Peck's granddaughter. She's my granddaughter, too."

Chapter Twelve

Edna sat motionless on her bed and stared at Glory Bee's tear-streaked face. Before she could speak, she gulped water from the glass on her nightstand to relieve her sawdust-dry throat.

When it came, Edna's voice squeezed up from her lungs. "Glory Bee, I . . . I don't know what to say. I'm . . . I'm so sorry."

Glory Bee sniffed and blew her nose. Her deep breath quivered when she exhaled. "Since then, Miz Peck's oozed meanness like a festering sore. Once those kids snuck off and got married, she hopped right on board with the whole town wantin' ta run 'em off on a rail. She dismissed Olivia, who worked here, too. Jeremy lost his job workin' at the mill. Miz Peck threatened ta dismiss me, but she knew nobody else would put up with her."

Edna could not hide her astonishment. "So you choose to stay with her and to care for her."

The hint of a mischievous smile crossed Glory Bee's face. "Yes, Ma'am," she said, her voice firm with conviction. "I'm a reminder ever' day o' the hurt she caused. And I ain't gonna let her ferget it. Miz Peck can blame the law against mixed marriages in Florida all she wants, but she's gonna hafta' account fer her part . . . right along with the townsfolk . . . fer drivin' those kids away. An' I pray ever' day she wakes up and asks the Lawd fer fergiveness fer what she done ta our babies. Like I said, she's a sick woman."

Edna sensed rage burning deep in Glory Bee. "I don't know

how you do it . . . coming here every day looking after Mrs. Peck as if nothing happened. You have to be so angry."

Glory Bee snorted. "Oh, I'm angry alright . . . and a big part o' my anger is her actin' like nothin' happened . . . that she picked up her life like she and me never had no family. Long as she could pretend nothin' happened, all her friends and most o' the town went right along with it. Won't even talk about it. Drifted off just like the tide." Her eyes widened. "Ya know what though? Tides drift back in. Ever' day they come back, and sometimes they bring some unexpected surprises." She smiled. "Jus' like you."

Edna smiled back. She hesitated asking, afraid of causing Glory Bee any further distress . . . even more afraid of the answer. But she had to know. "Where are they?"

"Up north. Way up in New York. Some little place up in the country called Peterboro. Workin' on a farm up there.

Glory Bee peered at Edna. "'O' course ya know slavery was abolished a long time ago, but that don' mean nothin' fer Colored folks travelin' from place ta place 'specially in the South." She cocked her head. "Ever hear o' Jim Crow laws?"

Edna shook her head. "No, I haven't."

"Well, that's somethin' fer another time. All's I can say now is Tom and me worried ourselves near sick wonderin' if those kids were gonna make it to a safe place. Most states in the South don't take ta Coloreds and Whites mixin'. When we finally heard from Olivia, she said Jeremy would only travel by night 'til they got ta Pennsylvania. She and Priscilla hid in the back o' the buckboard durin' the day while he looked fer food an' water. Prayed ta Heaven that baby didn't cry and give 'em away."

Glory Bee's shoulders sagged as she rested against the chair back. Tears reappeared and she pulled out her handkerchief. "Prob'ly won't never see 'em agin."

So overwrought with the retelling of her loss, Glory Bee said she would be leaving for home earlier than usual. "There's some hard-boiled eggs, 'maters, and cold chicken in the larder. Oh, and biscuits, too. I'm sorry ya have ta look after yerself the rest o' t'day."

"Glory Bee, please don't worry about me. I'll do just fine." Edna wrestled with adequate words to soothe such raw pain. Customary expressions seemed to minimize Glory Bee's unthinkable heartbreak. Still, something was better than nothing, so she said again, "Glory Bee, I'm so very sorry."

"Oh, I'll be fine, too, Miss Edna. It's the re-rememberin' that cuts like a razor." She raised her skirt to the calf of her leg revealing a pink slash against her dark skin. "Like this ugly scar. Much as I try ta cover it up and fergit it's there, it won't never go away. Sooner 'er later, I just hafta' accept it's there and learn ta live with it."

Edna cringed looking at the jagged, poorly mended scar. "You didn't have stitches?"

Glory Bee shrugged her shoulders. "No docta' ta stitch it, so my Mam stanched it."

Edna grimaced. "How did it happen?"

"Fell on broken glass when I was a young'un." She lowered her skirt. "Cuts heal, ya know. Even like this one . . . down to the bone. It aches and twinges now and then ta let me know it ain't goin' nowhere. Just like my anger. Once I git back up ta Lizey's Hill, take a walk in the trees up there, I'll forget bein' angry again. Eats away the spirit.

She stood and placed the chair back against the far wall. "We haft'a get along, Miss Edna. Don't matter how many cuts and scars."

Hours later, lying on her bed, Edna stared at the ceiling shaken and stunned by Glory Bee's heartbreaking account. She could not ignore the glaring contrasts. Glory Bee grieved over the loss of a cherished daughter and a granddaughter she would never see grow up, of circumstances in which she and Tom had no choice but to let them go. Edna, however, chose to abandon her sons, her family. The irony of her own and Mrs. Peck's abandonment of those closest to them was not lost on her.

Her gaze drifted to the trunk against the far wall, filled with monogrammed infant clothing.

"Named her Priscilla Porter Peck," Glory Bee had explained. "If it was a boy, they'd o' named him Patrick Porter Peck." She shook her head. "Near killed Miz Peck havin' her last name on that grandbaby's birth certificate."

Searching for anything to say to ease Glory Bee's hurt, Edna had commented, "It's a beautiful name." She added, "But they left all the clothing here."

"Had ta leave a lot o' belongin's. Took a satchel o' clothes, enough food ta get'em up the road a piece, jug o' water. That's about it. Didn't have room fer all them clothes."

When Edna asked who made them, Glory Bee had replied, "Olivia and me made some before her time come. Few o' the church ladies made some others . . . 'til Miz Peck found out." Glory Bee had lowered her voice. "It don't matter. Priscilla's almost three years old. Already grown out of 'em anyways."

"And Jeremy's artwork?" Edna had asked. "Where did it all go?"

Glory Bee had raised her head and moaned. "I can still hear the crackle of them flames out yonder in the back yard." After several moments, as if still in disbelief, she spoke barely above a whisper. "Afta' Jeremy and Olivia left, Miz Peck burned 'em."

Edna now understood the basis for the tension between Glory Bee and Mrs. Peck. It was quite another thing to understand Mrs. Peck's total rejection of her only son . . . and her only grandchild. Embarrassment over his indiscretion and love for Olivia resulting in an illegal marriage surely, but what else could cause such angst?

She recalled Glory Bee's stormy remark, "Ya jus' can't stand thinkin' we almost . . ." Mrs. Peck's aversion to kinship with her housekeeper and of her grandchild, a Mulatto, bearing her last name undoubtedly ate away at her.

Poor Jeremy and Olivia. Love is such a powerful force. So resistant to judgment. How well I know. It's like a pervasive, insidious illness that alters rational thinking. How easily I succumbed to it with Robert. How blind I became to my own affliction.

In the sultry heat of the late afternoon, Edna dozed. When she woke, the setting sun was casting long shadows on the wall from the tree outside her window. She decided it was a good time to make her way downstairs for a bite to eat.

As she walked into the kitchen, Mrs. Peck emerged from the pantry carrying a plate overflowing with fried chicken and biscuits. The two women stopped in their tracks and stared at one another.

Mrs. Peck's initial icy stare quickly transformed to chagrin as she looked from Edna to her heaped plate. Lifting her head, the icy stare returned. With unmistaken insolence, she asked, "What do you want?"

Edna averted her eyes as best she could from the abundant portions of food and especially from Mrs. Peck's appearance. Perhaps she used the same moisturizing concoction of lard and aloe Glory Bee had prepared for Edna. In any case, Mrs. Peck had smeared the greasy layer thick as cake icing over her entire face. A towel-like turban wrapped her hair. Her white robe, frayed, stained, and yellowed with age, did little to camouflage her stout frame.

Aware she might be causing Mrs. Peck embarrassment, Edna quickly moved toward the pantry door. "I . . . I thought I'd get a bite before retiring." She mumbled, "Just an egg and some tomato slices."

Mrs. Peck appeared rooted where she stood holding her plate of food.

Edna attempted a smile before stepping into the pantry. When she emerged with her plate of food, Mrs. Peck was gone. In moments, the slamming of her bedroom door reverberated throughout the house.

Relieved to be alone and resistant to returning to her stifling bedroom, Edna decided to eat on the back porch. Sitting down on the top step, she set the plate on her lap. She pushed up her sleeves and unbuttoned the top two buttons of her dress allowing a refreshing breeze to cool her moist skin.

While nibbling her supper, she reflected on Mrs. Peck's cold demeanor. Equally or perhaps more concerning was an apparent lack of regard for her health . . . if her prodigious size and the amount of food she was consuming were any indication.

Glory Bee had affirmed in an earlier conversation, "I believe Miz Peck grieves and hides her grief in her eatin'. I can give her little portions when I'm here, but I can't stop her goin' ta the larder after I leave."

Edna considered that possibility.

I imagine people handle grief in different ways. If Mrs. Peck is grieving, maybe food is like a tonic for her. If her grief is driven by shame and embarrassment, rejection of her granddaughter, as well as a son whose choices proved too much, maybe her way to cope is through self-destruction. If this is true . . . well, I pity her.

She swatted a fly that had landed on her arm and mumbled, "I guess self-destruction can come in many forms."

Edna set her plate aside, stood up, and walked down the steps. Curiosity moved her to walk to the side of the house to the tree where Penelope had sat when they first met. She continued to the front yard and the front porch where she sat down on the top step. Evidence of the house's decay . . . of the rotting floorboards on the porch and the railing, of peeling paint, of water stains on the white clapboard siding suggesting a roof leak . . . supported Mrs. Peck's financial straits.

More reason for her disagreeable temperament. Yet she wears her arrogance and pride like an invisible mantle.

Pink clouds floated across the darkening sky from the setting sun as dim lights appeared in neighboring windows. Edna left the porch and walked to the street. Gazing down a fairly steep hill, more lights appeared in buildings suggesting the location of the town. Her legs, while still a bit weak, had become stronger over the past several days.

Perhaps the hotel is down there. I'll try for a walk tomorrow. Maybe Glory Bee will go with me . . . just in case.

Returning to the back porch, Edna sat down and wrapped her arms around her knees. Peeping insects of some kind, or maybe tree frogs, filled the air. Staring at the sky, she wondered what her sons might be doing at that moment.

If they remember me, do they miss me? How long before young children forget a parent altogether? Had anyone tried to search for me?

As Edna's body healed and her mind cleared, she delved deeper into her psyche, into all the reasons why she had chosen to commit the act that would have ended her life.

I was so desperate to . . . what? Forget? Forget what? That I was an adulteress? That I'd allowed myself to risk everything and then to be left alone with . . . She shook her head but could not clear the painful reminder.

If I'd managed to drown, I'd have taken not just my life but yours, too.

Light glowed across the yard from an upstairs window. Mrs. Peck had not yet retired for the night. Rising from the step, Edna went into the kitchen and closed the back door. Exhaustion had settled in, and her legs strained to climb the stairs. Grateful to be back in her room, she changed into her dressing gown. After splashing water on her face, she climbed into bed.

The breeze separated the curtain panels at the window now revealing a totally darkened sky unhindered by pollution of city lights such as she knew in New Orleans. Through the tree branches, a Cheshire cat moon smiled at her. Above it, a large bright star winked amid clusters of other heavenly bodies. So silent was the evening, she could hear the waves sloshing along the shore far below. Somewhere down there, Penelope stored her boat.

***

"I tol' ya, Miss Edna. Ya ain't ready ta be doin' no trekkin' up and down this hill yet." Glory Bee halted her agonizing trudge and looked up the hill. "Almos' there," she wheezed.

Edna's lungs felt ready to burst, and the muscles in her thighs were most certainly on fire. She could only manage a gasping "I'm sorry" as her legs gathered their last bit of strength.

At last, the exhausted women reached the top of the hill. Nearly stumbling to the front porch, they dropped onto a step and gulped air into their heaving lungs. Grateful for shade the front yard's massive oak tree provided against the blistering sun, they slowly regained normal breathing.

"C'mon, Miss Edna. Let's git ya inside and out o' this heat. Yer pale as the inside of a clam shell." With the help of the wobbly step railing, Glory Bee stood up. "C'mon now. We need water."

The heat and exertion of the laborious walk left Edna weak, nauseous, and unable to get her feet under her. She shook her head and slumped against the step behind her.

"I can't," she whispered. Edna looked up at Glory Bee's perspiring, concerned face. "I'll be fine. I . . . I just need to sit here a bit longer."

Without wasting a moment, Glory Bee heaved herself up the remaining steps and into the house, calling over her shoulder, "Be right back."

Edna wiped the moisture off her face with the hem of her dress and closed her eyes. Shaking her head, she mumbled, "How could I be so stupid? Dragging Glory Bee out in this heat, down that hill and back. And me barely recovered . . ."

"Who're ya talkin' to?"

Edna's eyes popped open to find a man standing in front of her. Tousled blond hair framed a pleasant, slightly unshaven face. Forcing herself to sit up, she adjusted her skirt and ran her fingers through her damp hair.

"Oh, well. I . . ." She took a deep breath. "Glory Bee and I . . . we just went for a walk and . . ."

"That's why I'm here. Heard from a couple of folks down below you two were struggling to get back up here." He glanced behind him then back to Edna. "A bit soon for ya to be tackling that hill, don't ya think?" He tilted his head and scowled causing tiny wrinkles around deep-set coal-dark eyes. "You alright? Where's Glory Bee?"

Puzzled by his comment and questioning, Edna nodded. "I'm fine. We're both fine. Glory Bee is in the house. I think she's bringing me a glass of water." She fidgeted with a button on the front of her dress.

Why does he keep looking at me like a bug under glass?

"Thanks for your concern. It was my idea to take that walk. A foolish one, of course." She attempted an apologetic smile. "I'm Edna by the way. I'm staying here for . . ."

He interrupted her. "Oh, I know who you are." He reached out to shake her hand. "I'm Nathan. Nathan Walker."

Edna hesitated before taking Nathan's hand in hers. Something about his smile that reached his eyes, though amiable, unnerved her a bit. He no doubt had heard about her rescue, but something else, as if he knew her, puzzled her even more.

"A pleasure to meet you, Nathan."

The screen door opened and Glory Bee stepped onto the porch holding a glass of water, which she handed to Edna. "Mr. Nathan, we ain't seen you in days. I expect ya been trollin'."

"Oh yeah. And repairing nets." Nathan grinned. "Always somethin' to keep a poor fisherman out o' trouble. Oh, and helping

Penelope mend her crab traps. That useless father of hers is never around. Least I can do for her."

As Edna drank, she vaguely recalled Glory Bee telling her of the fisherman, a "Mr. Nathan," who carried her from the beach to her room in Mrs. Peck's house. An awkward clumsiness overcame her, and her face flushed with embarrassment.

Of course, he knows who I am.

Edna handed the empty glass to Glory Bee. "If you'll both excuse me, I'd like to go to my room now." Using the railing, she slowly pulled herself to her feet and was instantly overcome by a wave of dizziness.

Nathan's quick reaction saved her from tumbling down the steps. "Whoa there!" he shouted as he grabbed Edna under her arms. "Sit yourself back down there before you hurt yourself. Glory Bee, let me help you get her inside. She doesn't look so good."

"Yessir. I just don't know if she can make it up those stairs."

"Well, I carried her up those stairs once. Guess I can do it again." Shrugging off Edna's protests, Nathan helped her stand and climb the two remaining steps to the porch. He then scooped her up as Glory Bee held open the door.

Annoyed, embarrassed, and extremely lightheaded, Edna could only accept the help. She simply was too weak to argue.

At the top of the stairs, Nathan set her on her feet but held onto her arms. "You're pretty wobbly, ma'am." He turned to Glory Bee. "I'll let you take over from here."

Edna mumbled, "Thank you, Nathan." She added sheepishly, "I guess I should say 'again.'" She could think only of removing her garments and bathing her hot skin with cool water. "I think I'll be fine now. I'd like to lie down and rest."

Glory Bee gripped her arm. "Oh, yer gonna get in that bed alright, and I'm gonna see to it. Docta' B comin' day after tomorra' an' he's expectin' ta see ya feelin' a whole lot better'n yer lookin' right now." She turned to Nathan. "Ya go on now, Mr. Nathan. And don't make yerself so scarce."

As Nathan trotted down the stairs, Glory Bee steered Edna into her room. After helping her undress and bathe, Edna gratefully crawled into bed.

"Glory Bee, I'm so sorry. I never should have expected you to take that walk in this heat. That hill! Going down didn't seem that difficult. But coming back up!" Edna took a deep breath.

Glory Bee chuckled. "Kind o' like life, ain't it? Fallin's easy. Takes every ounce o' pluck ta crawl back up." She opened the bedroom door. "Git some rest now, hear? I'll be back up later ta check on ya an' bring ya somethin' fer yer lunch."

Alone and staring at the ceiling, Edna mulled over Glory Bee's ingenuous comment. Her comparison of the disastrous walk to Edna's disastrous choices over the past year could not be more obvious.

Could my circumstances fall any lower? Penniless, homeless, with no idea what's to become of me?

She knew much of her despair came from exhaustion. Even so, she could not suppress giving in to emotion. Pressing her fists against her eyelids, she struggled against threatening tears.

How do I crawl out of this? What on earth will I do? I have to get to the hotel. Like Mrs. Peck said, I could work there. Earn enough to rent a room. I just have to get stronger. No more walks down the hill for a while.

Edna turned onto her side and faced the window. A sturdy breeze blowing into the stifling room helped to cool her damp skin. As she closed her eyes, ready to succumb to sleep, she was alerted to a sound outside . . . the crunch of wheels on gravel and the whinny of a horse.

Gingerly, Edna got out of bed and made it to the window in time to see Reverend Albright helping Mrs. Peck step out of a buggy. He reached to the rear seat and retrieved a cloth satchel, which looked to be quite heavy, and handed it to her.

The breeze carried Mrs. Peck's piercing voice to the window. "Thank you, Reverend. I'll see to it Glory Bee has these things polished in time for next Sunday's communion service."

"That's right generous of you, Birdie." With a tip of his black broad-brimmed hat, he added, "Hard to believe it'll be the start of September.

Picking up the reins, Reverend Albright gave them a shake. "Now don't forget to tell Miss Edna if she needs to get into town, I'll be glad to take her when I come back for that bag."

"Rest assured, Reverend," Mrs. Peck replied. "Good day."

"Good day, Birdie."

Edna left the window and crawled back into bed, heartened that she might have a way to get to the hotel after all.

I'll ask Glory Bee when Reverend Albright expects to be back. I need to be ready and to feel better. Maybe I can even help polish the communion items. Maybe Mrs. Peck won't have such ill will against me . . . for whatever her reasons.

Too inspired to sleep, Edna got up again and took the sketch pad and pencil from her bureau drawer. Her drawing of Penelope's face was nearly finished and needed only a few touches. She used a finger to smudge a bit of lead to highlight the cheekbones. She drew wispy lines away from the face giving the hair a windblown effect. She was holding the drawing at arm's length when Glory Bee tapped on her door and walked in.

"I had a feelin' ya prob'ly weren't sleepin'. Imagine ya heard Miz Peck and the Reverend outside yer window." She set a tray of food on the bureau and walked over to Edna. "Now what ya got there?"

Edna handed the sketch pad to Glory Bee. "It's been a while since I've done any artwork." She raised her eyebrows. "Do you recognize the face?"

Glory Bee stared at the drawing. "My, my, my. Why that's little Penelope." She looked at Edna and smiled. "Ya shore know how ta do a likeness, Miss Edna. This look jus' like her."

Edna stared at the drawing. "I guess it looks like her. I haven't seen that much of Penelope, so I had to try to recall her features.

A thought suddenly struck Edna, and she groped with how to make the suggestion. "If you'd like, well, if you would be willing to share your memory... you know, of how you remember Priscilla, I'd be happy to do a drawing of her."

From the stunned look on Glory Bee's face, Edna regretted the suggestion. Perhaps it was too painful, too difficult for Glory Bee to conjure up those last moments as her daughter and granddaughter rode out of Pine Cove forever.

"Glory Bee, I'm sorry. I just thought that maybe having a picture of..."

Glory Bee held her hands to her bosom, her eyes round as saucers.

"Oh, Miss Edna. Ya don't need ta be sorry. Oh my, yes. I'd be so grateful if ya would do that. All I got o' that baby is in my head, and that mem'ry is fadin' more'n more every day." She pulled a handkerchief from her apron pocket and dabbed her tearing eyes. "Ya jus' let me know when it feels right, an' I'll tell ya all I can about my grandbaby's face as best I know how."

Edna released her breath and smiled. "Very well then! When you have the time, we'll do it." Relieved her suggestion had not distressed Glory Bee, she turned to a clean page in the sketch book. "This will be Priscilla's page."

After Glory Bee left the room, Edna pulled the chair to the window and nibbled on her lunch. Pondering the events of the morning, she again thought back to Glory Bee's comparison of the hill with life's ups and downs.

I surely have many hurdles to overcome. At least now, if I can get work at the hotel, maybe I'll be able to begin climbing out of the hole I dug for myself.

Having finished her lunch, Edna placed the tray on the bureau. Lying down on her bed, she closed her eyes against the sultry afternoon.

Day after tomorrow. I must talk to Dr. Bartlett. I must tell him . . . And it won't hurt to ask if . . . if there are options. And what if there are? Could I . . . would I . . . ?

Resting her hands on her abdomen, Edna drifted into a restless slumber weighted with a burden of ambivalence too heavy to bear.

Chapter Thirteen

Edna buttoned her dress and re-pinned wisps of hair that had escaped her chignon during her physical.

Dr. Bartlett closed his medical bag, set it on the floor, and stood up from the chair he had placed at her bedside. Shoving his hands into his pants pockets, he peered out the open window at a brilliant sunshiny afternoon.

"Weather ought to start cooling down a might pretty soon least ways at night." Leaving the window, Dr. Bartlett walked slowly to the opposite side of the room and back again, his head lowered, his brow furrowed. At the bureau, he rested an elbow on its top. He seemed ready to speak, but something on the bureau caught his eye.

"What's this?" Dr. Bartlett picked up Edna's sketch pad and stared at the drawing. "Why, this is a picture of Penelope." He looked at Edna. "Isn't it?"

Relieved at least momentarily of the forthcoming conversation, Edna smiled. "Yes, it is. I'm glad you recognize her."

"This is awfully good." He came back to the chair carrying the pad and sat down. "You're an artist."

Edna shrugged. "I guess you could call me an artist. This is the first drawing I've done in a while, but I did paint regularly before . . . well, at one time.

She lowered her head then looked up again. "I love to paint.

My friends in New Orleans said some of my works were quite good. I just never felt confident enough to pursue the art world."

Dr. Bartlett continued staring at the drawing. "I see. Well, maybe you should work on that. If your works are anything like this one, I'd say you're an excellent artist and should consider it seriously."

He laid the pad on the bed and leaned forward, the creases between his eyes growing deeper. "Now, Edna, about your health. Your lungs appear clear and your skin looks much better. Keep applying aloe though to keep it moist. Aside from needing to regain your strength, I believe you're doing quite well. After all, it's been only a week since I last saw you."

Edna nodded. "It seems much longer ago than that." She smiled. "That walk Glory Bee and I took on Monday wasn't a good idea. I never should have attempted it."

Dr. Bartlett shook his head. "No, and Glory Bee neither. What in the world you two were thinking . . . in this heat and in your condition. Well, no apparent harm, but you know not to do it again, at least until this weather cools down."

Edna nodded. "Of course. I understand."

Outside the window, a cacophony of squawking gulls halted furthering the conversation. The birds finally flew off leaving a heavy silence in the room.

Edna looked down at her hands and toyed with her bare ring finger. She clasped her hands on her lap. After several moments, she looked up and took a deep breath.

"Dr. Bartlett, I don't know what to do. Surely you recognize the hopelessness of my situation. The simple truth is I have no means to support a child." She lowered her head again. "I can't even support myself."

The doctor nodded and raised his bushy eyebrows. "I do understand. But do you understand that what you're suggesting is illegal?" Without waiting for an answer, he continued. "I shouldn't even be having this discussion with you. Not only that but as I said earlier, to terminate this pregnancy would not only kill the fetus, it might kill you, too. Oh, there's ways to do it, of course, and a few, shall I say, persons of questionable repute in the area to do it. Concoctions have been around since ancient times. Pennyroyal, tansy, and the like. Pills, some pretty grizzly surgical procedures . . . some work, some don't. And like I said, some are often lethal to the mother as well as the fetus.

Dr. Bartlett stood and walked to the window again. Mopping his brow with a handkerchief he pulled from his pocket, he added, "Frankly, I don't think you have the strength to take the risk."

Edna sat quietly staring at the tear drops spotting her dress. Looking up, she sniffled and wiped her nose with her handkerchief. She raised her voice as more tears streamed down her face.

"I understand that! But don't you see the position I'm in? If I can't find work, if getting a job at the hotel doesn't work out, I have nowhere to go. No way to earn an income." She buried her face in her handkerchief then looked up at Dr. Bartlett with a tearful scowl. "Isn't it worse to bring a child into such a hopeless situation?"

Dr. Bartlett returned to the chair and sat down. "Edna, do you believe in God?" Raising his eyebrows, he stared into her eyes.

Edna wiped the tears from her face. "I beg your pardon?"

"I said, 'Do you believe in God?'"

Edna thought for a moment. She saw herself in the water, thrashing, screaming, crying, praying to God she would not drown. "I believe I do. When I thought I would drown, I called out to God to let me live. And I have prayed since coming here."

Dr. Bartlett chuckled. "I knew a couple of atheists who were on their death beds. They called out to God to save them, too. So, you aren't an atheist."

"My goodness. No!" She dabbed away more tears with her

handkerchief. "I mean . . . well, I do believe there's a higher power out there somewhere." She waved an arm above her head. "I guess I just never put much thought into what, or who, a higher power might look like."

Dr. Bartlett nodded and muttered, "You have lots of company." He rested against the chair back. "Edna, life isn't easy for most of us. I think you know that. We fall and we pick ourselves up and we fall again. The thing is no matter how many times we fall, something compels us to get up and try again. Ever think why that is? If you have faith in God . . . I mean real faith . . ." He patted his chest. "In here." He tapped the side of his head with his knuckles. "And up here. If you have real faith, which I believe you do, you can keep on falling as long as you at least try to pick yourself up and try again. Those who don't try again . . . well, it's the giving up that disappoints God. That's when He sees a lack of faith, a lack of belief that whatever we put in His hands, He will take care of.

Dr. Bartlett shook his head. "We may not have any idea how. The future may look grim and the solution may look as you say 'hopeless.' But I can tell you it isn't. You just have to believe that something is going to work out for you. Don't try to control it. Just trust and be ready for whatever He has in store for you."

Edna closed her eyes. A memory . . . of her and her sisters as young children playing games at their grandparents' farm . . . of running and falling, of cuts and bruises on knees and elbows, and of jumping up and running and crying to their grandmother. Once she took away the hurt and the grime, they were on their way again ready to tackle the next adventure. As Edna opened her eyes, a sense of calm . . . perhaps submission . . . overcame her.

Dr. Bartlett was staring at her face. "Have I lost you?"

Edna shook her head. "No. Not at all. The fact is I've pretty much known all along I couldn't go through with it. I guess I just needed to hear the cold, hard truth before I could be sure.

Whether I believe in God or not, I know if I terminated this life and perhaps even my own, then I haven't learned anything. And all my pleas to live while struggling to keep from drowning . . ." She shook her head again. "They would have been kind of pointless, don't you think?"

Dr. Bartlett stood and placed the chair back against the far wall before returning to pick up his medical bag. Standing before Edna, he said, "Yes. I do think. Do I also think you have some hurdles to jump? Sure, but I also know that anyone who could survive what you've survived can handle this hurdle.

At the door, the doctor turned to face Edna. "Day at a time, Edna. It's no coincidence you're here. Give yourself a chance to find out why. I'll be back next Wednesday, and we'll talk again. Meanwhile, you need to focus on regaining your strength. Get outside for some fresh air, but don't let me hear you've taken another jaunt down that hill." He raised his eyebrows. "Hear?"

Edna nodded. "Yes, I hear. And thank you, Dr. Bartlett. I mean it sincerely. Thank you."

The hour or so session left Edna wilted with relief. A difficult decision was made with no alternatives. She picked up the tablet from her bed and lay down. Voices downstairs slowly drifted away as she gave in to a deep sleep thankfully free of dreams. She awoke sometime later to a tap on her shoulder.

"Miss Edna?" Glory Bee was standing over her holding a tray of food. "Miss Edna, I'm sorry, but I didn't want ta just leave without bein' sure yer alright."

Edna blinked her eyes and forced herself to sit up. "Yes. Yes, of course. I'm just fine." From the shadows of the tree on the wall, she knew she had slept several hours. "I'm glad you woke me." She looked at the tray of food. "And I'm starving. Those greens look delicious."

"Oh, just some collards I cooked up with a little bacon. Tom's been gettin' some good vegetables in our garden now summer's almost over. He thinks sweet 'taters and corn ought ta be ready soon." She handed the tray to Edna. "That fried chicken's cold, but I figured ya'd be okay with that." Glory Bee crossed her arms and wandered to the window.

Munching on a forkful of greens, Edna looked up. "Glory Bee, are you alright?" She swallowed and set the fork on the plate.

"Oh yes. I'm fine. I was just thinkin' about that picture ya said ya'd make of Priscilla." She turned from the window. "I was wonderin'. Do ya think we could do that tomorra'? Maybe for a little while on the back porch?"

Edna smiled, delighted with the thought of a distraction from her current worries. "Oh, yes, by all means! Let's do!"

Glory Bee beamed. She raised herself up to her full height and headed toward the door. "Alright then! I'll see ya in the mornin'. I'll make a pitcher o' tea and maybe make some cornbread an' . . ." Opening the door, Glory Bee turned back to Edna, her face filled with happiness. "Miss Edna, ya done made my day. I'll see ya in the mornin'."

Edna bid a good evening to Glory Bee. After finishing her supper, she considered taking the tray to the kitchen but was in no mood to risk running into Mrs. Peck. Retrieving the sketch pad, which had slipped onto the floor while she slept, she flipped over the page of Penelope's face and stared at the blank page that would become Priscilla's.

She had not drawn or painted a baby's face before. Her thoughts went to Mary Cassatt's works, filled with cherubic children's faces.

She did this so easily . . . so naturally. I'm not sure . . . I'll simply have to rely on Glory Bee, on her description of her granddaughter, before I can even begin.

She set the pad on the bed and walked to the window. A setting sun against a vermilion sky cast a rosy glow in the bedroom. As a light breeze cooled her moist skin, she glanced across the room at the trunk. Edna had not opened it since first discovering the infant clothing folded neatly inside. Lifting the lid, she carefully removed each item and laid it on her bed. Many were monogrammed with the same "PPP" . . . bibs and blankets as well as clothing.

Toward the bottom of the trunk, she discovered a Bible covered with stains as if retrieved from a trash pile. She sat down on the chair, opened the cover, and read the printed inscription inside. "To our precious Priscilla Porter Peck. We will love you until our dying day. From your Granny and Granddaddy Glory Bee and Tom Porter." It was dated July 22, 1902. Edna turned the page where she found a partially completed family tree that included the Porters and Priscilla's parents, Jeremy and Olivia Peck.

Edna peered closer at another name, which had been crossed out. Although nearly illegible, by turning the Bible this way and that, she was able to make out the printed letters. The crossed-out name was that of Winifred Roberta Peck.

**

"That's what I remember Priscilla's face looks like. Same shape as that chicken egg. Same rosy pink color mixed in with that sandy brown shell.

Glory Bee reached into her apron pocket and pulled out a black button the shape of half a marble. "And this here button. It's her eyes. Big 'round as this button and just as black.

Leaning forward in the wicker rocker, she pointed to an oleander tree in the far back yard. "And that tree back yonder? Her mouth just as pink as them flowers.

Lifting her face skyward, Glory Bee smiled. "That's how I 'member my grandbaby."

Edna cupped the egg and the button in the palm of her hand. "She sounds like a beautiful child, Glory Bee. I know you must miss her terribly."

The sadness on Glory Bee's face was complete. "There ain't nothin' more I can say 'bout that. But I sure am glad ya can make a picture o' Priscilla I can hold onto."

Edna picked up the pencil. "You know I'll do the best I can, but until I have the proper tools to make Priscilla look like how you've described her, I can only sketch with this."

"Oh, I know it. But once I see her face ya make with that pencil, I can picture her colorin'.

Glory Bee hoisted herself out of the rocking chair. "I almost forgot. Her hair take after her Daddy's. Soft and smooth as butter. Color o' sweet molasses." She grew thoughtful. "It sparkled. Looked like gold thread runnin' through it. Eyes sparkled, too. Like she was born with a star in each one."

The screen door creaked as Glory Bee opened it. "No baby I ever saw look like my grandbaby, Miss Edna." She stepped into the kitchen and closed the door. Through the screen, she added, "I gotta make a cake fer Miz Peck's Bible study t'night, so I'll let ya be fer now. I thank ya again, Miss Edna."

As the egg and the black button grew warm in her hand, Edna looked beyond the yard at the profusion of delicate pink oleander petals.

If only I had some means of creating colors.

She allowed herself a few moments to reminisce over the paints, brushes, and myriad other art materials stacked on shelves in her studio in New Orleans. Shaking away the memory, she spoke to the pencil. "You will have to do for now."

Between sips of tea and nibbles of cornbread, Edna began the sketch of Priscilla. Before long, she grew tired of sitting on the hard porch steps. Placing aside the pad and pencil, she stood and stretched her back.

Strolling to the side of the house, Edna leaned against the tree outside her bedroom window savoring its shade. A hush had fallen over the town in the sultry midday heat. Even the gulls had ceased their cacophonous screeching. She considered going to her bedroom for a nap before resuming Priscilla's sketch, but the coolness of the tree's shade was too welcoming. Gazing at the twinkling sunlight through the leaves, she marveled at the enormity of space the sun's rays reached.

Etienne and Raoul were likely outside playing right now . . . perhaps with their puppy . . . a gift from their father.

At that moment, as she pictured her sons romping with their little dog, Edna heard a whimper then felt a nudge against her thigh. A panting Bell stared up at her, her tail wagging.

"Bell!" Edna knelt down and scratched the dog's head. "Where did you come from?" She looked around. "Where's Penelope?" Concerned over the child's whereabouts, knowing she and her dog were inseparable, Edna stood and walked toward the street. "Where is she, Bell?"

The dog barked and ran to the back yard. Puzzled, Edna followed. Beyond the oleander, a blond head appeared rising above the yard's gentle slope.

"Here Bell!" Penelope called.

"Penelope!" Edna hastened across the yard. Reaching out her arms, she hugged the frail child. "I'm so glad to see you."

"Mr. Nathan said you weren't feelin' too good so I should wait before comin' ta see ya. Him and me was fixin' my crab traps and school started up so I've been kind o' busy." She patted Bell's head. "Are you feelin' better?"

Edna nodded. "Oh yes. I'm feeling much better. Thank you for asking." She turned toward the back porch. "Would you like some cornbread? And maybe a glass of tea?"

Penelope's eyes grew wide and she grinned. "Yes ma'am. Teacher let us out a little early cuz o' the heat. I was gonna go paddle around in my boat, but I got hungry and, well, . . ." As her voice trailed off, she averted eye contact with Edna then looked back and smiled. "I sure would like some cornbread and tea."

When Edna returned from the kitchen with the glass of tea, Penelope was holding Edna's sketch pad.

"This is a picture of me." She looked up at Edna. "Did you draw this?"

Edna sat down on the step next to Penelope. "Yes. Do you like it?"

"It's really me." Penelope ran her fingers gently over the drawing. "Yes ma'am. I like it a lot." Without taking her eyes off the picture, she asked, "Can I have it?"

Edna set the glass of tea on the porch floor. "Here. Let me have the pad." Very gently, she tore out the page of Penelope's face and handed it to her. "Of course, you can have it."

Penelope beamed as she stared at her likeness. "Thank you, Miss Edna. I'm gonna show this to my teacher. Only thing we draw in school is birds and animals and stuff we see here on the island.

Setting the drawing aside, Penelope gulped a mouthful of tea. "I really like drawin' on my chalkboard at school. I tried ta draw a picture of Bell but it didn't look too good. I didn't have the right color chalk for her fur."

Edna raised her eyebrows. "You have colored chalk at school?"

Penelope swallowed a large bite of cornbread then wiped her mouth with the back of her hand. "Yes ma'am. Lots o' colors. Just not the right one for Bell's fur." She gulped another drink of tea. "Miss Edna, when are ya gonna feel like comin' ta see my boat?"

Edna pointed at the back yard. "Well, let's see. I think you said your boat is down that way . . . the way you came here today, right?"

"Yes ma'am. Not far. I been sittin' here longer than it took me ta get from there ta here."

Edna stifled a chuckle at the child's sense of time and distance. "It doesn't look as steep as the street. Maybe on Saturday. You won't have school then, right?"

Crumbs of cornbread stuck in the corners of Penelope's smile.

"Nope. No school on Saturday. I'll come and get ya in the mornin' when it's still a little cool. Will that be alright?"

"I think that will be perfect. I'll ask Glory Bee to pack us a little lunch to take with us. How does that sound?"

Penelope jumped up nearly toppling her glass of tea. Handing the glass to Edna, she quickly picked up the drawing. "Thank you for the tea and cornbread.

Penelope hopped down the steps, her blue dress billowing in a swift, light breeze. "And for my picture." With a skip, she trotted across the back yard. "I'll see you on Saturday, okay?" she called over her shoulder. "I'm glad you feel better! C'mon, Bell!"

Edna returned the leftover cornbread and the pitcher of tea to the pantry. A clatter of dishes coming from the dining room reminded her of Mrs. Peck's Bible study scheduled for that evening. Edna hurried to the dining room hoping she could be of help to Glory Bee. She stopped in her tracks at the doorway, startled to find Mrs. Peck hovered over the table muttering to herself as she counted out silverware.

"Oh! I . . . I thought I'd help Glory Bee prepare . . ."

Looking up, Mrs. Peck scowled and pursed her lips. "Glory Bee went home," she grumbled. "She wasn't feeling well." Fumbling with an arrangement of linen napkins, she continued as if talking to herself. "Of all days."

"Is she alright? I wish she had told me."

Mrs. Peck snorted. "She was fine this morning. Never said what was ailing her. Just that she didn't feel well."

Edna put aside for the moment her concern for Glory Bee and stepped further into the room. "I know this is an inconvenience. I'm quite good at preparing for parties and dinners. If you'll let me . . ."

Mrs. Peck cut her off with her sharp tone. "This is not a party or a dinner! It's . . . it's just dessert. Cake. That's all I do for Bible study. Just cake."

Edna stepped around the table and picked up a napkin. She unfolded it then slowly began to refold it. When finished, Edna set the napkin on the table. It was the perfect shape of a crown.

Mrs. Peck stared at the finished napkin then at the remaining napkins stacked on the table. "Well. I suppose." She raised her head and peered down her nose at Edna. "Alright. May as well make yourself useful. I need eight of those. And I need eight dessert plates. They're in the buffet. And I'll need eight water goblets for the tea." She pointed to the end of the room. "They're in the China cabinet.

Raising her skirt, Mrs. Peck headed for the hallway. "I'm expecting Reverend Albright and the ladies to be here at 6. Please have everything ready by then.

At the doorway, she turned to Edna. "The cake is in the larder. Don't set it out until after everyone has arrived." With that, Mrs. Peck disappeared up the stairs.

Edna pulled a chair from the table, sat down, and folded the remaining napkins into crowns, a technique she had learned from her mother. She gathered the dishes, goblets, silverware, and various other items on the table. An hour later, satisfied with the results of her arrangements, she retired to her room.

As Edna lay on her bed, she tried not to worry about Glory Bee.

She hadn't complained of any ailment in the past few days, and she appeared perfectly fine this morning. The heat, of course, can make anyone feel ill. But Glory Bee is so accustomed to Florida's summer weather, it seems unlikely that would cause her to abandon Mrs. Peck on an important day. Well, I'm just glad I could finally be of help.

Relishing the breeze drifting through the window, Edna succumbed to drowsiness. She slipped into a deep sleep only to be awakened by the sounds of voices and the clatter of dishes. Leaping out of bed, she splashed water on her face and slipped on the best of the two dresses and her shoes. She tucked loose strands of hair into her chignon, pinched her cheeks, and headed down the stairway.

A woman's voice carried up from the dining room. "Why, Birdie, the table is positively elegant! When did you learn to make your dinner napkins into crowns? And the candelabra!" Another voice chimed in: "Everything is just stunning, Birdie." More complimentary comments followed.

Edna slipped into the kitchen and retrieved Glory Bee's cake from the larder. Arriving at the doorway to the dining room, she took a deep breath. "Hello, ladies." Bobbing her head to Mrs. Peck, Edna placed the cake in the center of the table.

The dining room glowed with candlelight. On the buffet, a profusion of pink oleander blooms cascaded out of a crystal vase. The crown-folded napkins, gold-rimmed China dessert plates, and an aligned row of silver forks completed the elegant presentation.

Aware that all eyes were on her, Edna moved to the end of the table and proceeded to pour tea into crystal goblets from a matching pitcher.

When Reverend Albright arrived, he stopped and gazed at the table. "My goodness! How lovely! Birdie, is this some sort of celebration?"

Mrs. Peck came out from behind the table. "Good evening, Reverend. No, just . . . well, I thought it was time . . . actually, Glory Bee fell ill and went home and my . . . house guest . . ." Mrs. Peck nodded to Edna. "My house guest offered to take care of the table setting."

"Well, I hope Glory Bee is alright." Reverend Albright smiled at Edna. "Nice to see you looking so well, Edna. And you certainly have a flare for . . ." He waved his arm over the table. "This is beautiful." He picked up a napkin. "And you made these? Almost too pretty to unfold."

Edna set the pitcher of tea on the tray. "Thank you, Reverend. I was happy to help Mrs. Peck."

Attempting to overcome an awkward silence, Mrs. Peck picked up a knife. "Alright, ladies, please get a piece of cake and let's get started with our Bible study." Placing a slice of cake on a plate, she handed it to Reverend Albright. "Here you go, Reverend. I'm sure you're anxious to share your words with us."

* * *

"You weren't really sick yesterday, were you?" Edna handed Glory Bee a handful of dried silverware then reached for the freshly washed pitcher to dry. She followed Glory Bee into the dining room.

Glory Bee busied herself with putting away dishes and serving pieces. "Goodness me, Miss Edna, I don't know what yer talkin' about. I felt a chill come over me an' if I was catchin' somethin', I didn't want ta be spreadin' it ta nobody." She closed the buffet drawer and looked past Edna as she left the dining room.

In the kitchen, Glory Bee draped wet towels over a drying rack and sat down at the table. Picking up a knife, she cut into the remains of cake and placed a slice on each of two plates.

"Now, how 'bout ya sit down and tell me when ya expect Rev'rend Albright ta come fetch ya."

Edna pulled out a chair and sat down. "Well, since the silver items for the church were nowhere to be found, he has to come back before Sunday's service. He said he'd be here today, probably early afternoon."

Glory Bee placed a hand over her mouth. "Oh my. Guess I did forget ta set that bag out fer him ta take last night." She shook her head. "Forgetfulness is an awful thing, ain't it?" She slid a plate of cake across to Edna. "Now, tell me what ya think o' this mango cake."

Chapter Fourteen

The carpet bag of freshly polished chalice, communion tray, and candle holders clattered and rattled on Edna's lap as the buggy bounced down the hill towards town.

"Maybe I can help in the hotel's kitchen. Or maybe help with cleaning the rooms." Edna glanced at Reverend Albright's contemplative face. "I only know I can't stay at Mrs. Peck's any longer."

Reverend Albright nodded. "I understand, Edna, but you're still recovering. Don't you think it's a bit soon to take on an actual job? And what if there's nothing for you to do at the hotel? Have you thought of that?"

Edna had thought about those possibilities, but she would not let them discourage her. She learned from Glory Bee that the tourist season would begin soon. Surely Lloyd Blauers, the hotel's owner, could use another employee in some way.

Reverend Albright reined in the buggy in front of the hotel. As he walked around to Edna's side to help her climb down, the door to the hotel burst open. A burly, coverall-clad man stumbled forward. If not for grabbing one of the porch overhang's posts, he most surely would have fallen off the edge of the board walk.

Once righted, the man peered at Reverend Albright through glassy eyes and slurred through his spittle. "How do, Rev'ren'.

He shifted his gaze to Edna. "Who'er you? Squinting his eyes, he took in her full length and appeared to focus on her dress's large stain. Jabbing a pointed finger toward her, he snarled, "Where'd ya git that dress?"

Taken aback, with raised eyebrows, Edna turned to Reverend Albright.

The man brought his scruffy unshaven face closer to Edna and scowled. "Eh? I said where'd ya git it?"

Reverend Albright took Edna's arm and steered her around the man and onto the board walk.

The man reached out and grabbed Edna's other arm. "Hey! Ya deaf?! I'm askin' ya agin! Where'd ya git that dress?!"

Edna yanked her arm from his tight grip, appalled not only by the man's abrupt assault but from the stench radiating from his body as well.

Reverend Albright pulled Edna closer to him and moved toward the hotel's entryway. Pulling open the door, he faced the man and spoke firmly. "Go home, Jasper. I'll be down to your house and check in on you later. Now do as I say. Go home."

Inside the hotel's foyer, as Jasper continued his rant outside, Edna recalled Glory Bee's reference to Jasper Worth. Aghast, she turned to Reverend Albright. "That's Jasper Worth, Penelope's father?!"

"I'm afraid so. Let me ask you something. Did you by chance get that dress from Penelope?"

Edna nodded. "Yes. And another one. They belonged to Adelaide. I had nothing to wear. It was so kind of her to let me have her mother's . . .

Recalling all she had learned from Glory Bee about Penelope's father, Edna held a hand to her bosom. "That man could barely stand up, yet he recognized Adelaide's dress?!"

"It would appear so, Edna . . . and probably the stain more than the dress. It is quite prominent.

Reverend Albright cautioned. "For God's sake, stay away from him. As you can see, when he's in town, even at this hour of the day, he tends to spend his time at the bar until he either runs out of money or Lloyd's willingness to offer him credit. When he's this intoxicated, well . . ."

He led Edna toward the registration desk. "Just be careful. Best thing for everybody, especially Penelope, is when he leaves town. Now, let's find Lloyd. I've got to get you back up to Birdie's before I make the delivery to the church." He grimaced. "And I'd best get down to Hungry Bend. I want to be sure Jasper goes home."

***

Glory Bee untied her apron and hung it on the hook behind the kitchen door. "Mind what Rev'rend Albright says about that Jasper Worth. He's nothin' but trouble. An' him seein' ya in that dress." She shook her head. "My oh my."

Edna looked down at the front of Adelaide's dress and ran her hand over the stain. "He was so . . . so agitated looking at this stain . . . like he knew how it got there."

Picking up a sack of vegetable peelings to take home for the chickens, Glory Bee scowled. "My guess he knows right where it come from." Her scowl deepened. "Not sure we wanna' know." Opening the door, she called over her shoulder, "I'll see ya in the mornin' before ya leave fer yer boat ride. We'll pack ya a little picnic when I get here."

Before stepping off the porch, Glory Bee turned back. "I sure am glad ya ain't gonna be needed at the hotel for a little while anyways. Cleanin' rooms'll take it out o' ya, so it's good ya got more time to recover."

Edna nodded and smiled. "You're right, Glory Bee. But at least I have a place to go before too long. It really is a load off my mind. And don't worry about my encounter with Jasper. I intend to stay clear of him, so I'm sure I'll be fine."

Glory Bee lingered as if contemplating another remark.

Returning to the moment, she took a deep breath. "Alright then. Have a good evenin' and I'll see ya tomorra'."

Back in her bedroom, Edna undid her chignon and ran her fingers through her hair. She took off the dress and hung it on its hanger. Holding out the skirt, she ran her hand over the large, rust-colored stain suspecting the likelihood it was blood.

Pulling her gown over her head, she then stretched out on her bed. A late afternoon breeze blew the curtains at her window nearly straight out. Shadows of the tree limbs bobbed up and down on the wall. She was hungry but too fatigued to bother with eating. She would go down to the kitchen later for a bite.

Edna reflected on her visit to the hotel, of meeting Lloyd Blauers, Molly, the cook, and Annie, the maid. There would be work for Edna, as well as a room, but she would have to wait until business picked up.

Mr. Blauers estimated at least two to three weeks and suggested she stay in touch. "Tourists don't start showin' up much before middle o' September, so it's perty quiet around here 'til then."

The only person Edna did not meet was Jean Murphy, who lived and, according to Reverend Albright, "earned her way in her room."

"But why wouldn't she work as a maid or in the kitchen?" Edna had asked.

Reverend Albright had grown thoughtful. "Well, when Jean's husband died, she was left penniless. It was the offseason and Lloyd didn't have any work for her. Nobody around town did. With no money to return home to Ireland, she really didn't have much choice.

Closing the hotel door behind them, Reverend Albright had continued explaining Jean's situation. "Abandoned and in despair over her husband's and her child's deaths, well, . . ." He shook his head and contemplated. "We can only imagine her state of mind. Hopelessness can drive people to do things they might otherwise never dream of doing." He had glanced at Edna and shrugged his shoulders. "Jean had to do whatever it took to survive."

Edna turned onto her side and stared out the window.

That poor woman. Through no fault of her own, she's had to resort to . . .

Closing her eyes, Edna shook off a sudden thought.

God help me! Deliver me from becoming that desperate!

Her thoughts turned to the confrontation with Jasper Worth. Edna did not want to even consider what Penelope's life must be like with her father. Recollecting Glory Bee's explanation of Adelaide Worth's disappearance, Edna could now better understand the suspicion hovering over Jasper.

Across the hallway, Mrs. Peck's bedroom door opened. The stairs creaked under her weight. A short time later, her heavy footsteps returned as she climbed back up the stairs. Several seconds of labored breathing elapsed before her bedroom door opened then closed.

At that moment, Edna pitied Mrs. Peck. With her poor health and her uncompromising attitude toward her family, her life appeared quite grim. Edna could only ponder.

What will happen to her?

***

The small skiff bobbed in the surf. A thin, frayed rope extending from its bow was tied to a scraggly pine tree on shore. Most of the white paint along its sides had peeled away, exposing gray, weathered wood.

Edna clutched the basket of food Glory Bee had prepared for their picnic lunch that morning. "It's . . . quite a small boat, isn't it?"

Penelope untied the rope from the tree and tossed it into the boat. "You can git in now." She grabbed hold of the pointed bow and pulled the boat further onto the sand. "It's safe. Ya don't haf'ta be afraid and I promise ta be real careful."

The tiny boat barely bigger than the wood companionway door Edna had clung to in the sea did not look sturdy enough to hold one person let alone two and a dog. Edna's stomach and throat muscles contracted, and her legs began to feel quite weak.

"Penelope, I . . . I'm not sure . . ." The last thing she wanted to do was to disappoint Penelope, but she also could not ignore the trepidation of climbing into this wobbly little craft.

"Ya really don't haf'ta be afraid. We're just gonna go up here a little ways right along the shore." Penelope pointed further up the shoreline. "The water won't even be over our heads." She brushed away wind-blown hair from her eyes. "I just wanna show ya somethin'."

Edna set the basket on the sand. She shielded her eyes and looked out over the water. "We won't go way out, will we? What I mean is, you must understand . . ." She pointed toward the open sea. "I can't go there."

Penelope giggled and pointed to her boat. "I wouldn't go way out there in this."

Edna smiled. "Yes. Of course. I should have known you wouldn't do that."

Taking a deep breath, Edna lifted her skirt and stepped into the boat's bow. Gripping the sides and stepping over a tin pail, a net, and a couple of rusted tin cans, she made her way to a plank in the stern that served as a seat. Bell leaped in behind her, whimpering until she found a spot on the floor and lay down.

With the basket in one hand, Penelope gave the boat a shove with the other and hopped aboard. After handing the basket to Edna, she took hold of two weathered oars and dropped the paddles into the water. Once the boat floated from the shoreline, Penelope pushed and pulled the oars, turning the bow away from the channel leading out to open water.

Edna maintained her grip on the boat's sides as she struggled to overcome the memory of her hours tossing in the sea on a flimsy piece of wood.

Penelope stopped rowing and pointed toward the shore. "See that buildin' up there? That's my school."

Grateful for the distraction, Edna nodded. "I'd like to visit your school one day."

A few minutes later, Penelope pointed again to a cluster of clapboard cottages. "See those houses up yonder? That's where Glory Bee lives."

Lizey's Hill rose higher than both the school and the street where Mrs. Peck's house was located. Small weathered-gray houses, more like shanties or cabins, dotted the hill. Many roofs sagged under the weight of rusted tin. Smoke swirled out of a few chimneys, and the smell of burning wood drifted down the hillside.

The rise sloped and flattened to the shoreline again, only closed and untamed. Overgrown vines snaked around deformed and gnarled trees and shrubs. Short, stubby palms fanned out of the ground like giant hands reaching skyward. Brilliant white egrets stalked the narrow shoreline. Gulls and pelicans darted and dove into the water. Tiny crabs skittered sideways along the sand, disappearing into holes as they dodged scurrying sandpipers.

The overgrowth thickened even more when Penelope announced over her shoulder they would be getting out. She turned the bow toward the shore. As the boat's bottom scraped on the sand, Bell leaped over the side. Penelope followed and pulled the boat as far onto the shore as she could.

"Come on." She waved a thin arm at Edna. Bell had already disappeared into the bushes.

Edna sat for a moment and stared with discomfort at the thick growth. She slowly made her way forward and took hold of Penelope's extended hand. Stepping out of the boat, her feet instantly sank into wet sand. Her unease at foraging through a jungle was now replaced with possibly losing her shoes.

Dashing into some shrubs, Penelope returned with a board. She dropped it at Edna's feet.

Raising her skirt, Edna pulled each foot out of the wet sand and stepped onto the board. She resisted Penelope's tug on her arm to follow her. The dog's whimpers and barks had grown faint.

"It's all right. Bell an' me come here all the time."

Edna looked into Penelope's celestial blue eyes. Placing her trust in the child, she took a deep breath and stepped onto dry sand. "All right," she said, preparing herself to be consumed by vines and more overgrowth.

When Penelope pushed aside a curtain of green, Edna pressed her hands to her breast and exhaled a relieved and appreciative "Oh!"

Stepping through the opening, she found herself in the twilight of a sheltering pine grove. The shaded ground, carpeted in a thick layer of pine needles and cones, emitted a pungent resin aroma that surged into her nostrils.

Penelope had run ahead and called over her shoulder. "Come on!"

Edna stood spellbound for a moment, taking in the magical scene. To her left, two rabbits bounced into a clump of bushes. Overhead, birds chirped and sang among the thick pine branches that blocked out the heat and brightness of the sun. Among the tall columns of trees, Penelope's blue dress appeared as a trail of vapor. Following the child's footsteps and inhaling the wonderful pine scent, Edna had the sensation they were the only beings on earth.

Up ahead, Edna noticed a formation taking shape, a kind of foundation, about two feet tall. Approaching, she saw it consisted of stacks of various sized rocks.

Penelope busied herself inside the foundation, which came up to her waist. Shooing Bell away from an apparent entrance, she said, "Come inside. Ya can even sit down."

The foundation formed a square, each side measuring four or five feet in length. Four perfectly straight pine trees formed the corners. Two smaller trees acted as a door frame forming the entrance. In one corner, a log, set on its cut end, was anchored around the bottom with rocks, its top covered with pine needles.

"Ya have to sit on the needles so ya don't get sap on yer clothes," Penelope said.

Edna stepped over to the upturned log, spread her skirt, and sat down.

Penelope picked up a handful of pine needles, sprinkled them on the cut top of another log, and sat down. Then she stood, spread her dress like Edna had done, and sat down again.

Lifting her face to the tree tops, Edna closed her eyes and inhaled. She looked at Penelope and smiled. "This is the most beautiful house I've ever been in, Penelope."

Penelope's face beamed. "Nobody else knows this is here. It's a secret."

Edna nodded. "I understand. I promise never to tell anyone."

Penelope smiled again. "You look perty in Mama's dress." She hesitated then added, "You look a lot like her." She shrugged her shoulders. "Leastways how I remember her."

Edna recalled the shadowy image of her own mother, the struggle to put form to her features, to her eyes, her mouth, the way she wore her hair. From pictures, Edna knew she folded her hands on her lap and crossed her ankles the same way her mother had. Other characteristics of her mother were vague or unknown.

She looked at Penelope. "I lost my mother when I was a little girl, too."

Penelope's eyes grew wide. "Ya did? What happened to her?"

"She got very sick. I was too young to remember anything about her illness, but I was told there was nothing anyone could do." Edna smiled. "I barely remember her at all, but I did see pictures of her."

Penelope gazed steadily at Edna. "I don't have no pictures of my Mama." She tilted her head. "Do ya ever visit yer Mama's grave?"

Shaking her head, Edna said, "No, I'm afraid I don't. You see, her grave is far away and it wasn't easy to get there." She turned her palms up and shrugged. "I'm sad to say I haven't been there in a very long time."

Chewing on her lip, Penelope tilted her head seeming to ponder a thought. Her gaze shifted from Edna to another cluster of smaller pine trees not far from the rock walls.

After a few moments, she stood and looked at Edna with raised eyebrows. "Wanna see my Mama's grave?"

Chapter Fifteen

Small stones encircled the bases of two stick crosses spaced roughly two yards apart. Penelope pointed to one of the crosses. "That one's my Mama's." The dark, loose soil around it looked as if an animal had disturbed it in search of something it had buried.

Penelope pointed to the other cross. "That one's for Bell One." She turned to the dog sprawled on the ground behind them. "That's Bell, too." She held up two fingers and grinned. "Get it? Bell Two?"

Surprised, Edna asked, "You had another dog? What happened to Bell One?"

"Pa shot her." Penelope's voice revealed no emotion ... only the deadpan tone of acceptance.

Edna gulped, struggling to keep her voice calm "Why did your father shoot your dog?"

Penelope shrugged her shoulders. "He got mad 'cause she ate his food so he got his gun and she tried to run away and he shot her." She recited the words as if she had said them a thousand times.

Frightening images of Jasper Worth waving a gun blended with the encounter at the hotel the previous day. "Was your mother still ..." Edna bit her lip. "I mean ... how long ago did this happen?"

"Mama was there but she couldn't do nothin' about it. She helped me get Bell in my boat an' we brought her here." Penelope pulled on Edna's skirt and pointed to the lengthy stain. "That's Bell One's blood."

Edna ran her hand over the stiff and faded rust-colored stain. Words seemed pointless. Still, she could not let the moment go without offering some form of comfort.

"Penelope, I'm so sorry." She looked at Bell Two behind them. "But I'm glad you have another dog. Where did you get this one?"

"Found her roamin' around the school. Some o' the boys were bein' mean to her, so I took her. She don't look nothin' like Bell One, but she's a good dog just like Bell One was."

Staring at the dog's grave, Edna asked, "What did Bell One look like?"

"She was almost all black." Penelope raised her foot. "All o' her feet were white, an' she had white on her chest." She grinned. "She wagged her tail a lot, too. Jus' like ringin' a bell."

Edna stepped toward the other grave marker where the earth appeared disturbed. "Penelope, your mother isn't really buried here."

Gazing at the grave, Penelope shook her head. "I just like ta pretend this is where she is so I can come and talk to her."

Glory Bee said Adelaide died when Penelope was four or five years old. That would be about four years ago. Edna placed a hand on Penelope's shoulder and pulled the child to her side.

Penelope leaned into the curve of Edna's arm then looked up and opened her mouth wide. She pointed a finger inside.

"I lost a tooth this mornin'. I put it under my pillow with the other ones." Penelope scowled. "Glory Bee said tooth fairies know where all the pillows are with teeth under 'em and that one day, a tooth fairy will come and leave me a penny for every one of 'em.

Penelope slipped out of Edna's embrace. "I gotta check my crab traps. Wanna eat our lunch first?"

Staring at Penelope's hopeful face, Edna nodded as she tried to remember if Etienne or Raoul had lost any baby teeth.

* * *

Penelope assured Edna the boat ride to the crab traps would add but another twenty minutes to their excursion. She also said they would stay very close to the shoreline.

"The traps are real close to shore. We don't have ta row out very far ta get to 'em," Penelope promised.

Edna loosened her hold on the sides of the little boat and dipped one hand into the water. Tepid and crystal-clear, it rippled around her fingers. "We shouldn't stay too much longer. I don't want Glory Bee to worry."

Penelope nodded as her arms worked the oars. "This won't take long."

The overgrowth along the shore and the pine grove thinned to open marsh engulfing them in the stench of rotted seaweed. Around the shoreline's curve, three white buoys bobbed in the water.

Penelope pointed. "There they are!"

Rowing the boat close to one of the buoys, Penelope pulled the oars into the boat. She stretched over the edge allowing water to pour over the side flooding the littered floor. She grabbed the tether attached to the white ball and pulled, tipping the boat further toward the water's surface.

Convinced she would topple into the water, Edna gripped both sides of the boat and leaned heavily toward the high side.

Penelope shouted, "No, Miss Edna! Ya can't do that! It's how I git the traps!"

"I'm sorry," Edna muttered and reluctantly shifted her weight back to the center of the seat. She pulled a handkerchief from the dress pocket and mopped her perspiring face.

Penelope worked the tether until a wood cage rose to the surface. Round protruding eyes peered between the slats and wire holding the cage together. Balancing the trap on the edge of the boat with one hand, Penelope reached for the pail in the bottom of the boat with the other.

Gulls flew in closer from all directions, soaring and darting toward the boat, their screeches echoing off the water. Pelicans appeared out of nowhere and hovered overhead. The creatures inside the cage scurried from one end to the other as their hard claws clicked against the wood.

Edna had never seen a live crab this close. She cringed as she looked into their beady, bulging eyes. "They look terrified!" she exclaimed.

Penelope held out the pail. "Miss Edna, here! Put some water in this and hold it over here so I can dump these crabs in it."

Grabbing the pail, Edna dunked it into the water filling it to its brim.

"That's too full. Ya gotta dump some out or the crabs'll float out of it."

Edna poured some of the water overboard and held the pail out for Penelope. "Here you go."

"Jus' hold it right there while I slide 'em in."

"Um. Alright." Edna scooched forward on the plank and held the pail as steady as she could while the boat rocked side to side.

As Penelope tipped the trap, one crab clamped a claw onto the other, and they slid as one into the pail. "Okay. Put the lid on it."

Edna pressed the lid on the pail and set it on the boat's floor. She shuddered at the sound of the trapped crabs clawing and scratching inside the pail. "Poor things," she muttered.

After shoving the trap back into the water, Penelope picked up the oars again and maneuvered the skiff to the other buoys. Aside from chicken necks tied to the traps, both were empty.

"There's usually more crabs than that, but I emptied the traps yesterday. I took 'em to Molly and traded 'em for more chicken necks. They make good bait."

Edna scowled. "That's it? Chicken necks . . . for the crabs you give to Molly?"

"Oh, she let me have a bowl o' soup, too."

"Oh, well, good. I'm glad you got something to eat, too." Edna hoped Penelope did not detect her note of sarcasm.

"And she gave Bell a big bone that still had a little meat on it. Boy, did Bell tear into that bone."

Edna recalled Etienne and Raoul's little dog begging for morsels. "Dogs do like chewing on bones. Are these all the traps you have?"

"Yeah, but they ain't mine. They're Mr. Nathan's. He lets me use 'em." Penelope bobbed her head toward the open water. "He's got lots more out yonder, but he don't want me goin' out there."

"Mr. Nathan sounds like a very wise man."

Penelope's eyes grew round as blue pools. "He knows everything! 'Specially about fishin'." She dropped the oars into the water and began to row. "Do yer little boys fish?"

Ashamed to admit she did not know if her sons ever fished, Edna's face warmed.

What else don't I know about my sons?

"Well, certainly not like you do." She changed the subject. "What will you do with these crabs?"

Penelope grew thoughtful. "Two ain't enough for Molly to do anything with. I'll give 'em to Glory Bee." She smiled. "Fer fixin' our picnic."

Water gurgled behind the boat followed by a snort and a gush. Bell sprang to her feet, and in the skirmish, toppled the pail of water sending the crabs scurrying across the floor of the boat.

Edna screamed and lifted her feet to avoid the escaped crabs. She turned so quickly to see what the sound was coming from behind the boat, she nearly slipped off the wood bench.

Penelope pulled in the oars and dove for the crabs and the pail. Amid Bell's barks and the boat wobbling as if perched atop a rock, she managed to recapture the crabs. She refilled the pail and shouted at Bell to stop barking.

Islands of Women

Edna regained her balance and stared at the swirling water off the stern. Within seconds, a gray hairy cow-like snout rose into the swirl. Two silver-dollar size nostrils dilated and snorted again expelling water into the air before disappearing below the surface. Another smaller snout appeared, snorted, and sank.

Edna screamed again as she stared in horror at the water.

Penelope had regained the oars and quieted the dog. She threw back her head and laughed. "Miss Edna, they're just manatees!" she shouted. Her laugh turned into a rippling giggle.

Still clutching the boat's sides, Edna continued to stare at the swirls. "Will they turn us over?"

Once again, the nostrils surfaced and snorted.

Edna withered at the image of a long, leathery tail, glistening sharp teeth, and chomping jaws charging out of the water and toppling the flimsy boat.

"Oh dear! Penelope, row faster!"

Penelope had grown weak with laughter. "They ain't gonna turn us over, Miss Edna. They have ta come up fer air every once in a while just like we do."

"Manatees don't have teeth?" Edna's knuckles had grown white as she gripped the boat and stared at the water.

"Oh, they might have some teeth, but they don't eat people. Not like 'gators an' sharks. They got tons o' teeth! Gators'll drag people, animals, all kinds o' stuff under water to get soft and then eat 'em."

Could that be what happened to Adelaide in the river?

Edna shuddered. She shook off the grizzly thought.

Penelope pointed to the smallest sea cow as it floated away with its mother. "See that one? It's a baby. It's prob'ly still nursin' its mother. When they get big, they eat plants and stuff that grows in the water."

Edna relaxed on the bench as the surf slapped the side of the boat. She searched the water's surface for any signs of the manatees, but they were gone. *'They have to come up for air every once in awhile just like we do . . .'* She inhaled and filled her lungs with the salty air.

Watching anxiously for the familiar spot on the shore where she and Penelope began their journey, Edna reflected on the morning . . . on Penelope's secret place, a lovely sanctuary for her to escape to, and on her mother's and Bell One's graves. She glanced down at the blood stain on Adelaide's dress and shuddered at the horror Penelope must have felt when her father shot her dog. For Edna, the cruelty was unimaginable.

The morning and all she had learned had tired Edna. She longed for the quiet of her room and a nap.

* * *

The next three weeks rolled into September, and life became a routine for Edna. Dr. Bartlett arrived on Wednesdays to check on her recovery and the progress with her pregnancy. Every Thursday evening, she helped Glory Bee prepare the dining room for Mrs. Peck's Bible study. Every Saturday, Penelope and Edna rowed to the pine grove with a picnic lunch and to check the crab traps. And every day, Edna and Mrs. Peck did their best to avoid running into one another.

Meanwhile, as Edna began to show signs of an expanding waistline, she worried that she might not ever hear from Lloyd Blauers about a job at the hotel.

"Don't you worry, Miss Edna. Lloyd's a good man and true ta his word. Season's takin' a slow start this year. You be hearin' soon." Glory Bee handed Edna an apron. "Here. Put this on. Undo those two buttons 'round yer middle and nobody'll know the difference.

Glory Bee's eyes opened wide. "Come ta think of it, once ya start at the hotel, you'll be wearin' a uniform with a apron while yer workin', so won't nobody know what's under it." Glory Bee grinned. "If anybody says anything, tell 'em Molly's cookin's so good, ya just can't stay out o' the kitchen."

On the second Wednesday in September, Dr. Bartlett arrived with news. "Lloyd Blauers has a job for you, Edna. I can deliver you to the hotel today. How soon can you be ready?"

Torn between gladness and trepidation of moving to the hotel and beginning a new and unfamiliar job, Edna looked at Glory Bee then back to Dr. Bartlett.

"Today? I . . . I guess I can." She clasped her hands to her bosom and smiled. "Yes! Of course, I can!"

Dr. Bartlett continued with a cautionary tone. "You're in good health, Edna, so I don't see a reason you can't manage whatever Lloyd has for you. You do, however, have to be careful with overdoing it." He headed for the stairway. "Go collect your belongings. After I see to Birdie, I'll get you to the hotel."

With so few possessions, Edna was ready and waiting when Dr. Bartlett came downstairs. She sat at the kitchen table with a small carry bag on her lap.

Glory Bee assured Edna, "Miz Peck won't never miss that bag. Been collectin' dust fer years."

Dr. Bartlett placed his medical bag on the floor and turned to Glory Bee. "Mrs. Peck is feeling poorly. Her heart rate isn't good. After I take Edna to the hotel, I'm going to stop at the church and tell Reverend Albright he needs to cancel the Bible study tomorrow night. Birdie's having a fit, of course, but she's got no business even coming down the stairs."

Picking up his bag, he turned to Edna. "Looks like you're ready to go." At the door, he looked back at Glory Bee. "I know this puts a strain on you, Glory Bee. You be careful going up and down those stairs, hear?"

Glory Bee bobbed her head as Dr. Bartlett left. She turned to Edna. "I sure am gonna' miss ya, Miss Edna."

"Glory Bee, I don't know how to . . ."

Waving a hand, Glory Bee shook her head. "Don't be worryin' 'bout nothin', hear? Ya helped me in more ways than ya might think." She smiled. "That picture ya did fer me of Priscilla is all the thanks I need."

Holding open the back door, Glory Bee swatted at the never-ending flies as Edna stepped out to the back porch. "An' ya ain't seen the last o' me so don't go thinkin' jus' 'cause yer down that hill I can't get down there, too.

Swatting more flies, Glory Bee closed the door. Speaking through the screen, she said in her firmest voice, "Now go on. Once the season starts, it gits busy real quick in that hotel, and Lloyd's waitin' on ya."

Edna scurried down the porch steps. Before disappearing around the corner of the house, she shouted back to Glory Bee, "If you see Penelope, be sure to tell her where I am!"

Once aboard Dr. Bartlett's carriage, Edna looked back at Birdie Peck's house. Glory Bee would already be heading up the stairs to check on her mistress.

At Dr. Bartlett's slap of the reins on Bessie's behind, Edna faced forward and stared at the descent toward town. She clutched the bag containing her scant belongings closer to her. During the entire ride, she prayed that whatever the job Lloyd Blauers had in store for her, she could handle it. Most of all, she prayed she would not run into Jasper Worth.

Chapter Sixteen

The hotel's long-serving housemaid, Annie Blevins, tossed a wadded sheet onto the bed. The scowl on her face deepened years of wrinkles. She ran her fingers through steel-gray, closely sheared curls then perched her fists on generous hips. The jowls along her jaw line waggled when she spoke.

"Now do it again. I gotta' think the third time you'll figure out how to do those corners."

Once again, Edna spread the sheet over the double bed. She tucked it in at the foot and followed Annie's instructions for the corners. Perspiration trickled down the sides of her face. A growing ache ground at the base of her spine.

Straightening and arching her back, Edna looked at Annie with raised eyebrows. "Is this alright?"

Her fists still perched on her hips, Annie offered a slight nod. "It'll hafta' do. Boat's due at the dock soon so guests'll be arrivin' before long. Now do the same thing with that blanket and put the bedspread on. Fluff up those pillows as if this was a guest's bedroom and not yours.

At the door, Annie turned to Edna. "We got three rooms ta get ready so get into your uniform. I'll be in the room at the end of the hallway." She exited the room slamming the door behind her.

After making her bed, Edna changed into her uniform, a black dress and white apron. In the bathroom, she splashed her face with water. She looked longingly at the bath tub. Back in the bedroom, she surveyed her appearance in the mirror, grateful the apron camouflaged her thickening waistline.

Taking a deep breath, Edna opened the door and made her way down the dimly lit hallway. As she approached the last guest room, she recognized Annie's agitated voice.

"Lord'a mercy, Lloyd. That woman don't even know how ta make a bed! And you expect me to train her with no extra pay? It ain't right, Lloyd, and you know it."

"Annie, I don't think it's gonna take her long. Doc said she's been doin' household chores up at Birdie's. Just 'cause she had to remake that bed a couple times don't mean . . .

Lloyd turned toward the shadow falling across the entrance to the room. "Edna, come in and give Annie a hand."

Ignoring Annie's mumbles, Edna scooped up a stack of towels from the bed and took them into the bathroom. Returning to the bedroom, she picked up a cloth and began dusting the dresser, desk, and night stand. When she finished, she turned to Annie and Lloyd.

"If you'll tell me where to find clean linens and direct me to the other two rooms, I'll start making beds."

Annie pointed at the door. "Go out that door and turn left. Room next ta this one already has the linens in there. I'll be there after I finish up in here.

As soon as Edna left, Annie turned to Lloyd. "How much you payin' her on top of a room and meals?"

Lloyd pursed his lips. "All she's gettin' fer now is a room and meals. It ain't like it's one of our best rooms or that the hotel has maids' quarters.

At the door, Lloyd turned back to Annie. "What I normally charge for that room plus the puny little bit she eats don't come close to what I'm payin' you. When business picks up, if I need that room, I'll hafta' think about it. Fer now, be glad ya got some help." He left leaving a chagrined Annie staring at the closed door.

The afternoon wore on as Edna learned the routine of readying rooms for guests all the while reflecting on her former life. Never had she made a bed, even her own, at her home in New Orleans. Never had she given a thought to the care her staff took for her every need. She pondered the guests arriving at the hotel soon, weary from their trip, all of them anticipating the comfort of their rooms ... just as she and Léonce expected during their various travels.

"O' course when they leave, all the sheets and towels have ta' get washed," Annie said as she and Edna left the third guest room. She headed toward the stairway, Edna close behind. "I'll show ya that when the time comes. Right now, I'm leavin' fer home. A lot o' chatter down there, so folks'll be comin' up to their rooms. Then they'll go back down fer their dinner. Ya might want ta get somethin' ta take to yer room before the kitchen gets too busy."

Edna placed a hand on the woman's arm. "Thank you, Annie ... for all you're doing to help me. I ... I realize I have a lot to learn. I hope I've proven my willingness to do my share."

Annie peered at Edna's hand ... free of vein lines, wrinkles, and liver spots ... then to the young woman's unblemished, wrinkle-free face. She pulled away her arm and grumbled. "Ya did alright t'day.

Fighting the urge to bring up Edna's employment arrangement, Annie turned toward the stairway and called over her shoulder. "I'll see ya tomorrow mornin'. Yer shift starts at seven so no dilly-dallyin'."

Edna called after her. "I'll be ready. I ... I'll see if I can locate a clock."

Annie stopped mid stride and turned to Edna. "Good luck findin' one." With that, she stomped down the stairs.

Back in her room, Edna stripped off her uniform and opened

the window. A slight breeze cooled her warm, damp skin. Tempted as she was to take a bath, she decided instead to take Annie's advice and get something to eat. She pulled the pink dress over her head followed by Glory Bee's apron.

In the hallway, Edna walked close to the wall dodging weary guests toting travel bags to their rooms. Approaching the stairway, a door suddenly swung open in front of her and a woman stepped out of the room. The two collided, each grabbing hold of the other's arms. Collecting themselves, they both uttered, "I'm so sorry." It took a moment for the two to release one another and to overcome their awkward embrace.

Edna looked into a face framed with auburn hair. Recalling her conversation with Dr. Bartlett, she suspected this woman most likely was Jean Murphy.

She attempted a smile. "Hello. I'm Edna. I'm . . . working here now." She pointed down the hallway. "My room is down there."

The woman's bottle-green eyes round as coins scanned Edna's attire from head to toe. She raised eyebrows equally as red as her hair. "Aye?" She took hold of the edge of Edna's apron then let it go. "Workin' here ya say." She snorted. "An' what might ye be doin' here . . . all prettied up in yer pink dress?"

A distinct brogue convinced Edna this woman was indeed Jean Murphy, the Irish woman who Dr. Bartlett said earned her keep in her room. She detected a note of wariness in Jean's voice and was struck with a horrific thought.

Dear God, does she think I'm here to compete with her?

"Oh, I'll be cleaning rooms with Annie." She felt compelled to add, "That's all. Just cleaning . . . and preparing rooms for guests."

Another awkward moment passed as Jean continued to stare at Edna. At last, she smiled and spoke. "Aye, well. We all hafta' work, don't we now?" She held out her hand. "I'm Jean. Jean Murphy. Pleased ta meet ye, Edna." She glanced toward the stairway. "Now if ye were headin' to the kitchen fer yer supper, do ye mind if I join ye?"

"I'm happy to meet you, Jean. Yes. Please lead the way." She smiled. "It's been a long day and I'm quite hungry."

Jean hesitated before heading to the stairway. "Long day, eh?"

The irony of Jean's question was not lost on Edna . . . that Jean likely experienced some very long nights. Housekeeping seemed much more appealing when considering a very unappealing alternative.

Noise from the direction of the bar increased as the women descended the stairs.

"Sounds like a bloody fracas," Jean said.

Shattering glass added to the escalation of voices. Chair legs scraped across the floor.

Lloyd's voice bellowed, "Out, Jasper! I've warned ya fer the last time! Now get out!"

Having reached the main floor, Jean and Edna stepped out of the way as Jasper stumbled into the hallway.

"Well, hello ladies!" Spittle drooled from Jasper's nearly toothless mouth. He leaned against the door jamb. "Nice evenin' fer a walk. What'cha say?"

Peering at the women, he squinted his eyes at Edna. "I see'd you with Doc t'other day." He leaned closer, his gaze spanning her face to her feet.

Jean took Edna's arm. "Another time, Jasper. Come on, Edna. Let's go."

"Edna, huh? Pretty pink dress ya got there, Edna. Where'd ya git that dress?" Jasper followed the women as they headed toward the kitchen.

"You hear me?!" Jasper growled. "I said where'd ya git that dress?"

Edna scurried behind Jean and into the kitchen, her stomach in knots and her heart pounding. Holding her hand to her chest, she exhaled a deep breath. "Dear Lord."

In the distance, Lloyd once more ordered Jasper to leave.

Tilting her head, Jean scowled at Edna. "Wha' in bloody hell was that all about? Why's he askin' about yer dress?"

Edna shook her head and closed her eyes. She took another deep breath. "This dress and the only other one I wear belonged to his wife."

Jean snorted. "Wha' man notices a woman's dress? And wha' in the world are ye' doin' with Adelaide's dresses anyway?"

Edna shrugged her shoulders. "The other one . . . the one I was wearing when I came to the hotel to see about work has a huge stain. He recognized it. Penelope . . . Do you know his daughter, Penelope?"

"Ev'r'body knows Penelope. Sweet little ragamuffin."

"Well, she brought me the dresses and some other items that belonged to Adelaide because I had nothing . . ."

Jean's eyes widened. "Yer the woman Doc told me about, the one near drowned . . . stayin' up at ol' lady Peck's!"

Edna nodded. "I guess things spread quickly here. Never mind for now. Let's get a bite. I need something to settle my stomach."

Thanking Molly for their bowls of steaming fish stew, the two women hastened upstairs. At Jean's door, they both began speaking at once then laughed.

"You first," Jean said.

"Well, I was going to offer to have you join me in my room, but quite honestly, I think I'd best get some rest. Annie said tomorrow will be a much busier day. But if you'd like . . ."

Jean was already shaking her head. She looked at the floor then back to face Edna. "I canna' join ye anyway, Edna. Ye see, my 'day' is just beginnin'. Ye may as well know . . ."

Edna rested her hand on Jean's arm. "You don't have to explain anything to me, Jean. I . . . I understand." She smiled. "Like you said, 'we all hafta' work, don't we now'."

Jean's somber gaze seemed to extend far beyond the hotel and the island. She shifted from wherever her mind had taken her into a feeble smile.

"Aye. Things do spread quickly here. It's a small island." Placing her hand on the door knob, Jean looked at Edna. "It ain't every night. Go get some rest. We'll have ourselves a bit of a . . . a chit-chat soon." Jean grinned. "Molly says ye call it that." Turning the knob, Jean added with a knowing look, "I'm thinkin' ye got a story ta tell jus' like me."

A slow smile crossed Edna's face and she nodded. "Good night, Jean."

A few steps down the hallway, Edna turned back and caught Jean before she closed her door. "Jean, wait. You don't by chance have a clock I could borrow, do you? I'm afraid I'll oversleep."

"Aye," Jean said, disappearing into her room. She returned with a small windup clock. "It'll jangle yer nerves when the alarm goes off."

Edna laughed. "I don't think my nerves could be more jangled than they already are. Thanks, Jean."

Once in her room, Edna ate her supper. A hot bath eased her tense muscles and calmed her mind. She pulled on her dressing gown and sat on the edge of the bed. Fighting weariness over the day's events, she glanced at the clock that ticked its mesmerizing seconds to seven-thirty.

It's too early to go to bed.

With a groan, she stood and arched her back. At the desk, she sat down, opened the drawer, and placed her drawing materials in front of her. Poising the pencil over a blank page, she outlined details of Jean's face. Using the few pieces of chalk Penelope had brought her from school, she blended red and brown for Jean's hair and eyebrows. She smudged red chalk for her cheeks and lips giving them a pink tinge. The sage green chalk deepened Jean's penetrating eyes. Tiny flecks of brown highlighted her freckles against her rosy complexion.

As nighttime descended, Edna worked by the desk's lamplight. Deep in thought and in the detail of Jean's face, she lost track of time. Not until the chatter and footsteps of guests coming and going in the hallway had diminished did she glance at the clock.

"Dear me," she mumbled. "Ten-thirty!"

Dissatisfied with the finished drawing that did little to capture Jean's far-off, sad expression, Edna placed the sketch book back in the desk drawer.

I made her look like a school girl. How will I define that forlorn look I saw in her face today? Poor Jean. She's lost everything.

At her window, looking at the star-glistened night sky, Edna thought of Glory Bee and the painful loss of her daughter, Olivia, and granddaughter, little Priscilla; of Jean's heartbreaking loss of her daughter, of her husband . . . even her faraway home. Though by choice, Birdie Peck as well lost her entire family. Mostly, Edna thought of Penelope.

What does she do when her father comes home in the condition he was in tonight? If she leaves, where does she go? Surely not the pine grove at night.

Edna pondered when she would have time to go to the pine grove with Penelope now that she was working. Her window faced the south side of town . . . toward the area Glory Bee called Hungry Bend. Penelope . . . and Jasper . . . lived there.

I can't abandon Penelope. It's too soon to ask when I might have time off and if it might be a Saturday or Sunday. Surely those days are likely the busiest. But I must find a way to spend some time with her.

Tired as she was, it was too much to grapple with, to consider the ugliness of the child's existence. The ticking clock on the dresser and murmurs from Edna's neighboring room lulled her into a sleepy stupor. She crawled into bed and switched off her bedside lamp. Resting her hands on her abdomen, stroking its roundness, she stared into the room's dark space.

Before long I'll feel life. I feel so much tenderness toward this baby.

So different from when I carried my sons. Why is that? Why could I not feel the same toward my sons the way I feel toward you . . . even before you're born? I must protect you. I must do all I can to care for you.

Turning onto her side, she closed her eyes.

Before that can happen, I must get some sleep.

* * *

By late afternoon on Friday, Edna had learned the hotel's housekeeping routines. Exhausted and longing for fresh air, she changed into one of her two dresses. Out on the weathered boardwalk, she shielded her eyes from the late afternoon sun.

Across the street, two signs swung over store fronts . . . W. T. Green Merchandise and I. O. Anderson & Co. Beyond, gulls and pelicans swooped above a waterside dock constructed over a thick marsh. A white egret poked its head above tall, reedy green grass. Several small boats bobbed along the outer edge of the dock.

As the odor of fish and salty air filled Edna's nostrils, she began walking south toward Hungry Bend, her hope of finding Penelope overriding concern she might run into Jasper. Penelope would be out of school by now.

I need to let Penelope know I'm working and that I hope we can find time to spend together.

Several yards ahead a barefoot boy Edna guessed to be fourteen or so stood in her path, his head tilted, long arms hanging loose at his sides. Light-colored hair stiff as straw stuck out from under a black broad-brimmed hat. His stretched-out suspenders held up dirt-smudged, baggy pants.

Put off by the boy's blank, vacant stare, Edna stepped off the boardwalk to resume her walk in the street. When the boy did the same, Edna stepped up on the boardwalk again. When the boy stepped up on the boardwalk as well, Edna looked around for someone . . . anyone . . . she could appeal to for help. At that moment, a man and a woman emerged from the mercantile chatting over bags of items.

Edna raised an arm and waved. "Excuse me. Sir? Could you please . . ." She gestured toward the boy. "I can't seem to continue my walk."

The man walked to the edge of the boardwalk. "Elmer Truegood, git on home, hear? Or the café', one or t'other."

When the boy did not move, the man raised his voice. "Elmer, I said git on home. Now! Or I'll go git Sylvester ta come after ya."

Elmer stared at the man then turned to Edna. "You lookin' fer Penelope?"

Nodding, Edna replied, "Yes. I am looking for Penelope."

Elmer pointed behind him. "That's her house down there."

Thanking the man, who strode off with his companion, Edna returned her attention to Elmer. "Yes, I know her house is down there. Do you know if she's home?"

Elmer shook his head and began rocking back and forth. "I like Penelope."

Alarms rang in Edna's head. She gulped. "I like Penelope, too. I would like to see her."

Shoving his hands in his pockets, Elmer continued rocking back and forth. As he stared at Edna, tears filled his eyes and streamed down his face.

Stunned, Edna stepped toward Elmer. "What's wrong, Elmer? Tell me what's wrong."

Elmer ran his shirt sleeve across his eyes. His voice quivered when he spoke. "She's gone again. Penelope's gone."

Chapter Seventeen

"Edna! What'd ya do with the towels for Room 8?" Later, "Edna! Where'd ya leave the broom?"

Worried over Penelope's whereabouts, Edna wandered through her tasks in a daze. "I'm sorry, Annie," she repeated apologetically.

The next day, Annie's irritation, and her voice, escalated. "For the love o 'might, Edna! Do I hafta' follow ya around like a child? Not a bar o' soap to be found in this bathroom!"

Edna tried harder to focus, but her worry over Penelope festered with each passing day. She would spend as much time in the evening as her energy allowed pacing the boardwalk watching for the child. Before going to bed, staring out her window at the night sky, she prayed.

Dear Lord, protect Penelope. Please don't let any harm come to her.

The only diversion to the seemingly endless days was Wednesday morning when Dr. Bartlett arrived at the hotel.

"You're doing well, Edna, but I can see in your face you might be overdoing it. I spoke to Lloyd. You'll have Saturday afternoons and Sundays off. Guests arrive late Saturday mornings, so you and Annie will have the rooms already prepared."

"That's wonderful. Thank you. And I'll do better to pace myself," Edna promised. "But I am concerned about Penelope. She seems to have disappeared. I'm very worried."

Dr. Bartlett frowned. "Hmmm. Well, I'll be going up to see Birdie. Maybe Glory Bee knows something." He patted Edna's knee. "Penelope's a clever little girl and knows every inch of this island. Most of the other islands as well. Try not to worry. I'll be back this afternoon and let you know if I learn anything."

When Dr. Bartlett returned to say Glory Bee knew nothing of Penelope's whereabouts, Edna's worry increased. She checked with Molly in the kitchen.

"No, ma'am. Ain't seen Penelope fer days."

Thursday morning, Edna glanced out the bedroom window before reporting to work to see Jasper driving his horse and wagon away from town. Something was in the bed of the wagon, but he disappeared from view before Edna could make any sense of it.

That evening, drained from work, worry, and minimal sleep, Edna stumbled to her room, closed the door, and dropped onto the bed. She awoke Friday morning to the clang of the alarm clock and the aroma of fried bacon. Her stomach growled having missed dinner the night before, but thoughts of Penelope pervaded. Completing her toilette and quickly donning her uniform, she settled for only a cup of coffee and a biscuit before beginning the chores Annie had assigned her.

By mid-day Saturday, bleary-eyed from lack of sleep and sick with worry and lack of nourishment, Edna sought the bench on the boardwalk. She interrupted her vigil only to pace and once to fetch a glass of water.

By late afternoon, having decided to go to the kitchen to sate overpowering hunger, Edna caught a glint of blond hair from the direction of the dock. Shielding her eyes and squinting into the sunlight, she gasped. "Dear God!"

Adrenalin surged. Picking up her skirt, Edna ran across the street onto a wood walkway leading to the dock. Nearly breathless with relief, she felt her heart would explode.

With Bell on her heels, Penelope ran toward Edna, who

wrapped the girl in a warm embrace. "Where have you been?! I've been worried sick!"

Baffled over the child's appearance, Edna held Penelope at arms' length. Everything about her . . . skin, hair, dirt-smudged clothing . . . reeked of wood smoke.

Edna gingerly touched Penelope's smock made of something like animal skin. "And where did you get this . . . this dress?" She fingered the tiny beads braided through her hair. "And who did this to your hair?"

Penelope unwound a braided leather bracelet from her wrist and handed it to Edna. "I made this for ya."

Edna took the bracelet and held it in the palm of her hand. "You made this?" More questions arose as Edna gazed at the gift and scrutinized Penelope's appearance. "Where?" She tried again. "I'm trying to understand . . . your dress and your hair. Where have you been?"

"I went to see my friend." Penelope pointed to the bracelet. "She let me stay so she could show me how to make that. She made this dress, too."

"Your friend. Who? Where is she?"

"Oh, she's on a little island not far from Pine Cove Key. I can row to it without goin' out too far. I'll take ya there if ya want."

Edna nodded, still perplexed. "Penelope, you've been gone for days. Are you alright?"

"Yes ma'am. Just kind o' tired." She scratched her arm and attempted a weak smile.

Deciding to risk Lloyd's disapproval if he were to take issue with harboring the child and a dog, Edna took Penelope's hand.

"Come with me. I have a room at the hotel now that I'm working there. Let's get you bathed and something to eat. Maybe take a nap. Then you can tell me more about your friend."

***

"She's a Seminole Indian. Her name is Tepkunset Berry." Penelope crawled under the bed sheet and nestled her head into the pillow. Drowsy from the warm bath and hot soup, she closed her eyes. Before drifting to sleep, she mumbled, "She's really old."

While Penelope slept and Bell stretched out on the floor at her side, Edna washed the animal skin dress. Slipping out to the hallway, she made her way to Jean's room. After a few light knocks, Jean opened the door a crack. From the tousled hair and squinted eyes, Edna knew she had awakened her.

"Jean, I'm so sorry." Edna turned to leave. "I can come back later."

Jean opened the door further. "No. Yer fine. Are ye alright?"

Edna nodded. "Yes. Yes, I'm fine . . . but . . . well, I need . . ." Struggling with how to phrase her problem, her shoulders slumped. "Jean, Penelope is asleep in my room. She showed up having been gone for days. Her only clothing is some kind of animal hide and . . ." She took a deep breath. "I thought maybe you might have . . . I know you had a little girl and I thought maybe you might still have . . ."

Before Edna could continue, Jean pulled her into the room and closed the door. She pointed to a stuffed chair in the corner. "Have a seat."

After tightening her robe, Jean dragged a satchel from under the bed, opened it, and upended a bundle of items onto the rumpled bedspread. Slowly, she picked up each piece and gently folded it.

Edna could only imagine Jean's emotional restraint as she laid one item of clothing on top of another.

"These were me Kathleen's." Jean ran her hand over the top garment, a blue gingham dress trimmed in white bric-a-brac, and smoothed out the wrinkles. "Could'na bring meself ta get rid o' her clothes.

Jean sighed. "Kathleen was almost four when I lost her. Me

Mum made these clothes big fer her so's she could wear 'em a long time." She held up the dress and looked at Edna. "Ye think this might fit Penelope?"

Edna's heart was near breaking at the palpable sadness in Jean's eyes. She struggled for words. "Jean, I am so sorry. I don't know what to say."

Jean shook her head, her eyes growing moist. "Them words already been said, Edna. Kathleen's gone. Penelope's here.

Blinking away the threat of tears, Jean held out the dress. "Now if ye think Penelope can fit into these clothes . . . well, it's time they got used fer somethin' b'sides stuffin' a bag."

Edna marveled at Jean's resolute manner. She stood, reached across the bed, and took hold of the dress. "Penelope is so tiny, I'm sure this will work perfectly. And I doubt very much she will care how well it fits. Right now, she's lying in the bed naked with nothing but . . . well, very simply, she needs clothing, and whatever you're willing to let her use is greatly appreciated."

Jean stuffed the remaining items back into the bag and zipped it closed. "Take 'em. All of 'em. An' there's some under things in there, too. Now, what I wanna' know is what Penelope was doin' wearin' an animal hide dress." As soon as she said it, her eyebrows raised. "She's been out ta see that ol' Seminole crone, ain't she?"

Surprised, Edna nodded. "Yes! Do you know her?"

"Sure. Ev'r'body 'round here knows Tepkunset Berry. Her grandson, Joseph, too." Jean grew somber. "Sad wha' happened to 'em." She looked at Edna. "Ever hear o' Wounded Knee?"

"No. I don't know much about Indians. Is that where they're from?"

Jean shook her head. "No. From Florida." She picked up the satchel and moved toward the door. "It's a long story. We'll go visit 'em sometime so's ye can hear it from them."

Edna followed Jean to the door and took the satchel from her.

"I can't thank you enough. And I know Penelope will love these clothes. After her mother died, goodness knows she's not had anything like them."

Jean's weak smile conveyed unfathomable depths of sadness. By relinquishing Kathleen's clothing, she experienced another kind of death . . . of letting go of the only tangible connection she had to her little girl. She placed her hand on Edna's shoulder and gently moved her closer to the door.

"Jus' go now. Saturday night, ye know. Time to get meself tidied up for another . . . well, let's say it's time ta get ready fer work."

Back in her room, while Penelope slept, Edna inventoried the items of clothing and determined Penelope would be able to wear most of them. She sat down at the desk and took out the sketch pad. Flipping to Jean's face, Edna pondered again how to capture that forlorn yet steadfast look so evident in the woman's face today.

Her eyes. I think it's in her eyes . . . the sadness.

A rustling from the bed interrupted her thoughts. She turned to see Penelope sitting up in bed rubbing her eyes. Bell immediately leaped to her feet and commenced to whine.

Penelope looked around the room seeming perplexed before focusing on Edna. Her face grew sad, and she lay back on the pillow.

Edna left the desk and sat on the edge of the bed. "What's wrong, dear heart?" She laid her palm on Penelope's forehead. "Are you feeling alright?"

Penelope nodded. She appeared ready to cry. "Are you gonna make me leave?"

Edna had been giving a lot of thought to the possibility of Penelope staying with her. The reality, of course, was the likelihood Lloyd would not permit it simply because Edna would be working and unable to supervise the child. Then there was Jasper to consider. She cringed to imagine him in a drunken rage wreaking havoc in the hotel and inflicting harm on Penelope... and possibly herself. It broke her heart to have to tell Penelope that for now, she and Bell would have to go home.

"I don't have a choice right now, Penelope. I have to work. If you stay here, I might lose my job."

Penelope's eyes filled with tears. "But I don't wanna go home!"

Edna pulled the child to her and held her close. "I don't want you to go either. I just don't see a way to make it work for you to stay here.

Hoping to divert her attention, Edna stood and stepped to the bureau. "Penelope, look at these dresses." She held up one then another. "All yours. Aren't they lovely?

Placing the dresses back on the dresser, she held up a pair of pantaloons. "Even pairs of under things." She walked back to the bed. "Let's slip them on and see how they fit."

Only mildly mollified, Penelope crawled out of bed. Although a bit short, the blue gingham hung loosely on her tiny frame.

Penelope twirled. "This one's my favorite," she said with a hint of a smile.

Edna pointed out, "It's a perfect match with the blue beads in your hair." She folded the remaining items and placed them back in the satchel. "Penelope, did you know a little girl by the name of Kathleen who lived here?"

Penelope sat cross-legged on the bed. "Yes ma'am. She died."

"Yes, I know. Were you and Kathleen friends?"

Penelope shook her head. "No. Her Mama wouldn't let her play with me cuz'... well, she didn't like my Pa an'..." She shrugged her shoulders. "She wouldn't let Kathleen come to my house to play." Attempting to downplay the rebuff, she added, "She was younger'n me anyways."

Edna zipped the satchel closed. She could think of nothing to say to undo layers of hurt. "Well, Kathleen's mother wants you to have her clothes. That's who these belonged to."

Penelope looked at the dress spread around her legs. "Oh." A perplexed look crossed her face. "Do you think she'll be sad when she sees me wearin' her daughter's clothes?"

Edna sat down next to Penelope and took her hands. "Does it make you sad to see me wearing your Mama's dresses?"

Penelope grew thoughtful. "Sometimes. But I like seeing you in my Mama's dresses 'cuz it's like she's still here."

"Don't you think it might be the same for Kathleen's Mama?"

Penelope was quiet for a few moments then looked at Edna. "It's kind o' the same thing, ain't it?"

"I think so. It might make Kathleen's Mama a little sad at first seeing you in her daughter's clothes, but over time, I think it will make her happy.

Edna let go of Penelope's hands and patted her knee. "Now, how about I walk you to your house?" Hesitating, she added, "I . . . I'm pretty sure your father isn't home."

Penelope replied with a somber, "Okay."

Edna, Penelope, and Bell managed to slip out of the hotel undetected by Lloyd. Making their way to Hungry Bend, Edna spoke about the Seminole woman and her grandson, Joseph.

"I'd like to meet them one day. Do you think next Saturday would work?"

Penelope replied, "Okay."

The closer they got to Hungry Bend, the slower Penelope walked and the tighter she held Edna's hand. She eventually came to a stop before arriving at her house.

"I can go from here, Miss Edna." Penelope patted Bell's head. "We'll be okay." She took the satchel from Edna. "Tell Kathleen's Mama thank you for these clothes. They're real pretty. I like 'em a lot."

Reluctant to leave before seeing the child home, Edna knelt down. "Listen, if you need anything . . ." Realizing the emptiness of her remark in her current situation, she started over. "Penelope, please be careful. You know where I am. If you decide to go off again, please tell me so I won't have to worry." She tugged on Penelope's arm. "Okay? Promise?"

Penelope nodded. "I promise." With that, she turned and resumed her walk to her house.

With the weight of a stone in her heart, Edna watched Penelope for a few moments before turning to go back to the hotel. Not until she was nearly at the side street leading in and out of Pine Cove did a growing clamor of horse hooves and the rattle of a buckboard catch her attention. In an instant, the horse was nearly upon her as the driver shouted and slapped the reins.

In a cloud of dust, Edna lifted her skirt and ran for the boardwalk, managing to avoid being run over in the nick of time. Catching her breath while clinging to a boardwalk post, she watched the driver steer the horse toward Hungry Bend.

Chapter Eighteen

Dear Léonce,
    This letter will likely come as a shock. Much to your doubtless surprise, frankly as it is to mine, I am very much alive. Whether or not you care to share this news with our sons is entirely up to you. I do not wish to divulge where I am living and will only say I am comfortable and well cared for. My circumstances have provided significant amounts of time to reflect on my conduct over the past year or so. In some ways, I regret my actions that assuredly caused you embarrassment. In other ways, I can only say that desperation will drive an otherwise sane individual to commit insane acts.

    Edna's hand hovered over the letter as she struggled with how to close. Distracted by a knock on her door, she placed the letter into the desk drawer.

    Jean's voice followed another knock. "Edna, ye there?"

    "Yes," Edna replied. She quickly slipped on her apron, tying it loosely to camouflage her expanding middle. "Coming!" Upon opening the door, Jean stood before her holding her finished drawing Edna had completed the week before.

    "I was just wonderin'." In an imploring voice, she asked, "Will ye make one o' these o' me Kathleen? I can tell ya just wha' she looked like. I'd be so grateful . . ."

Taking hold of Jean's arm, Edna pulled her into the room and closed the door. "Of course, I'll do one of Kathleen. I should have thought of it sooner.

Picking up her sketch pad, pencil, and chalk from the desk, Edna opened the pad to a fresh page. "Let's sit on my bed and I'll draw while you tell me what she looked like."

For the next hour, Jean shared details of her daughter's looks. "Oh, how she fussed over one stubborn curl. Stuck straight up na' matter how much I plastered it down wi' water.

As Edna worked on Kathleen's mouth, Jean pointed. "Right there. Under her bottom lip, a little dimple . . . like the ones in her cheeks.

When Edna picked up the red chalk for Kathleen's hair, Jean shook her head. "It weren't that red. It was . . . well, I always said I must'a eaten a lot o' carrots when I was carryin' her. An' her eyes. Same color as mine, but they glowed . . . like dew on moss.

When Edna finished, Jean stared at the likeness of her daughter. "Me wee girl. Me Kathleen to a 't.' Her thick russet hair . . . devil of a time gettin' a brush through those curls, but she would'na let me cut it. The dimple in her chin . . . loved plantin' me pinky finger in it. The green o' her eyes . . . ye even got the wee fleck o' gold in 'em.

Jean smiled. "An' her freckles. Teased her I was gonna connect the dots with a pencil." She held the picture at arm's length and moved it side to side. "She's lookin' at me. She's followin' me.

Jean's eyes welled. Through her tears, she looked at Edna and whispered, "How'd' ye do it? How do ye bring a face ta . . ." She gulped. "How d' ye bring someone back ta life like this?" Setting the picture on her lap, Jean covered her face with her hands and released a sob.

"Oh, Jean!" Edna pulled a handkerchief from her apron pocket. "I didn't expect this would be so hard, that it would upset you so." Handing her the handkerchief, she reached for the picture. "Let's put it away."

Jean pushed Edna's hand away. She picked up the picture and held it to her chest. "No! Lordy, no! Ye don't know how hard... how ev'ry day, Kathleen's face faded more'n more. She was disappearin' from me." Jean sniffled, wiped her eyes, and gazed at the picture. "Ye've brung her back ta me."

Edna struggled for words to comfort her friend. To suggest Jean might have another child one day would do nothing to assuage her heartbreak over the loss of Kathleen. The idea that one child could replace another was unthinkable.

"Jean, I can't begin to know what you're feeling right now... the depth of grief over the terrible loss of your child... and your husband." Edna swallowed hard. "To see you like this... it breaks my heart."

Jean managed a weak smile and sniffled. "Ye know 'bout me Tim then, too." She shook her head. "Sometimes I canna' b'lieve it. Both of 'em. Gone.

"I want ta be a mother again," Jean said with longing. She held up the picture of Kathleen. "Meantime, this'll help so much... ye know, for those times when I'm missin' me wee girl the most. I can hold this ta me heart and feel she's right here wi' me."

Edna nodded and smiled. "That makes me happy, Jean. Truly."

Drying her eyes, Jean grew thoughtful. "Ye know wha'? Ye ought ta do these o' some o' the townsfolk." Her eyes grew wide. "Ye could sell 'em! Maybe even ask Lloyd if ye can hang 'em in the hotel. Edna, wha' if ye sat on the dock when the tour boats come in? Charge a wee bit. Ya did this one s' quick. It'd be a souvenir tourists can take home wi' 'em. And money in yer pocket!"

Edna tilted her head and smiled. "Hmmm. Well, I'll certainly think about it. Of course, I'd need more than this little sketch pad. Do you think Fred at the mercantile would barter a drawing for a larger sketch pad?"

Jean hopped up and headed for the bedroom door. "Well, we

still got most o' the day. Wha' d' ye say we go right now and find out? Ye got most o' the afternoon in front o' ye!"

To Edna's delight, along with a large sketch pad, Fred offered a packet of wax crayons that included more colors than the chalk Penelope had brought to her.

"Now I ain't the handsomest old dog in Pine Cove," kind but crusty Fred said as Edna and Jean turned to leave the mercantile, "so you make me look good as ya can in that picture now, hear?"

With Edna's promise to Fred that he would look quite handsome, she and Jean headed to the dock. Being a Saturday, a tour boat had arrived earlier in the day. Most passengers had left to register at the hotel, but a few lingered to watch the activity along the water. Some fishermen tossed remains of fish to squabbling gulls and pelicans hovering overhead. Others worked on repairing yards and yards of cast nets and crab traps while others worked on boat repairs.

Edna took in the austere weathered dock that included only one bench in need of repair. She turned to Jean. "I don't know if this will work. There's no place to sit."

Before Jean could reply, a voice from behind called out. "Hallo! What'r you two doin' down here?"

Nathan Walker stepped out of the café and greeted the women with a warm smile that spread to his eyes.

"Hi Nathan," Jean said. She bobbed her head at Edna. "Do ye know Edna's an artist? She's seein' if any passengers might like her to draw their picture. Maybe sell 'em. But there's no place for her ta sit."

Nathan's eyes grew wide. "Nope. Didn't know Edna's an artist."

"Hello, Nathan," Edna said, her discomfort growing over the idea of setting up business on a waterside dock. "I . . . well, Jean thought maybe tourists might like to have a souvenir and that maybe I could sell them their likeness for, oh, I don't know. I've no idea what I would charge for a drawing. And there's no place where I can sit to draw. I really don't . . . I mean I've never done anything like this, so maybe . . ."

Before Edna could finish, Nathan turned and dashed into the café. A few moments later, the café door swung open. Nathan emerged carrying a small table followed by Sylvester carrying a chair. After setting them down, they both stood with fists on their hips looking at the women.

"Alright, where do ya want 'em?" Nathan asked.

Following a short discussion among the four over placement of the pieces, Sylvester turned to go back into the café. At the door, he pointed and waggled his finger.

"Let me know when yer finished and I'll come fetch them things. I wouldn't'a offered ta do this, but like Nathan said. Might bring more business in the café while people wait on their picture.

He squinted his eyes and looked at the sky. "Afta'noon sun mighty hot right now. Too bad ya can't git down here in the mornin' when the tour boats come." Without waiting for an explanation or Edna's thanks, he turned and went back inside.

Edna set her sketch tools on the table and sat down. She, Jean, and Nathan looked from one to the other as if each was thinking the same thing.

Now what?

Nathan spoke first. "Well, I've got work ta do." As he turned to leave, he added, "Let me know if ya need anything."

Within moments, Jean shouted, "Nathan!" Motioning for him to come back, she placed her hands on the table and leaned close to Edna's face. "Look, ye got somebody right here ye can start drawin'. That's gonna' get anybody walkin' by wantin' ta see what yer doin'."

Before Edna could respond, Nathan had approached the women. "What, ya need somethin' else already?"

"Aye." Jean pointed to the café. "Go on an' get another chair. Edna's gonna' draw yer face."

"Aw, Jean. I don't have time for this. I've got nets ta mend and..."

"Ye got plenty o' time fer that an' this don't take that long. Edna needs our help so go on. Fetch a chair and git yer... git on out here and sit yerself down."

Grumbling, Nathan did as he was asked. A half hour later, as Edna put the finishing touches on the drawing of Nathan's face, a man and woman strolling from the far end of the dock approached the threesome. Their travel attire indicated they had no doubt arrived earlier on a tour boat.

"What do we have here?" the woman asked as she peered over the table. Stepping closer, she looked at the drawing then at Nathan then back to the drawing. "My goodness. That's a perfect likeness."

She turned to her companion. "Look, John. This is very good. Even his hair! And with a crayon no less!" Addressing Edna, she asked, "Do you draw for others, dear? I'm quite interested."

Setting the yellow crayon on the table, Edna forced a smile at the woman. *Dear?!*

"Yes, of course," Edna replied as congenially as she could muster.

"And how much do you charge, dear?" the woman asked in her patronizing voice.

"Oh, well..." Her face burning with embarrassment, Edna searched Jean's and Nathan's faces.

Jean stepped forward. "Three dollars! Miss Edna charges three dollars for each... um, each portrait."

Edna lowered her face to hide her shock. She picked up the pencil and signed her name on Nathan's picture.

Three dollars! What is she thinking?

Raising her eyebrows, Jean stared at Nathan. "There ye are, sir. Three dollars fer yer signed portrait. In color, too!"

Scowling at Jean, Nathan reached in his pocket, handed Edna

three one-dollar bills, and took the picture from her. "Thanks, *Miss* Edna." With that, he stalked off down the dock.

Jean stepped around to the chair Nathan had vacated. "Now, which one o' ye is ready fer Miss Edna ta do yer portrait? Only takes a few minutes."

"Why, I think that's more than fair," the woman said. She turned to her companion. "Let's have her do ours, John."

By the time the afternoon light began to fade, Edna had completed six drawings and pocketed eighteen dollars. With Sylvester's help, she and Jean returned the table and chairs to the café.

Walking back to the hotel, Edna reached into her apron pocket, pulled out three one-dollar bills, and handed them to Jean. "You more than earned this, Jean. Thank you so much."

Jean raised her hands deflecting the offer. "No, no, no. I didna' do anythin' ye couldna' o' done yerself. I'll not take yer money. Jus' glad ta' see ye got a way ta earn yer way out o' workin' in the hotel.

Her voice subdued, Jean added, "I'm always thinkin' wha' I could do fer the same reason." She took hold of Edna's arm. "Now let's get some supper. Me belly's starvin'."

Chapter Nineteen

"Climb in, ladies. Watch out for that string o' fish hangin' off the side. They're for Tepkunset and Joseph."

Nathan extended a hand first to Edna then to Jean. Once the women were seated in the stern of the Jon boat, he pushed off from the dock and dropped the oars into the water.

"Bit choppy now the wind's picked up," Nathan shouted. "Too bad ya didn't come to the dock earlier. Smooth as glass on the Gulf this mornin'."

Laying Penelope's animal skin dress on her lap, Edna gripped the sides of the boat. Taking a deep breath, she closed her eyes wishing to be anywhere but in another boat.

Jean tapped Edna on a knee. "Ye a'right?"

Edna gulped. "I'm fine. Or I will be if . . . when we find Penelope."

"We'll find her. Her boat's gone, so she's bound ta be back at the Seminole camp." Jean's voice saddened. "I still can't b'lieve Jasper dumpin' Kathleen's clothes in the hotel lobby. Man's crazy." She added, "At least he didna' burn 'em."

"I'm so sorry, Jean. I never should have let Penelope take the clothes home. Who would think . . . ?"

Jean shook her head. "No. Stop thinkin' like that. Jasper ain't right in the head, so no tellin' wha' the man might do."

Having made their way beyond the dock, Nathan stuck close

to the shoreline for a short distance then turned toward open water. He pointed to an island up ahead. "That's where we're headed. Hang on. Might get a little bumpy."

The boat pitched and rolled in the foamy surf as Nathan pulled and pushed the oars.

Edna swallowed a sickening urge and gripped her stomach. Closing her eyes against the rise and fall of the waves, she prayed she would not have to lean over the side. When she opened her eyes, Jean was staring at her with a smirk.

After glancing over her shoulder to be sure Nathan was out of ear shot, Jean leaned toward Edna and whispered, "When're ye due?"

Edna looked over Jean's head. "I don't know what you mean."

"Edna, yer face is green as grass an' I don't b'lieve it's all from the boat."

"I'm not fond of boats . . . or being out this far on the water."

"Well, then, tell me what yer hidin' under that apron. Yer always wearin' it an' somethin' tells me it ain't ta keep spills off that dress." Jean tilted her head and raised her eyebrows. "Well? Ye canna' hide it f'rever."

Edna lowered her head and relaxed her shoulders. Weary of the futile efforts to hide her pregnancy, with a sense of relief, she raised her head and faced Jean. "The baby is due in February."

Before Jean could respond, the boat scraped bottom. Nathan jumped out and pulled it up onto the shore. After helping the women onto the sand, he removed his hat and wiped his brow with a shirt sleeve. He pointed to some thick overgrowth.

"It isn't too far to the camp. Once we get through those cabbage palms and sea grapes, it's a pretty easy walk."

Maneuvering the women through the brush, Nathan led the way along a worn, pine-needle-strewn path.

Edna's and Jean's minds raced, Edna's for Penelope with hopes they would find her safe and unharmed at the camp, Jean's for the delight in Edna's revelation.

A baby!

Long-forgotten emotions and memories of her own pregnancy surged through Jean . . . movement inside her swelling belly as her baby grew, the smell of her newborn's breath, the touch of downy hair, of Kathleen's tiny fingers clutching her mother's breast as she nursed.

Kathleen would live forever in Jean's heart, but the loss of her daughter's physical touch had nearly driven Jean to the edge. Perhaps this new life, though not hers, might help to heal some of her brokenness. A revived sense of anticipation, an emotion Jean had not felt in a very long time, brought tears to her eyes. Smiling, she linked arms with Edna.

Nathan stopped and turned to the women. "The Berry's camp is right up ahead. Let me go first to be sure we're welcome." Carrying his string of fish, he disappeared into the brush, the pungent aroma of wood smoke filling the air.

Jean let go of Edna's arm, picked up a pine cone, and held it to her nose. "Kathleen loved pine cones. She liked their smell." She wandered a few yards down the path and picked up another. She turned to Edna.

"Ye told me about yer little boys and where ye come from. Still dunno how it is ye landed on the beach here, but I fig'ered ye'd get ta it sooner 'er later." She approached Edna and took her hand. "It ain't none o' me business but I was jus' thinkin'. Maybe ye wanna' talk about yer baby and why yer hidin' it."

Edna lowered her head as warmth crept up her neck and to her face. Releasing Jean's hand, she turned away. A few moments later, she turned back around and faced Jean. "I . . . I committed an indiscretion.

Taking a deep breath, she continued. "My husband is not the father of this baby. I tried to take my life, but, well, obviously that was not meant to be. I didn't expect to live, so here I am and . . ."

Voices in the distance grew closer. From behind clusters of

cabbage palms, a blond head emerged moving swiftly toward the women with Nathan and Bell not far behind. Still clad in the blue gingham dress, with beaded braids bouncing around her face, Penelope ran headlong into Edna's embrace.

Edna knelt down and wiped away dirt-smudged tears running down the little girl's face. Holding Penelope's shoulders at arms' length, she looked her over for signs of physical harm. Finding none, she pulled her close while choking back her own tears.

"You promised you would tell me if you had to leave!" She gently shook Penelope's shoulders. "Why didn't you come to me? I've been worried sick . . . wondering if something . . . wondering where you'd gone."

Penelope wiped her eyes with the back of her hand. "Ya said I couldn't stay with ya. An' Pa took my clothes . . . said if he found out I was goin' to the hotel, he'd do somethin'." She wrapped an arm around Bell's neck. "I was afraid he might shoot Bell." She started to cry again.

Pulling Penelope into a tighter embrace, with tears streaming down her cheeks, Edna whispered, "You poor girl."

Nathan stepped forward and knelt next to Edna and Penelope. "Listen, Tepkunset and Joseph have invited us all to their camp. They're cookin' the fish I brought, and they wanna' share it with us." He took Penelope's hand. "Maybe they'll let you stay here awhile 'til y'all can figure out somethin'."

***

While Tepkunset shuffled around the encampment removing the guests' plates and cooking utensils, everyone else but Joseph sat around the campfire on hand-hewn benches. Joseph sat cross-legged on a hand-woven mat smoking a pipe.

Edna marveled at the efficiency of the Seminoles' lives, the simplicity of their small cabin, and their ability to live off the land. Tepkunset, so hunched her feather-trimmed braids nearly touched the ground, was obviously quite old. Joseph, with his shock of thick blue-black hair, appeared ageless. His shirt, white as sun-bleached bones, cast a ghostly glow onto his flawless ocher-colored face. A primitive aura embraced the entire setting.

Penelope snuggled against Edna. "Mister Joseph, tell 'em about the shell mound." She looked up at Edna, her eyes round as the tin plates on which their fish was served. "There's ghosts!" When Edna appeared unconvinced, she added, "Really! Ain't there, Mister Joseph?"

Nathan nodded. "I've heard that, too."

Jean agreed. "Aye. Me, too."

Joseph tapped ashes out of his pipe against a tree stump. "Many spirits walk the shell mound. I've seen them many times." He lifted his face and closed his eyes for a moment. "Spirits of our Seminole family live there."

Tepkunset approached one of the benches. Bent and frail, her skeletal frame appeared brittle as dead twigs. Accepting Nathan's hand, she settled between him and Jean.

In a barely audible voice, as if breathing took more strength than her lungs could provide, Tepkunset spoke to her visitors.

"Many years ago, my family . . . me, my son, his wife, and their little boy . . ." She nodded toward Joseph. "We traveled with other tribes the government was forcing west. Many Seminoles stayed in Florida and fought for their land. My son did not want to fight and risk our family being slaughtered, so we chose to leave."

No one spoke for a few moments. Jean finally spoke up. "But you and Joseph'r here now. Ye both came back." She looked from Tepkunset to Joseph and back to his grandmother. "Where'r yer son and his wife?"

Her voice low and somber, Tepkunset gazed beyond the camp as if seeing again the horror that occurred so many years ago.

"After things settled down, many of us decided to return to Florida. Hundreds . . . all struggling to get back to our homes. We came to a place in South Dakota called Wounded Knee. We danced and begged our gods to return our lives to what they had been. The white men got nervous. Thinking we were getting ready to attack, they started shooting their guns at us." Tepkunset paused. "Men, women, and children."

Burning wood crackled in the fire pit as smoke coiled upward. A crow cawed on a pine tree branch far above.

Penelope was the first to speak. Her eyes wide with disbelief, she whispered, "They shot little kids?"

Tepkunset turned to her. "Yes, child. Almost no one was spared."

Bewildered, Jean spoke up. "I . . . I don't understand. You an' Joseph . . . ye both survived. How?"

Tepkunset nodded to Joseph. "My grandson will explain. I must rest now." Her eyes nearly closed with age, with Nathan's help, she shuffled to the cabin and closed the door.

Joseph relit his pipe. "My grandmother does not want to be haunted by the spirits, so she leaves it to me to tell what happened to my mother and father.

He puffed several times on his pipe, the embers in the bowl glowing brighter each time. "When the white men started firing their guns, my father threw himself on top of my grandmother and me. That's how we survived. My father and mother were slaughtered with the others."

Edna could only stare at Joseph in disbelief. Equally unimaginable as Joseph's account of the killing of his parents was his father's sacrifice of his wife . . . his son's mother . . . for that of an aging grandparent.

"Why?" Edna finally asked. "I mean no disrespect to your grandmother, Joseph. But why would he have not saved your mother?"

Horrified, Jean agreed. "Aye! Why not save yer Mum? Did yer Da na' have a choice?"

Joseph puffed on his pipe, smoke curling from the red embers.

"My grandmother says there is no future without a past. Only she knew the ancient customs and traditions of our family. If she had died, our past would have died with her. Since she lived, my grandmother passes on our family and tribal stories to me. I will do the same when I marry and have children."

Tepkunset and Joseph's tragic, sobering story left Edna pensive and light-headed. So absorbed with her own life, she never considered the story her young sons would tell one day ... of their mother who abandoned them and chose to end her life. Edna closed her eyes.

What a sad memory for them to live with. God forgive me.

Setting his pipe aside, Joseph stood up. "Penelope, go fetch more wood for the fire."

With Penelope out of earshot, Joseph addressed Edna, Jean, and Nathan.

"Penelope and Bell will stay with us for now. We ... the Seminoles ... know her father. He is a very bad man. We believe he killed his wife, and he is involved with a group farther north known to kill Coloreds and Indians. You are welcome here any time, but do not tell anyone you are coming or that Penelope is here. If her father finds out and comes for her, I will kill him."

Joseph's clear message sent chills through Edna. He left no doubt he meant what he said.

When Penelope returned and deposited an armload of firewood on the ground, Edna took her in her arms. "I promise we'll come back soon. For now, we're glad you have Tepkunset and Mr. Joseph to look after you.

Wiping away Penelope's tears, Edna pointed to the animal hide dress folded up on the bench. "I brought the dress Tepkunset made for you," she said tugging on the gingham dress's skirt. "Two should do for now."

Jean gave Penelope a kiss on the cheek. "An' ye'll get back the rest of Kathleen's clothes, too."

Joseph raised his arms. "Now, you may go. I must look in on my grandmother."

Promising again to return soon and that Nathan would take care of Penelope's crab traps, the trio said good-bye.

That night, as Edna lay in bed, she pictured a woman with long braided hair sitting outside a wood shack. Resting his head against her sunken chest, a little dark-haired boy listened to his grandmother's stories . . . of being forced to leave their home and traveling far away . . . of the misery and deprivation in an unfamiliar land . . . of how his father had sacrificed his life and that of the boy's mother in a strange, distant place . . . all so the little boy could someday tell that tragic story and others to his children.

A memory surfaced of a conversation with Edna's friend Adele' . . . that she "would never sacrifice herself for her children."

In the physical sense, no. But Adele' sacrificed herself in so many other ways . . . through her endless preoccupation with her children. She was rarely without them . . . always responding to their every need. And if they were not with her, she worried constantly about them. Why could I never be that way with my sons, yet it's exactly what I'm doing with Penelope? But why her and not them?

The answer was not long in coming.

My sons didn't need me.

Closing her eyes, Edna reflected on Joseph's remark about Penelope's father. *'He's a very bad man . . . I will kill him.'*

Once again, Edna did not doubt for a minute that Joseph meant it. And if he . . . or anyone . . . was to kill Jasper, where would that leave Penelope? To lose her father as well as her mother seemed the ultimate cruelty.

But she's as good as parentless as it is.

Edna recalled Dr. Bartlett's comment following one of her physical examinations: *'. . . I don't believe in coincidence. There's a reason you're here.'*

She never considered whether or not fate had brought her to Pine Cove. If that was the case, if a higher power had orchestrated the events leading to her arrival on the island, then perhaps Penelope was the reason. But with the birth of her child mere months away and with no plan as to how to care for it, the prospect of caring for two children seemed insurmountable.

Too weary from the day's events to think more about it, Edna switched off her lamp. At that moment, a flutter rippled through her abdomen.

Chapter Twenty

Jean stood up from the bench in front of the hotel and stretched her arms over her head. "That bench is too hard. Let's go for a walk. Get yer mind off o' worryin' about Penelope."

Looking toward the dock, Edna shook her head. "I doubt a walk will make a difference. It's been three weeks since we were at the camp. I can't get there without Nathan, and he's off fishing for who knows how long."

Jean took hold of Edna's arm and pulled her up. "Ye know good 'n well she's with Tepkunset and Joseph, or she'd be right back here lookin' fer ye. Come on. A walk'll do ye good."

Edna stood and arched her back. "How do we know that's where she is, Jean? What about Jasper?"

"Wha' *about* Jasper?" Jean stepped off the boardwalk and reached for Edna's hand. "Easy wi' ye."

Taking Jean's hand, Edna stepped onto the dusty street. "No one's seen him. What if he went to the camp? What if he snuck into the camp in the middle of the night? What if Joseph didn't hear Jasper and he grabbed Penelope?" Edna stopped in her tracks. "What if she couldn't come looking for me?"

Jean glanced at Edna. "Don't ye think Bell would o' barked her head off once he tried somethin' like that?"

"I suppose. But he did shoot Penelope's other dog."

"An' Joseph would o' heard it. Ye saw that rifle he keeps next ta him. Jasper wouldna' get out alive if'n he tried somethin'."

"That makes sense," Edna conceded. "I'll try to put that out of my mind. If I could just get there to be sure."

Dust from the street plumed around the women's feet. More of the dry, powdery dirt swirled into the air as a horse-driven surrey rolled past.

Jean propelled Edna away from the dust cloud and toward the walkway. "We ain't been to the dock in a few days. Maybe Nathan's back."

Grateful for the cooler temperature ushered in with late fall breezes, Edna scurried to keep up with Jean. "Let's hope," she muttered.

A walk of the entire length of the dock revealed no sign of Nathan or his boat.

"Ain't no tellin' when he'll be back, 'specially if mullet's runnin'," Sylvester said as he handed Edna and Jean glasses of tea. "Sorry it ain't cold. Ice won't git here 'til the weekend."

The pungent smell of cooked swamp cabbage mingled with cigar smoke from a nearby customer.

Edna's stomach turned. She leaned close to Jean and whispered, "I need to get back to the hotel."

Recognizing Edna's distress, Jean nodded. "Thanks fer the tea, Sylvester. We'll try again in a day or so."

As the women stood to leave the café, Sylvester shouted from behind the counter. "Now hold on there. I plum fergot ta tell ya." He pointed to a wall. "Since I hung up that picture, people been askin' when the lady whut does the drawin's is comin' back."

So consumed with worry over Penelope, Edna had not noticed her drawing of Nathan.

"Sylvester, that was awfully nice of you to do that." The distraction along with standing eased the threatening nausea.

Sylvester grinned. "Thing is, yer picture-makin' sure brought more people in here waitin' their turn fer ya to draw theirs. People ya drew pictures of took 'em home and told others if they come here, look fer the lady what draws yer picture." He scowled. "What'd ya quit fer?"

Edna stared at the drawing.

Why indeed! The waiting, the wondering, the worrying. I can't think . . . can't focus when every waking hour is filled with Penelope.

"Sylvester, I guess I've let my concern for Penelope and my job at the hotel interfere." Edna smiled. "I'll come this Saturday for a few hours."

"Tour boat gits here 'bout 'leven. Ya ought'a be here in time fer those folks gittin' off." Sylvester grinned. "An' they'll be hungry."

Jean piped up. "Well, ye better make a bigger kettle o' that cabbage patch stew ye been makin' lately. Had a bowl t'other day. I could smell garlic 'n tomatoes 'n cabbage before I even opened the door."

"Yup, yup. Been doin' real good," Sylvester said. "Folks like dunkin' biscuits in the broth. I'll crank my batch up a notch."

On their walk back to the hotel, Jean patted Edna's arm. "Ye look like yer feelin' better. Nathan'll be back soon. That boat can't hold but so many fish, so he can't stay out in the Gulf f'rever."

"The fresh air is making me feel better," Edna said. She glanced at Jean. "Maybe by Saturday, Nathan will be back. At least I have something else to think about. I do need more drawing supplies though. Let's stop at the mercantile before we go to the hotel."

***

The following Saturday proved lucrative for both Edna and Sylvester. With the season in full swing, the tour boats were booked. Throngs strolled along the dock waiting for a seat in Sylvester's café. While they waited, many stood in line for Edna's artwork. By the end of the afternoon, she had completed a dozen drawings.

"If ye had more daylight, ye could o' done more," Jean commented while helping Edna gather her supplies.

Islands of Women

"True, Jean, but I'm not sure I can sit much longer than four hours. This was fine. But I still think three dollars is too much for these drawings."

Jean scoffed. "Are ye kiddin'? Bet if ye charged four er five dollars, ye'd still have a line o' people. Comin' here from the big cities, these tourists ha' got money."

"I suppose," Edna slipped the handle of her satchel over her arm. "Well, I'm happy to see Sylvester so busy, too."

"I was thinkin' he'd be askin' fer his table and chairs back, but he knows what yer doin' is helpin' him, too."

With the table and chairs returned to the café, Edna and Jean began their walk back to the hotel. They had not gone far when they heard a shout from the dock.

"Edna! Jean!"

Edna was the first to turn around. "Nathan!" She handed Jean the satchel and hurried to Nathan. "I'm so glad to see you! You were gone so long!"

Nathan grinned. "Good haul this time. Just docked." He bobbed his head at Jean. "Howdy, Jean."

"Good ta see ye, Nathan. Edna here's been a'wonderin if ye were ever comin' back." Jean's voice grew somber. "Ain't seen Penelope in weeks. She's worrit and hopin' ye . . ."

Nathan was already nodding his head. "I can take ya but not 'til tomorra' afternoon. Where is she?"

Edna took a deep breath, her shoulders relaxing. "We think . . . we hope she's still at the Seminole camp. Tomorrow afternoon will be fine. Thank you, Nathan. Thank you so much."

The following afternoon, the threesome met at the dock. Holding onto Nathan's and Jean's hands, despite her expanding girth, Edna managed to climb down the ladder and settle onto a seat in the Jon boat. With a gift of several mullet for Joseph and Tepkunset, Nathan rowed the anxious women to the remote island camp.

With Nathan having gone ahead with the fish, Edna scurried beside Jean along the pine-laden path. "I hope and pray Penelope is here and she's alright."

"I'm bettin' she's just fine," Jean said. She pointed ahead and shouted, "Look! There she is! And Bell!"

With arms outspread and running swift as a fawn, Penelope yelled, "Miss Edna! Miss Edna!"

Edna scooped up the little girl in her arms. Tears of relief welled as she hugged Penelope to her.

"Oh, my girl! How I've missed you!" Edna held Penelope at arms' length. "Let me look at you! I think you've grown an inch!" She lowered herself to her knees and hugged her again. "Are you alright? Is everything . . . I mean . . ."

"I'm okay." Penelope's smile did not reach her eyes. "I just wish I didn't have ta stay here."

Edna nodded. "I wish that, too. For now, let's have a nice time together."

Penelope's smile broadened. "Okay." She tugged on Edna's arm. "I got somethin' ta show ya!"

When Edna, Jean, and Penelope arrived, Nathan's fish were already sizzling over a bed of hot coals.

Joseph welcomed the women, but Tepkunset was nowhere in sight. "My grandmother is not well. She is resting in the cabin." He offered Edna and Jean the bench. "Please sit down. When the fish are ready, we will have a meal of it with stewed tomatoes and onions." He pointed to a kettle hanging over another bed of hot coals.

While they waited to eat, Penelope beamed as she showed everyone her new possession, a cedar wood carving of a bird.

"Mr. Joseph made it for me. It's a raven. He said it's a totem spirit animal." She pointed to the sky. "He's been teaching me about the stars. The raven is in the con . . . the conselta . . ." She turned to Joseph and scowled. "I can't say that word."

Joseph smiled. "Constellation. The constellation Corvus."

Edna took the realistic image of the bird from Penelope and traced a finger over the fine details. "It's beautiful, Joseph." She handed the carving back to Penelope. "Are there other spirit animals?"

"Oh, yes," Joseph replied. "Many. The wolf, the owl, the otter, the falcon, and more. They all have traits we recognize in people born under each totem symbol."

"Spirit animals'r tied to when people were born?" Jean asked.

Joseph nodded. "That's correct. We believe people are born under spirit animals' signs. Each one aligns with a month on the calendar."

Holding the carving close, Penelope squeezed onto the bench between Edna and Jean. "I picked the raven 'cuz Mr. Joseph says I'm a survivor and . . ." Her brief frown turned into a smile. "Oh yeah! And 'cuz he says I'm in harmony with the island!" Her smile broadened. "Jus' like the raven!"

Joseph tossed a small log onto the fire. Red embers shot into the air. "It's an intelligent bird able to adapt to its environment." He chuckled. "The raven can also be very demanding . . . like Penelope when she teases to go home."

Struck with the realization that she had no idea when Penelope was born, Edna peered at the carving and turned to Penelope. "Well then, now you can tell me when your birthday is."

Penelope gazed up at Edna. She shrugged her shoulders. "I dunno when it is."

The fire crackled in the fire pit. Nathan turned the fish over the hot coals and added a few more small logs to the fire.

Joseph relit his pipe. Smoke from the bowl spiraled into the air. He cleared his throat. "According to the raven totem, Penelope's birth date would be between September 23 and October 22. It is up to her to pick a day."

Taking Penelope's hand, Edna stared at the child's upturned face.

Is it possible she doesn't know when she was born? Surely her mother would have done something for her daughter on her birthday. But Penelope was so young when Adelaide disappeared and with no one else to care, I guess she wouldn't remember.

Releasing Penelope's hand, Edna placed her arm around the child's shoulder and pulled her close. "Well, since it's now the beginning of November, you have a whole year to decide on a day." With increased enthusiasm, Edna added, "And we have a whole year to plan a birthday party."

Penelope's eyes widened. "A birthday party?"

The disbelief on Penelope's face tore at Edna's heart. She recalled her sons' parties and those of her friends' children in New Orleans. Dozens of rambunctious children, games, even pony rides followed by birthday gifts, treats, and, of course, a birthday cake.

Edna raised her eyebrows. "What's a birthday without a birthday party? Yes! A real birthday party."

***

By the time the meal was over, Nathan was anxious to leave. "Hate ta rush everybody, but I got a lot o' nets ta mend and cleanin' up ta do on my boat before headin' out again."

Joseph and Penelope, along with Bell, walked the trio to the beach. A tearful Penelope buried her face in Edna's embrace. "Please come back soon," she whimpered.

Gathering Penelope in her arms, Edna did her best to console her. "We'll return as soon as Mr. Nathan can get us here, darling."

All the way back to the dock, Edna fretted over her thoughtlessness.

Penelope cannot wait a whole year before celebrating her birthday.

By the time Nathan docked the boat, Edna had a plan.

***

Islands of Women

Two weeks passed before Nathan was free to take Edna and Jean back to the encampment.

"Sorry about the ropes an' nets. Just kick 'em to one side," Nathan said as he pushed off from the dock with an oar. "Watch out for that string o' mullet though. They're under them nets." He looked overhead at the brilliant late morning sky. "Gotta keep 'em out o' the sun."

Once settled, Jean wrapped her arm around Edna's shoulders. "Water's choppy t'day. Ye a'right?"

Edna leaned toward Jean. "I'm fine. Just glad it's not that far. Any longer than the twenty minutes it takes to get there, and I could be in trouble."

Following a joyful reunion with Penelope, Nathan and Joseph prepared a lunch of fried fish and roasted potatoes and corn.

"My grandmother apologizes once again that she is unable to join us," Joseph said as he stoked the flames in the campfire. "She and Penelope picked red mulberries early this morning, which made her very tired."

While the food cooked, Edna, Jean, and Penelope sorted through the mulberries discarding leaves and twigs.

"The Grandmother crushes the berries and makes a tea," Penelope explained. "She says it helps her sore joints."

After their meal, Jean showed everyone how to play a game she learned as a child. "Make a fist with both yer hands," she said. "I'll start." Tapping each fist with one of hers, she recited, "One potato, two potato, three potato, four, five potato, six potato, seven potato more."

Penelope giggled. "When's it my turn?"

"Yer next," Jean said. The last fist she tapped was one of Edna's. "Put that arm behind yer back, Edna."

The game went on, over and over and round and round, for nearly a half hour. Penelope's infectious laugh rippled throughout the camp, echoing above the soaring longleaf pines.

Finally, the dreaded moment came for Edna, Jean, and Nathan to depart.

Heartbroken to be left behind again, Penelope begged, "Please! Can't I go with you?"

Edna knelt down and held the little girl close to her. "Oh, sweet girl. I can't. Not yet. You have to stay here until . . .

Until what? And when?

"We need to be patient, dear. I know that's very hard for you. It is for me, too, but at least I know you're safe here with Mr. Joseph and Tepkunset." Edna pressed her lips together before adding, "And I think we all know it's best you don't go home, so promise you'll stay here?"

Penelope lowered her head and nodded. "I promise," she mumbled through her tears.

* * *

Back in her room in the hotel, Edna relived the cries of a despairing, tearful Penelope. She turned from the window and began preparing to go to bed. Pulling on her dressing gown, she mulled.

She can't go home. I can't bring her to the hotel.

Edna crawled into bed, switched off the lamp, and rested her hands on the roundness of her abdomen. Staring into the darkness, she recalled Dr. Bartlett's prophetic words: '. . . something is going to work out for you.'

Dear God, I pray he's right. I want to hear Penelope laugh again.

* * *

With Nathan off fishing, monotonous, seemingly endless days escalated Edna's worry for Penelope. Making and remaking beds, cleaning floors and bathrooms, and sorting and folding piles of laundry put her mind in a state of helpless indifference. Evening chats with Jean, two occasions to do portraits at the dock, and Dr. Barlett's Wednesday visits were her only diversions.

The Monday before Thanksgiving, Glory Bee paid Edna a visit. She dropped onto the boardwalk bench and mopped her brow.

"Needed a few things from the mercantile. Had ta rest before headin' back up that hill."

"You need to take it easy. That hill is steep." Edna patted Glory Bee's hand. "I'll be right back." She returned with two glasses of iced tea. Settling back on the bench, Edna asked, "How's Mrs. Peck?"

"Lawd a' mercy, Miss Edna. That woman lay up there in her bed howlin' like a wounded animal. Keeps sayin' 'jus' let me die' over and over. I keep askin' her if she's in pain. Jus' shakes her head an' tells me ta leave her be."

"That's terrible. What does Dr. Bartlett say could be wrong?"

"Says maybe it's her weak heart. Grievin' maybe lookin' back over her life. People do that, ya know. Prob'ly thinkin' o' Jeremy knowin' she won't never see him again. When Docta' B examines her, nothin' else appears ta be causin' so much pain ta make her carry on so."

**

On the Wednesday following the hectic Thanksgiving rush, as Edna stacked folded sheets and pillow cases in the linen closet, she was alerted to footsteps hastening up the stairway. Dr. Bartlett hurried toward her.

"Edna! Thank God!" He took her by the arm and pulled her toward her room. "Come. Gather your things. I've already cleared it with Lloyd for you to leave. We must hurry."

Perplexed by Dr. Bartlett's apparent distress, at her bedroom door, Edna pulled her arm free. "Wait! What do you mean you've cleared 'it' with Lloyd? Cleared what? Where are we going?"

Opening the door, he grabbed Edna's arm again and pulled her into the room. He frantically looked around. "Glory Bee's had an accident. Where's something to put your belongings in?"

"An accident?! What kind of accident?!"

"I'll explain on the way! Now hurry!"

Minutes later, after helping Edna into the carriage, Dr. Bartlett climbed aboard. "Those damnable stairs!" he shouted, snapping the reins on Bessie's rump.

As the carriage whisked the two up the hill to Birdie Peck's house, Edna struggled to control the hammering of her heart. Clutching her satchel stuffed with her belongings against her expanded girth, she prayed.

I never should have left her. Please be alright. Please be alright. Lord, give me strength.

Chapter Twenty-One

With her right arm bound up in a plaster of Paris cast, Glory Bee did the best she could to adjust the bed pillows with her left arm. She needed to use the chamber pot, but with her right leg also in a cast, she could not manage by herself.

"Tom!"

The back door squeaked open then slammed shut. Glory Bee's husband, Tom, hustled into the bedroom mumbling, "I'm a'comin'. I'm a'comin'. What ya need now?"

Glory Bee pointed to the chamber pot. "Ya know I can't do this by m'self an' I ain't been once since last night."

"Well, you was sleepin' when I looked in on ya', so I was gatherin' eggs ta take ta Miss Edna. She ran out o' eggs yesta'day an' Miz Peck is gonna want her eggs fer her breakfast."

Tom raised Glory Bee to a sitting position. Following the arduous undertaking of helping Glory Bee relieve her toilet needs, he returned her to her bed.

Before leaving, he scolded, "Won't be long takin' those eggs, so don't be tryin' anything like ya did yesta'day."

Glory Bee mumbled, "Figured I could'a gotten m'self a glass o' water."

"Well, now ya know ya can't. Lucky ya didn't break another arm or leg. I'll bring ya a glass o' water before I leave an' fix our breakfast when I git back."

"How's Miss Edna doin'? Glory Bee asked. "Been weeks since she's been lookin' out fer Miz Peck."

"She's doin' jus' fine. Church ladies still poppin' in every now an' then, an' Miss Jean is spendin' more'n more time helpin' out.

Tom grinned as he scratched his graying chin whiskers. "Who'd o' thought them ladies and the likes o' somebody like Miss Jean would be caught workin' side by side. And o' course, Miz Peck ain't likin' bein' stuck in bed, but ain't nothin' she can do about it."

"Time comin' on for that baby," Glory Bee said, her voice filled with concern.

"Miss Edna says she don't mind bein' there by herself in the night," Tom said. "With her belly gettin' bigger an' bigger, jus' needs help durin' the day."

Glory Bee slumped against the pillows. For the umpteenth time, she shook her head and grumbled, "If I'd o' only taken the time ta fix the hem o' that dress."

Tom stepped into the kitchen and returned with a glass of water. "Well, too late ta be frettin' over spilt milk. Fact is, like Doc said, with a tumble like you took down those stairs, you won't be fit ta be workin' least ways climbin' stairs for a long time, so ya may as well git used to it.

He set the glass of water on the night stand. "I asked ya t'other day. What if ya broke yer neck? Like I been sayin', far as I'm concerned, Miz Peck's gettin' taken care of jus' fine, so mebbe it's time fer ya to fergit goin' back there anyways."

After Tom left, Glory Bee gazed out the bedroom window. With the weather turning cooler, she longed to be outside tending her garden.

Them radishes, carrots, an' collards goin' crazy. Need ta get some to Miss Edna. Maybe Tom's right. Maybe I should give up workin' for Miz. Peck. Plenty ta do 'round here, an' I ain't gettin' any younger. Miz Peck's needin' more an' more care ... more'n I can do by m'self.

Recalling the years caring for Mrs. Peck, despite the tension between them over Jeremy, Olivia, and their shared granddaughter, Priscilla, Glory Bee could not imagine her life without her work at the Peck house.

I'll think about it. Christmas next week. Can't do no preservin' or decoratin'.

Snuggling deeper into the pillows, Glory Bee chuckled.

That piece o' cake Tom brought me last week looked like a mud pie. Miss Edna got a lot ta learn.

* * *

Edna leaned into the sink's edge as close as her pregnancy would permit and pumped water into the kettle. She hefted it onto the wood stove and dropped a dozen eggs into the water. Pressing the ache in her back with her fists, she pondered whether to sweep or to wash the breakfast dishes. Instead, she pulled a chair from the table and sat down.

A voice chirped from the back porch. "Yoo-hoooo! Mornin' to ye!" Jean let herself in and stared at Edna. "Ye a'right?"

Edna forced a smile. "I'm fine. It's . . . well, my back is troubling me right now, but I'll be fine once I lie down awhile." She frowned. "You're awfully early. I wasn't expecting you until later."

Jean grinned. "Aye, well, got a good night's sleep." Pulling a chair from the table, she sat down. "Knowin' none o' the church ladies could be here t'day, figured ye'd need help wi' chores. More comfortable when they ain't here anyways. Caught a couple of 'em in the larder t'other day talkin' behind me back. Not as bad as t'was at first, but if t'wasn't fer lookin' out fer Miz Peck, prob'ly wouldn't bother helpin' either one o' us." She nodded toward Edna's belly. "How's the wee one this mornin'?"

Edna arched her back then slumped against the chair. "He's very active. I'm having trouble sleeping."

"'He' eh? Ye keep sayin' 'he.'"

"I guess from having two sons, it seems natural to call this one a 'he.'" Placing her palms on the table, Edna pushed herself up with a grunt. "I'm glad you're here, Jean. If you don't mind, I'll go lie down a while."

"Ye g'w'on. I'll do up these dishes and take care o' whatever's in that kettle. Anythin' else needs doin'?"

"Sweeping and dusting as always. Maybe debone the chicken carcass in the pantry. A little cold chicken with tomato slices and a hard-boiled egg will be plenty for Mrs. Peck's lunch. Ours, too, for that matter." Edna placed her hand on Jean's arm. "Your being here means the world. I hope you know that."

Jean scoffed. "Bein' here instead o' day after day in the hotel means the world ta me, too, don't ye know! Now g'w'on wi' ye. Get some rest. I'll be up ta check on ye later and peep in at Mrs. Peck. Sometimes I think she fakes sleepin' when I go in her room."

Lifting her head, Jean sniffed. "Jus' might pour me a cup o' that coffee and sit on the back porch a spell before tacklin' the chores." She giggled. "Bu' first, I'm gonna watch ye waddle ta the stairs."

Holding onto the door jamb leading to the hallway, Edna laughed and called over her shoulder. "Don't choke on your coffee, Jean!"

As the baby rolled and punched her insides, Edna turned side to side in her bed to find a bit of comfort. She groaned against the ache in her back.

If only I could lie on my stomach. Two months to go . . . at least if Dr. Bartlett's calculation is accurate. Maybe I'll know more when he comes tomorrow.

Desperate for sleep, Edna closed her eyes and willed her body to relax. Eventually, exhaustion drove her into a fitful sleep fraught with disturbing dreams . . . her sons calling for their mother and Jean screaming for Kathleen. She woke with a start as Penelope's boat began to sink with the little girl in it.

Gasping for breath, Edna struggled to sit up then stand. At the window, she pushed up the sash and breathed in the cool ocean air.

It's been too long . . . since Thanksgiving. She'll think I've abandoned her. Christmas is next week. I must go see her.

Following a tap on the bedroom door, Jean called, "Edna, ye 'wake?"

Edna turned from the window. "Yes. Come in."

"I peeked in at ye 'while ago. Ye were sleepin' so I let ye be."

"I did manage to get some sleep." Edna sat on her bed. "Jean, I need to see Penelope. I wonder if Nathan could take me to the camp again."

"Aye, s'pose he can. Come Saturday, when ye go to the dock ta do yer drawin's, he'll prob'ly be 'round ta ask."

Edna shook her head. "I don't want to wait that long. I want to find him . . . to see if he could take me today. I'm worried, Jean. I haven't seen her since Thanksgiving, and she was so distraught last time we were there. I . . . I need to know she's alright."

"Well, we can't leave Miz Peck alone. And I don't like ye tryin' to get down ta the dock by yerself."

"I'll be fine. Are you okay staying here for the day?"

"Aye. Nothin' 'til the weekend."

Edna sat on the edge of the bed. She looked up at Jean with a hopeful smile. "I don't suppose you would mind helping me with my shoes, would you?"

Kneeling, Jean reminisced. "Comes back ta me watchin' ye. Wee things git harder an' harder ta do." She tugged both shoes onto Edna's swollen feet and laced them both. Standing, she perched her fists on her hips and looked at Edna. "Come ta that, Miz Peck can fend fer herself awhile 'cuz I'm goin' wi' ye."

At the bottom of the hill, Edna convinced Jean she could make her way to the dock on her own. Laboring her way toward the waterfront, she spotted Nathan sitting on the dock's edge seemingly buried in a pile of fishing net.

He tossed the net aside when he spotted her and jumped up. "What in the world . . . ?" Nathan drew closer and took Edna by the arm. "What're you doin' down here by yerself?" Looking around, he asked, "Where's Jean?"

Over the past few months, a brotherly camaraderie between Edna and Nathan had developed. Taking Nathan's hands in hers, Edna implored, "I was hoping to find you. I need to see Penelope. Can you take me?" She raised her eyebrows. "Today?"

"Today? What's the rush?"

"Well, it's been since Thanksgiving that I last saw her. And I'm worried. Something tells me . . . I just need to know she's alright."

Nathan stared at Edna for a few moments. "I guess the nets can wait a few hours." He gripped her arm. "Let's go."

The sun was reaching its zenith by the time Nathan and Edna arrived on the shore leading to the Seminole's camp. The smell of wood smoke permeated the overgrowth.

Once out of the boat, Edna hustled over the forest floor, her hands beneath the fullness of her pregnancy bearing its weight.

Nathan attempted to restrain her. "Slow down. We don't need you fallin' before we get there."

At last, the encampment came into view, smoke spiraling from the wood fire. No one appeared to be about as they approached.

Edna made for a wood bench and sat down to catch her breath.

Nathan skirted the camp. "Hallo!" he called.

The door to the cabin opened and Joseph came toward them.

Edna peered at his face that appeared frozen with . . . what? Worry? Sadness?

His hand outstretched, Nathan approached Joseph. "It's good to see you." He looked around the camp then back to Joseph. "We've come to see Penelope. Edna felt bad that she hadn't seen her since Thanksgiving, so I offered to bring her today. We hope we haven't disturbed you and your grandmother."

Joseph shook Nathan's hand then glanced toward the cabin.

"I'm sorry my grandmother isn't well enough to see you today." He turned to Edna. "Greetings, Miss Edna. You are becoming great with your child."

Edna sensed a delay tactic. "Yes, I certainly am. Joseph, I want to see Penelope. Where is she?"

Joseph looked down, hesitating as if searching for the right words. He faced Edna, who by now was becoming fretful. In a flat voice, he said, "Penelope is not here."

A buzzing sound escalated in Edna's head. Convinced she would swoon, she gripped the edge of the bench. Nathan was instantly by her side holding her upright. Edna could only stare at Joseph.

"Three days ago, when I woke, Penelope was gone." Joseph nodded toward the nearby shoreline. "As was her little boat. She took a few strings of smoked fish, oranges, and some loaves of bread.

Shaking his head, Joseph's long blue-black hair shimmered in a stream of sunlight. "I have taught her well the ways of the Indian. We heard nothing." He sat down on another bench. "She had been crying and asking to go home. I could not do that and could only comfort her with promises you would be back soon."

Edna could barely catch her breath. The buzzing was subsiding, but her limbs had gone weak.

I knew it. I knew I should have come sooner.

Choked with heartbreak and mostly fear, Edna's tears streamed down her face. She turned to Nathan. "We have to find her."

Nathan nodded. "We do, but where? The hotel?"

"She may have gone there looking for me." Edna wiped her tears and scowled. "No. Jean would have seen her or at least learned from Molly that she'd been there." She held her hand to her chest. "I suppose she could have gone to her house."

Several silent, gut-wrenching moments passed before a hint of a smile crossed Edna's face. Turning to Nathan, she used the strength of his arm to stand up.

Perplexed, Nathan stared up at her. "What?"

"We need to get back to your boat. I know where she is."

Chapter Twenty-Two

Penelope unrolled a blanket woven in varied shades of blue, red, green, and amber. "Tepkunset made it for me." She settled cross-legged on one end of it. "I roll up in it at night."

Edna lowered her knees onto the blanket and ran a hand over the knobby texture. "The colors are beautiful."

"Tepkunset makes dyes from all kinds o' stuff." Penelope giggled. "She got mad at me 'cuz I kept eatin' the berries she was usin' for the red dye."

Gathering the abundant fabric of her oversized dress, Edna stretched out on her side then rolled onto her back.

"Mrs. Peck's dresses are a bit loose, but I'm beginning to fill them out." She turned to Penelope, a look of mock concern. "I hope you can help me get back up again."

"I'll help ya." Having rolled onto her belly, Penelope propped her chin in her hand. "Do you want yer baby ta be a boy or a girl?"

Lately, Edna frequently asked herself that same question, especially when thinking about Etienne and Raoul. Her longing to see her sons had gradually diminished with the passing months. She would think of them fondly, but as for their presence, she had to admit she did not miss their raucous play and ceaseless squabbling. When she would grow irritated with them, their nanny would scurry them away from her.

Edna stared up at the canopy of swaying pine boughs, their

pungent resin scent filling the air. As pine needles floated and drifted across the ground, she again recalled Cassatt's familial paintings. Edna would feel like an outsider when looking at the engaging interaction between little children and their mothers. The physical act of giving birth to her sons was just that . . . a physical act without the maternal connection she observed between other mothers and their children. With no responsibilities for her sons' care from the time they were born, her disconnect with them became more acute.

Unlike her previous confinements, which she could not wait to end, during this pregnancy, Edna hummed lullabies and rubbed her hands over her abdomen hoping the infant would move. She pondered who the baby would look like, praying it would favor her dark hair and blue eyes.

One day, she opened the trunk in her room filled with baby clothes meant for Glory Bee's and Mrs. Peck's granddaughter, Priscilla. Holding up a monogrammed gown, Edna pondered names using the three P's. The child's last name would, of course, be Pontellier. For first names, she always liked Paulette for a girl; for a boy, perhaps Paul. Whether or not she could use the clothes for her baby, knowing she would be fully responsible for its care sparked feelings she had never experienced with her sons.

No matter what this baby is, I want to be a good mother. I will be a good mother.

Edna turned to face Penelope. "Well, since I don't have any say in the matter, I'll be happy with whichever one it is. I only want it to be healthy. Now, I have a question for you."

She took Penelope's hand. "Why did you leave the camp? Tepkunset and Joseph were taking such good care of you. They . . . we don't understand."

Penelope pulled her hand away and rolled onto her back. Several moments passed before she spoke.

"I wanted . . . I missed my Mama. She called this our safe place.

I used ta pretend it was jus' me 'n her livin' here." She turned to Edna. "I couldn't stay away any longer."

"Couldn't you have come for a while and then gone back to the camp?"

Penelope gnawed her lower lip. "I was ... I didn't want nothin' ta happen to Tepkunset and Mr. Joseph if my ... if Pa came lookin' for me."

In the months since meeting Penelope, Edna assumed the child's avoidance and palpable fear of her father was due solely to his alcoholic often gun-toting violence. Her resistance to go to her home in Hungry Bend seemed so obvious.

Who wouldn't be afraid of a father like that? After all, the whole town avoided him.

Over time, Edna attributed Penelope's small bruises and scratches to her near-vagabond existence. Then there was Penelope's vacant, sad look, much too discerning for a child her age.

Could I have been so consumed with my own troubles that I didn't notice ... or if I did, chose to avoid asking how she got them? Adelaide called it their 'safe place.' Safe from what exactly?

An array of puzzle pieces began to coalesce, and Edna was overcome with a sickening chill. Taking hold of Penelope's hand, Edna thought hard before speaking.

"Penelope, is that the only reason you're afraid of your father ... that he might harm Mr. Joseph and Tepkunset?"

Only the surf washing ashore in the distance and the rustle of an escalating breeze through the pines broke the deafening quiet.

Penelope turned onto her side and curled herself into a ball, her back to Edna. Bell, waking from her slumber next to the blanket, crawled on her belly toward Penelope and whimpered. Several moments passed.

Edna laid a hand on the child's arm. "Penelope?"

Penelope began to shake with a choking sob.

Alarmed, Edna pulled Penelope to her and stroked her head. "Penelope, tell me. What did he do? What has he done to you?"

Shaking her head, Penelope answered with a strangled "Nothin'."

"Penelope, look at me. Tell me what he's done."

Grief that had piled up during Penelope's short life seemed on the verge of exploding through uncontrollable shaking and sobbing.

Bell crawled closer to Penelope, laid a paw on her arm, and whimpered.

Penelope wrapped her arms around the dog's neck and buried her face in Bell's thick fur. She finally ceased sobbing but kept her back to Edna. At last, she spoke in a quivered voice. "I don't like my Pa touchin' me."

It took some effort for Edna to sit up. Shaken, she pulled Penelope onto her lap. Cradling the little girl, she rocked her side to side, her soothing shushes gradually calming her.

Penelope slowly grew limp in Edna's arms.

Several minutes passed as Edna continued to rock the child. Eventually, she rested her chin on Penelope's head. "I have a question," she said quietly.

Penelope stiffened and tried to pull away.

"No, no," Edna said as she tightened her grip. "Not about . . . not about your father. Not now anyway. Something else. Look at me please."

Penelope turned her head toward Edna but remained downcast.

Placing her fingers under Penelope's chin, Edna lifted the girl's head. "I want you to look at me. This is important."

Penelope wiped smudged tears from her face and looked at Edna through red-rimmed, tear-filled eyes.

Though her heart was breaking, Edna smiled. "There you are," she said as she held Penelope by the shoulders. "I have some news. I'm not working at the hotel any longer."

Penelope sniffled. "You aren't?"

"No. I'm living at Mrs. Peck's house while Glory Bee . . . well, we'll get to that. I'm working there now, and my question is what do you think about coming there to stay . . . at least for a while?"

Penelope gawked at Edna. She licked her lips and swallowed. When the question finally registered, she flung her arms around Edna's neck.

"Oh, Miss Edna! Can I?" She let go and looked at Edna with disbelief. "Really? I can come live with you?"

Edna smiled. "I think it's a grand idea, don't you?" Her voice grew serious. "Of course, you must understand we'll have to do our best to keep from disturbing Mrs. Peck. She's nearly bedridden now, so we'll have to be very quiet especially when we're upstairs. Do you think you can do that?"

Penelope nodded then looked at Bell. "What about Bell?"

"Same with Bell. We have to remember this isn't my house. I'm only working and staying there for, well, for as long as I'm needed, so we'll have to keep Bell very quiet."

Penelope patted Bell's head. "She's a good dog. She'll be quiet."

"One other thing," Edna said, her voice taking on a more serious tone. "You must go to school. You can start back after Christmas. Agreed?"

With scant enthusiasm, Penelope said, "Yes, ma'am."

Edna tugged on Penelope's deerskin dress. "We'll ask Miss Jean if we can get Kathleen's clothes back. Now, let's gather up this blanket and anything else . . ." She looked around Penelope's haven. "I guess there isn't much else to bring, is there?"

Penelope's gaze shifted from Edna and lingered for several moments over the two grave markers. Kneeling beside her mother's, she adjusted the stones and rocks she had piled in front of the cross. When she stood up, she stared at the marker all the while chewing on her lower lip. Picking up her blanket, she scooted past Edna.

"No. Nothin' else," she mumbled.

Not for the first time Edna puzzled over Penelope's attention to Adelaide's grave . . . a grave that was not a grave at all but simply a touching memorial to her mother. She recalled another occasion, before Penelope added the stones and rocks, when Penelope had piled more dirt on the small area in front of the cross.

"Do you have something of your Mama's buried there?" Edna had asked.

Penelope had avoided looking at her and only shook her head.

Now, once again, Edna found herself pondering Penelope's wary behavior.

Is she hiding something?

Racing toward the water and her boat, Penelope yelled, "Come on, Miss Edna!"

Edna glanced one last time at the grave marker. "Coming!" she called. Having caught up with Penelope, Edna said, "Miss Jean will be wondering where I am."

"Miss Jean's at Miz Peck's house, too?"

"Only to help me with chores. She isn't staying there."

"Where's Glory Bee? Is she okay?"

"Glory Bee's fine. Come along. We'll talk about that when we get to the house."

Once again, Edna cringed as she climbed into Penelope's little boat. A light chop on the water did nothing to assuage her discomfort, but Penelope deftly maneuvered the boat close to shore. Before long, they were back to the same beach where Penelope had discovered Edna months before.

As they trudged up the hill, a stiff, chilly December wind off the water rustled the sea oats and whipped up sand off the dunes. In her labored walk through the sand, Edna cast off worries of upsetting Mrs. Peck.

If she discovers Penelope and Bell staying in her house, so be it. What could she do about it in her condition anyway?

Far more concerning were the grotesque images of Penelope's monstrous father and the physical and emotional harm he inflicted on his young daughter.

How could he? How could a father do this to his child? I'll talk to Dr. Bartlett when he comes tomorrow. But if I do, what will happen to Penelope? Would she be taken away . . . somewhere? I can't let that happen. But neither can I ignore what her father has done to her. Surely there are laws . . .

Having raced ahead to the top of the hill, Penelope waved an arm and shouted, "Hurry, Miss Edna!"

Though warmed by Penelope's evident excitement, Edna wrestled with her thoughts.

Maybe she'll be alright. If she has a real safe place to live, maybe in time she'll forget the ugliness in her life. But who am I to be offering Penelope a home when I don't have one for myself and this baby?

It was too much to unravel. For the time being, she would provide Penelope with as much love and care as was possible in Birdie Peck's house.

At the top of the hill, Edna took Penelope's hand and smiled at the child's eager face. "Let's go home."

* * *

Edna stared out her bedroom window, her arms crossed above her round mid-riff. Sunbeams winked through tree branches bobbing in a stiff wind off the Gulf. She turned to Dr. Bartlett. "So, what you're saying is nothing can be done to that man?"

Dr. Bartlett leaned back in Edna's bedroom chair. "I'm sad to say the law would protect Penelope's dog before it would protect her. If Bell was abused, there's an animal abuse law protecting that dog. Is it right? Of course not. But that's the law.

Placing his medical bag on his lap, Dr. Bartlett continued. "Don't get me wrong. I love animals much as the next man, but I'd like to think that one day, children will rise above the importance of animals in terms of protection in the eyes of the law."

Shaking her head, Edna returned to her bed and sat down. "People had to know."

Dr. Bartlett snorted. "Oh, I suspect more than a few around here had an inkling of what's gone on in that shack down yonder. Not many will venture near Hungry Bend. Bottom of the barrel, you know. Maybe an attitude if I don't see it, it isn't happening. That is if they even spent any time concerned about it.

He stood and placed the chair against the far wall. "And what if they did know? Reverend Albright does his best, but only so much can be done when there's no law supporting him."

Dr. Bartlett moved toward the bedroom door. "Another thing you might not have heard about Adelaide's disappearance. Speculation among a few is she discovered what Jasper was doing and probably threatened him.

He opened the door. "Nobody wants to mess with Jasper Worth, Edna. It's sad Penelope's had to fend for herself. Like I said, if Penelope was a dog . . . Now, I've got to go check on Birdie. And you need to rest. You said Penelope's napping in her room, so get those legs up for a spell. The baby's doing fine, but keep an eye on your ankles. Drink lots of water and stay away from the salt. We don't want that swelling to get out of hand. I'll see you next week. Have a Merry Christmas."

Edna stretched out on her bed woozy and sickened by Dr. Bartlett's revelation of Adelaide's possible demise and Jasper's treatment of his little daughter. She could only shake her head with disgust.

Christmas next Monday.

Closing her eyes, Edna recalled images of resplendent holiday festivities. Endless parties and galas, elegant carte du jour, candlelight glowing in every room, layers of wrapped packages tied with glittering red and green ribbons and bows stacked around a ten-foot tinseled and garlanded Christmas tree in the parlor of her home. Pine Cove's humble holiday events, most of which centered on church activities, could in no way compare to the mind-boggling extravagance of her former life.

The baby poked Edna's ribs, and she turned onto her side. Gazing out the window, once again, her thoughts drifted to the father of her unborn child, Alcée Arobin. Her face burned with the memory of their affair.

Oh, Alcée. Knowing the philanderer you are, how could I . . . ?

Edna had given up caring what Pine Cove's town gossipers might be saying about her pregnancy.

They can only speculate, so let them talk. It's certainly no worse than the gossip I brought on myself back home.

Reverend Albright, who had visited recently, reminded her that everybody makes mistakes. "We learn from them," he said, adding, "Isn't it amazing how without struggles we wouldn't discover our strengths?

In reply to her self-admonishment of her thoughtless and reckless actions, he reminded her, "You're human, Edna. Be grateful you've been given another chance for a new beginning. Ask for God's forgiveness and move forward."

Edna had replied, "I can't even seem to forgive myself."

Scowling, Reverend Albright had leaned close to Edna's face. "And you think your forgiveness of yourself is a higher standard than God's forgiveness?"

His comment had jolted Edna. She finally replied, "I never thought about it that way."

Edna's unfinished letter to Léonce, which she had started while at the hotel, lay in a drawer beneath her under garments. She had taken out the letter numerous times with the intention of adding to it but each time returned it to the drawer. Over and over, she reached the same conclusion.

Léonce, my sons, my friends . . . all believe me dead. Letting them know I'm alive would only raise questions. I certainly can't go back with a child that Léonce would know isn't his. And what about Penelope?

Edna turned onto her other side and stared at the bureau drawer.

I have a chance at a new beginning here. But how will I live? How can I provide Penelope with the home she deserves when I've no idea how I'll take care of this baby?

With Reverend Albright's words fresh in her mind, Edna left her bed and retrieved the unfinished letter from the drawer. Rereading the few words telling Léonce she was alive, she again wrestled with her dilemma.

No matter what, I can't go back. I must move on. I'll resume my artwork once the baby comes. Maybe Lloyd will let me work at the hotel again. Will it be enough? Only God knows.

Edna hesitated but a moment before tearing the letter into shreds and dropping the pieces into the pocket of her dress.

I'll toss them in the stove later.

Returning to her bed, she breathed in deeply and rested her hands on her abdomen. Outside the window, the jingle of bells from the street presumably from a horse and carriage brought Edna back to the present. The merry sound made her smile.

I wonder if Penelope has ever made paper snowflakes or strung popcorn.

Chapter Twenty-Three

"Don't be lettin' that fire go out in the stove, Miss Edna. Ya got plenty o' firewood on the back porch now, so y'all be alright 'til this snap passes." Tom rubbed his hands together over the stove. "An' don't be messin' with that fireplace in the livin' room. No tellin' how much soot an' pine tar up in that chimney. Don't need riskin' settin' the house on fire."

Edna wiped her wet hands on a towel. "Thank you, Tom. Happy New Year." She followed Tom to the door. "Please tell Glory Bee how glad we'll be to see her."

"Yes, ma'am. Said this mornin' next week can't come soon enough ta git back here." Tom tipped his hat. "Happy New Year to y'all."

Opening the kitchen door, he was met with a blast of frigid air. "Cold 'nough ta freeze a bucket o' saltwater," he muttered before closing the door.

During the coldest months, with most homes on Pine Cove Key heated with coal and wood, chimney fires were fairly common. In the night, when temperatures dropped even colder, the sky occasionally would glow from a roaring blaze somewhere on the island. Along with the town's lone fire truck, bucket brigades would form but often did little to save the old and dry wood structures.

On New Year's Eve, as clocks approached midnight and Pine

Cove Key quietly prepared to bid farewell to 1906, the fire truck siren alerted residents of a fire in Hungry Bend. A crowd of townsfolk gathered, grew, and only watched as Jasper Worth's clapboard shack burned to the ground.

No one had seen Jasper and his horse and wagon for weeks. With Penelope living in Birdie Peck's house, it was safe to say the shack was unoccupied when the fire started. As for how it started, no one knew . . . or cared.

Edna and Penelope, wrapped in heavy quilts, stood in Mrs. Peck's front yard gazing down the hill as the flames died.

"I didn't get my book." The rattle of wind-blown palm fronds nearly drowned out Penelope's voice.

Wrapping an arm around Penelope's shoulder, Edna bent down to hear better. "A book, you said?"

"My princess book."

Edna pulled Penelope closer. "What was the book about?"

Penelope shrugged. "It was about a princess. Most o' the pages was ripped out. I just liked her dress."

"I see. What was her dress like?"

"It was long and pink and had ruffles." Gazing up at Edna, Penelope pulled the quilt tighter. "It had sparkly things on it. I like things that sparkle."

"I like things that sparkle, too," Edna said. "Like how the stars sparkle at night and the sparkles on the water when the sun shines on it."

Penelope's long stare disarmed Edna.

She has to be in shock over yet another loss.

Penelope continued to stare at Edna. Twice she opened her mouth as if to say something. Instead, she pressed her lips together and looked back at the smoldering rubble of her home.

Edna's instincts suggested Penelope's withdrawal might be attributed to more than the loss of her home and her book.

"Penelope, this has to be awfully hard seeing your home

destroyed. And your book, of course. If something else is wrong, you'll tell me, won't you?"

Moments passed before Penelope nodded. "Yes, ma'am."

The two continued to stare at the smoking remnants of Penelope's home for several minutes. Edna finally broke the silence.

"Well, a princess usually wears a robe." She pulled the quilt tighter around Penelope. "This works pretty well, don't you think?"

Penelope shrugged. "I guess." She pulled away from Edna's embrace and turned toward the house. "I wanna' go inside now. C'mon, Bell."

Since moving into Mrs. Peck's house, when not in school, Penelope spent most of her waking hours in the warm kitchen with Edna and whoever else was there to help with chores. She seemed content most of the time doing her homework or drawing, but when Edna would catch Penelope staring at her, the child would quickly look away.

"I'm trying not to make anything of it, at least not yet," Edna told Dr. Bartlett during his visit the second Wednesday in January. "She's been through so much. Sometimes, she acts . . ." Edna pondered. "I guess I would say wary. When she acts like that, she seems sad and won't even look at me. Maybe it's too soon to expect her to overcome . . ." Edna sighed. "Maybe it's too soon for her to act like a . . . like a normal child."

"You might be expecting too much too soon. How's she doing in school?" he asked.

"She doesn't want to go. The kids make fun of her and joke about her father and where she used to live. Elmer Truegood follows her wanting to kiss her."

Dr. Bartlett scowled. "I'll speak to Sylvester about Elmer again. I've told him over and over he's got to rein in that boy." He shook his head. "Body too big for his age and a brain too damaged for . . . well, you get the idea. As for the other kids making fun of her, I guess that's just kids. They'll pick on the weakest of the lot."

"I suppose you're right." Edna's thoughts shifted. "How's Glory Bee? Tom said this morning she's ready to come back to work next week. He didn't appear too happy about it."

Dr. Bartlett chuckled. "Can't keep that woman down. Her arm and leg have mended just fine. It'll take time to work out the stiffness, but she can get around mostly on her own. Tom's been after her for a while to give up working here. Now with you here . . . you and Jean and the ladies from the church looking out for Birdie, he's all the more determined she stay home.

Dr. Bartlett looked around the bedroom then to Edna. "This house is a big part of who Glory Bee is." He raised his eyebrows. "I suppose you know all about Olivia and Jeremy."

Edna nodded. "And Priscilla. Glory Bee told me a few months ago. Very sad."

"Sun rose and set on that baby. Nearly killed Glory Bee when they got run off. And then when Birdie stood with the rest of the townsfolk . . . well, as you say, very sad."

Edna nodded. "Do you think they'll ever come back?"

Dr. Bartlett shook his head. "They'd be risking their lives if they came back here. Probably wouldn't even make it through the Carolinas. No tolerance in the South for Coloreds and Whites marrying."

In the coming weeks, Mrs. Peck's health deteriorated significantly. With Edna's pregnancy nearing its term and her swollen ankles forcing her to spend more time lying down, Jean and the church ladies spent more time at the house.

"Don't ya be worryin' about Miz Peck an' these chores," Jean said as she set a kettle of water on the stove. "Me an' the church ladies'r takin' turns. The Rev'rend pops in almost every day, too. He goes up ta say prayers with Miz Peck and reads ta her out o' the Bible.

Jean pulled out a kitchen chair and sat down. "Edna, ye know wha' Miss Lydia did? Ye know, the one that always brings her Bible wi' her? We had occasion ta talk an' I told her about me Tim an' Kathleen dyin'. She got so choked up, when she come back next day, she brought me a Bible.

Jean shook her head. "Never had a Bible o' me own." Reaching across the table with a laugh, she tapped Edna on her hand. "Next thing ye know, I'll be gettin' invited ta Bible study."

On Monday of the third week of January, Tom brought Glory Bee with him when he made his delivery of more firewood and eggs.

Using Tom's arm as a crutch, Glory Bee limped up the front steps and hobbled into the kitchen. "Land sakes, Miss Edna! You look ready ta pop any minute!"

Shaking flour dust off her hands, Edna set the bowl of biscuit dough aside and pulled a chair from the table. "Glory Bee! I'm so glad to see you! Sit down! Let me fix you a cup of tea."

Tom rested a hand on Glory Bee's shoulder. "I'll be back this afta'noon ta bring you home. Don't let me hear ya been climbin' those stairs now. Hear?"

By mid-morning, Jean and the church ladies had arrived. Jean took immediate control.

"Glory Bee and Edna, you two handle the cookin'. The rest o' us'll take care o' laundry, cleanin', and carin' fer Miz Peck."

During the last week in January, Reverend Albright and the church ladies held candlelight vigils for Mrs. Peck. Gathering around her bed, they read from the *Book of Psalms*. They sang *Amazing Grace, How Great Thou Art, Go Tell It on the Mountain,* and other hymns they knew to be Birdie's favorites.

On January 27, Winifred Roberta Peck breathed her last breath.

"God rest her soul," was all Glory Bee said following Dr. Bartlett's conclusion that Birdie died of a massive heart attack.

Other than gratitude to Mrs. Peck for harboring her in her time of need, Edna could only feel great sadness for a woman who, to her last breath, chose to reject her family. Try as she might, Edna could not censor the small voice mulling in her head.

How can I judge her? Didn't I do the same with my own family?

Edna could only speculate Glory Bee's myriad emotions in processing Mrs. Peck's passing. Forgoing sentiments that might have appeared shallow or perhaps trivialized the decades-long relationship between the two women, Edna simply said, "Glory Bee, I'm so sorry."

The following few days brought countless residents to Mrs. Peck's house for her wake. Platters and dishes of food covered every inch of the kitchen and dining room tables. Edna, Jean, and the church ladies alternated in making and serving iced tea. The church pews burst at the seams with tearful residents attending the funeral service of Pine Cove Key's grand matriarch.

A few days after Mrs. Peck's funeral, Elmer Truegood ran into his father's café. Hopping up and down in a frenzied fit, he pulled on Sylvester's arm. "Ya hafta' come!" he shouted over and over.

As Sylvester pulled off his apron, he called to Nathan, who was sitting at a table eating his lunch. "Nathan, keep an eye on things, will ya? Just 'til I git back." Sylvester ran out the door to catch up with his son.

Arriving at a remote part of the island where Elmer had been scavenging the beach, the boy pointed to a Live Oak tree several yards ahead. "See?" Elmer whispered.

Sylvester did see, and on approach, knew instantly whose bloated, grotesque body dangled by the neck from a rope tied to an outstretched branch. Jasper Worth's arms had been bound by the wrists behind his back. His shredded coveralls revealed his body had been slashed multiple times presumably with a knife. Birds had pecked his eyeballs clean leaving hollow black holes. The body had to have been hanging there for days . . . perhaps longer. There was no sign of Jasper's horse and wagon.

With no known kin, other than Penelope, and no obvious suspects or witnesses, Levy County law enforcement closed the case.

"Menace to society, he was. No great loss," said the county sheriff. "Word has it Jasper raped and killed a Seminole girl up north o' the Suwannee." He spat a stream of tobacco juice onto a cabbage palm then shoved his hands into his jacket pockets. "Indians don't take kindly to that kind o' rubbish."

The sheriff spat again. "Tracked down a few o' the gang members he was involved with up north o' the river. Might all hang." Shrugging, he walked back to his buggy and called over his shoulder. "Jus' sayin'."

Outrage arose among both Coloreds and Whites over which cemetery to bury Jasper in.

Glory Bee's husband, Tom, ranted. "Ain't no way that heathen's gonna rot anywhere near our kin!"

Voices among the White community mirrored Tom's feelings over their hallowed ground. A few shouted, "Drag his body out ta sea."

In the end, Jasper was buried in a remote uninhabited part of the island far from either cemetery. No one, not even Penelope, chose to be there when the body was interred. Reverend Albright stood over the grave for a brief moment, presumably praying for Jasper's soul. No one was willing to pay for a grave marker.

Speculation as to who killed Jasper ranged from thugs he was purported to be involved with and who he may have owed money, to a member of the Seminole Indian tribe, to someone from any one of several Colored communities spanning Pine Cove Key, the Suwannee River, and beyond.

The day Jasper was buried, Edna whispered to Jean as they peeled hard-boiled eggs. "Do you suppose it was Joseph?"

Jean raised her eyebrows. "Would'na be surprised knowin' how he felt about Jasper. From what I hear, ain't nobody that cares."

* * *

The day after Jasper's body was buried, Penelope did not come home from school.

Edna paced the kitchen, her worry growing with each passing minute.

"Ye got ta sit down," Jean urged as she pulled out a kitchen chair. "Like Glory Bee said before she an' Tom left fer home, there's prob'ly a good reason she ain't home yet." Jean grew thoughtful. "Prob'ly checkin' her crab traps. Or maybe she had ta stay after school."

Edna sat down, perched her elbows on the table, and laid her forehead in the palms of her hands. "When Penelope stayed with Joseph and Tepkunset, she couldn't take care of the crab traps, so Nathan took them back. As for staying after school, Penelope's teacher, Miss Treeter, has to leave right after school to care for her ailing father.

Edna took a deep breath. "As I said, Penelope's gone to her safe place. I'm sure of it. It's where she goes when she's feeling . . . oh, I don't know. With all she's been through, who knows what she's feeling?" She looked up at Jean. "I need Nathan."

"I'm bettin' she'll be home," Jean said before leaving. "I'll try ta find Nathan, but meanwhile, ya know Bell won't let no harm come ta her. I'll see ye in the mornin'."

A few hours later, as the winter sun descended into the horizon, Edna sat alone at the kitchen table shivering despite the warmth from the wood stove. Too consumed with worry to eat anything, she sipped a cup of tea. Concluding that Jean could not locate Nathan, she stood and walked to the window praying she would see Penelope and Bell coming up the hill.

With the sky darkening, Edna sat down again, her worry heightening as she recalled Reverend Albright's recent observation: "Children long for their parents . . . even if the child is mistreated."

Realizing she's an orphan now, Penelope may be longing for the only parent she had left. Would she feel such despair that she would do something . . . ?

Edna's heart skipped a beat with an unsettling image of Penelope rowing her tiny boat out to deeper parts of the Gulf, whether willingly or accidentally.

No! Penelope would never harm herself! Would she?

Edna knew well the crippling and desperate effects of loneliness and despair. She came to recognize she had brought those emotions on herself through self-indulgence and lack of self-control. Her circumstances could hardly compare to Penelope's misfortune.

Lightning flashed followed by the rumble of thunder in the distance. With the onset of rain and chilly nighttime temperatures, Edna's concern intensified. Feeling helpless, she could only pray. "Lord, protect her."

As the night wore on, Edna roamed Mrs. Peck's house, eerie and strange in its emptiness. Upstairs, she looked in Penelope's room. The blanket Tepkunset had made for her was folded on her bed. She so wished Penelope had it with her for protection and warmth.

At Mrs. Peck's bedroom door, feeling like a trespasser, Edna hesitated before turning the knob. Since she and Glory Bee had not yet sorted through Mrs. Peck's belongings, the room and everything in it remained as if still occupied. A hair brush, makeup, and a few pieces of jewelry cluttered the dresser; a pair of slippers sat askew on the braided rug by the bed. Her faded, nearly threadbare robe lay over the rose print stuffed chair. The unmade bed appeared as if Mrs. Peck had just risen from it.

Closing the door behind her, Edna went to her own room, turned on her bedside lamp, and lay down on her bed. Looking around the room, an unexplained tranquil feeling came over her. The room, the bed, the bureau . . . all had become . . . She searched for a word. *Comfortable.* In fact, the whole house had become comfortable to her. Allowing herself a moment of respite from worry, she reflected on her recent conversation one morning with Tom.

"Miz Peck had no notion o' Jeremy claimin' ownership o' this house. Understandin' was when Miz Peck died, me an' Glory Bee could live here long as we wanted, no strings attached.

Tom had chuckled and shook his head. "Can't see her reasonin' since Jeremy could claim it for his own, but there weren't no arguin' with her. Bein' we got a mess o' chickens an' a big ol' garden up on Lizey's Hill, I don't see us movin' here, but we don't see no reason fer you ta be goin' somewheres else neither. No sense boardin' up the place an' I kin do some fixin' here an' there. Ya got Miss Jean lookin' in on ya, an' I kin tell ya right now, ya ain't gonna be rid o' Glory Bee. She's gonna be here cookin' an' cleanin' prob'ly every day so's you kin take care o' that young'un when it comes."

Edna closed her eyes and embraced the comfort in knowing she and her child . . . and Penelope, of course . . . had a place to live for the time being. Hurdles, not the least of which was how to make a living, plagued her thoughts. She could not expect to live here without helping to cover household expenses. Short of resuming her artwork and possibly returning to work at the hotel, she had no other ideas.

I can't worry about that right now.

She prayed again. *Lord, please let her be safe.*

As Edna lay quietly, feeling the movement of her baby and continuing to pray, a remarkable realization dawned on her. In a matter of months, as if awakening from a long, deep sleep, every one of her senses had sharpened. Along with aroused levels of emotion . . . fear, anger, joy, sadness, worry, among others, her heightened awareness of colors, smells, tastes, sounds, even touch had elevated her mind and spirit to a whole new dimension. With her existence purged of self-absorption, Edna's heart swelled with intoxicating sensations she could not recall experiencing, at least not in her adult life.

Overwhelmed with newfound tenderness, love, and compassion, she was struck with another revelation.

For so many years, I only 'observed' these emotions between mothers and their children in Cassatt's paintings . . . and between my sons and their nanny. I felt excluded from their lives . . . all because of my own self-centeredness.

Another revelation surfaced and Edna almost laughed.

Because of Penelope, I haven't had time to worry about myself. Penelope has changed my life . . . has become part of my life.

Tears sprang from Edna's eyes. As they trickled down her face, she tried to recall the last time her emotions had moved her this deeply. She sniffled and groaned.

I am tormented with the euphoria of love and the agony of worry.

Chapter Twenty-Four

A clamor of footsteps on the stairs accompanied by voices and aromas from the kitchen roused Edna from a deep sleep.

"Edna! Ye 'wake?" Jean opened the bedroom door a crack then stepped inside. "Edna?"

Her head dulled from only a few hours' sleep, Edna mumbled, "I think so." She rolled to her side and squinted at Jean through the bright morning light. "Yes. I'm awake."

Her mind cleared, Edna tossed aside her quilt and sat up. "Penelope." She looked at Jean with dread. "Did she come home?"

Jean nodded. "Aye, she's home a'right. Muddy mess."

Edna's shoulders slumped. "Thank God." Scowling, she asked, "What do you mean 'muddy mess'?"

"Well, from the looks o' her, she spent the night wallowin' in the mud. Bell, too. We got her face and hands cleaned up best we could." Jean wrinkled her nose. "She needs a bath."

"Who's 'we'?"

"Me an' Glory Bee. She's fixin' Penelope some porritch now."

Edna heaved herself out of bed and pulled on her robe. "Has she said anything? Does she seem alright . . . other than needing a bath?"

"Seems okay. Said Bell kept her warm all night. Hasn't said much more since Glory Bee an' Tom brought her in the house. Spotted her an' Bell walkin' up the hill on their way here."

Edna gave her hair a hasty brush and made her way down the stairs as quickly as her awkward weight and bulk would allow.

At the bottom of the stairs, Jean took hold of Edna's arm. "Jus' thinkin'. Ye might wanna' give her time ta get rested before askin' her too many questions." Jean raised her eyebrows. "Know wha' I'm sayin'? Let her be . . . maybe even let her come ta you when she's ready. Fer now, jus' let her know how glad ye are ta see her and that she's home."

Edna considered how Penelope's life and her own compared . . . not in terms of parental loss and ill-treatment certainly, but definitely in terms of grief and hopelessness. As the two spent more time together and their relationship developed, Edna had come to believe Penelope trusted her with her own feelings of despair, particularly the chilling circumstances of her young life. She trusted Edna with the sanctity of her "safe place" and willingly shared her longings and fears.

Over the past few months, however, something in Penelope's demeanor changed. Edna had sensed more than once that Penelope was withholding something. On each occasion at her safe place, Penelope seemed guarded when Edna came close to her mother's grave marker. The last time she and Penelope were there, just before leaving for Mrs. Peck's house, Penelope lingered over the grave rearranging the pile of rocks.

Most recently, while they watched her house burn, Penelope only stared at Edna when asked about her princess book. She would skirt Edna's questions when asked if there was something else wrong. "Nothin'" was Penelope's typical reply. Edna speculated that these moments were all due to so much sadness and trauma in the child's life. Now she wondered if that was all they were about.

Edna laid a hand over Jean's. "You're right, Jean. I'll . . . I'll try to be careful."

When Edna walked into the kitchen, it took all of her

convictions to withhold a gasp. Caked, dried mud on Penelope's legs and feet, through her hair and covering her dress perfectly described someone who had wallowed in mud.

Edna pressed a hand to her chest and whispered, "Penelope."

Penelope looked up then quickly back to her bowl of porridge.

"Mornin', Miss Edna." Glory Bee swept clumps of dried mud into a dustpan, opened the back door, and tossed them off the porch. Back inside, she asked, "Ready fer some breakfast?"

Edna took a deep breath, pulled out a chair, and sat down. In her cheeriest voice, she said, "Good morning, Glory Bee. Yes. Yes, of course. Thank you."

Sensing wariness in Penelope, Edna cautiously reached for one of her hands. When Penelope pulled it away, Edna glanced at Jean, who gave a slight shrug of her shoulders.

Edna leaned a little closer to Penelope. "I'm so happy you're alright. You must have gotten quite chilled out in the rain all night. I bet a warm bath will feel good. How about I get another dress from your room, and we'll get you cleaned up, and then . . ."

"I'll do it," Penelope mumbled into her bowl. Pushing herself from the table, she set the empty dish in the sink and headed for the stairs.

Puzzled, the three women looked from one to the other.

"Don't you want to have your bath first?" Edna called out as Penelope's footsteps raced up the stairs.

Slumped against the back of her chair, Edna shook her head. "I don't understand." She looked from Glory Bee to Jean and repeated, "I don't understand."

Jean pulled out a chair, sat down, and laid a hand on Edna's forearm. "She's hidin' somethin', Edna. Dunno' wha' it is, but no way she'd be actin' like this if there wa'n't somethin' she don't want us ta know."

"Won't even look us in the eyes," Glory Bee said. "Sure sign she's keepin' somethin' ta herself."

Edna nodded. "I agree. But what?" She glanced at Bell. "I wish you could talk."

Pushing herself from the table, Edna headed to the staircase. "Why would she spend a whole night out there, probably at her safe place, in the pouring rain no less? I'm going upstairs to see if I can get some answers. Penelope needs to know that whatever the problem is, we can fix it."

Jean stood up from the table. "I'll go up wi' ya." She turned to Glory Bee. "Nobody's touched Miz Peck's bedroom, an' you and Edna ain't in any condition ta tackle it. Thought I'd go up and strip the bed, clear out the closet, maybe start on the dresser drawers. Tha' be alright, Glory Bee?"

"Lawdy be, Miss Jean, I been dreadin' that job like ya don't know, so ya jus' go on an' do what ya can. Might as well clear out them desk drawers, too. I'll have Tom bring some boxes or bags or somethin' we can put stuff in. Rev'ren' Albright likely be comin' one o' these days. He can cart it all off to the church for the rummage sale come spring. Maybe they can use some o' her clothes an' shoes and whatnot."

At the top of the stairs, before going into Mrs. Peck's bedroom, Jean pulled Edna close to her and whispered. "Like I said before, let Penelope tell ye in her own good time what's goin' on wi' her. Whatever's wrong, she's troubled about it an' if ye push her, she might not never tell ye."

"I'm sure you're right, Jean. I just hope she feels she can trust me."

Leaving Jean to deal with Mrs. Peck's belongings, Edna approached Penelope's closed bedroom door and tapped lightly. "Penelope, may I come in?" With no reply, she tapped on the door again. "Penelope?"

Penelope opened the door a crack. Wrapped in Tepkunset's blanket, she turned and sat on the edge of her bed. Her mud-caked hair fell in clumps hiding her downcast face. The wadded-up mud-stained dress lay on the floor.

Opening the door wider, Edna stood in the doorway for a few moments struggling to understand Penelope's strange behavior. She kept her distance when she sat down next to her. Folding her hands on her lap, Edna gazed around the room taking in the shadows developing on the bare walls and floor from the morning light. She stood and walked to the window.

"The view of the water from here is so lovely. Come see how it sparkles in the sunlight." With no response, Edna came back to the bed and sat down, this time a little closer to Penelope. "We should do some drawings to hang on your walls. Would you like to do that?"

Penelope sat motionless, her head still lowered.

Edna turned toward Penelope and took one of her hands surprisingly without resistance. "Penelope, my sweet girl, what is wrong? Have I done something, have I said something to hurt you? Please talk to me. I . . . I need to understand why you're . . . why you won't even look at me."

Edna stroked Penelope's hand, fighting the urge to pressure her to speak.

Be patient. Don't push her. In her own good time.

After a minute or two, she let go of Penelope's hand, stood, and walked to the door. "I'll come back a little later. Maybe you'll be ready to tell me what's . . ."

Head still lowered, with a resolute tone, Penelope asked, "Would you ever leave?"

Startled, Edna returned to the bed and sat down. "Leave? Penelope, look at me." She placed her hands on each side of Penelope's face. "Look at me. Do you mean leave Pine Cove?"

Penelope pulled away. Still wrapped in her blanket, she stood to face Edna. "Yes!" She promptly demanded, "Would you?!"

Penelope's disturbing behavior both puzzled and alarmed Edna. "Whatever . . . why ever would you ask me that?"

"'Cuz I heard ya talkin' ta Miss Jean and Glory Bee about needin' money. That ya might go back ta work at the hotel and do more o' yer drawin's down on the dock ta make more money." By now, tears brimmed in Penelope's eyes. "I figured ya might be missin' yer little boys an' if ya had a lot o' money, you'd go back to 'em." Her lower lip quivered. "Well, would you?! If ya had a lot o' money, would ya leave when yer baby comes?!"

Edna never considered the effect her conversations with others might have had on Penelope. Recalling talks with Jean and Glory Bee, even a time or two with Dr. Bartlett and Reverend Albright, all within Penelope's hearing, she had indeed shared her concern for income.

But Penelope never heard me say those concerns included her.

As for Etienne and Raoul, in Penelope's experience, Edna had abandoned her sons . . . something the child knew all too well. She had to have wondered . . . obviously did wonder . . . how Edna could have done that without remorse, without thoughts of going back to them.

Edna took hold of Penelope's arms and held her close. "Oh, my dear. Some things are difficult to understand . . . and to explain."

How can I make this abused, neglected nine-year-old child understand? I certainly can't discuss the reasons for trying to end my life. That because of those reasons, especially the one I am carrying, I cannot return to my former life. Whatever I say has to make sense to her in some other way.

Pulling Penelope to sit next to her, Edna chose her words carefully. "Yes, sometimes I miss my sons. But . . . well, to be honest, I doubt they miss me because . . . well, because they have a nanny who always looked after them. I . . . wasn't with them very much, so we didn't do things together too often. Even when I tried to do things with them, they preferred running outside with their little dog or playing in the nursery with their little friends or going on outings with their nanny. I believe both of my sons are very happy doing the things they love to do, and I believe if I went back to them, I might spoil that happiness."

Edna stared at the floor a moment to consider the concession she felt was necessary for Penelope to better understand. Raising her head, looking directly into Penelope's face, Edna's calm voice conveyed the truth she had struggled to acknowledge to herself for months.

"Penelope, the thing is, I wasn't a very good mother."

Penelope appeared to ponder Edna's explanation. "Do you love 'em?"

Do I love them?

Forced to confront Penelope's question, Edna struggled to define her feelings for her sons, for the children she gave birth to just as she would give birth to the child she currently carried.

Such different circumstances.

So swiftly were Etienne and Raoul whisked away from her at the time of their births, so swiftly was her role as their mother replaced by a nanny, so swiftly did Léonce insist on resuming their extravagant lives following the boys' births, Edna never got to know them, never experienced the binding kind of "love" she knew Penelope envisioned . . . and longed for.

Edna took Penelope's hands in hers. "Penelope, there will always be a place in my heart for Etienne and Raoul. That might not sound like love to you, but I believe that's a kind of love that can happen even though the people aren't together.

"Think about Miss Jean and her little girl, Kathleen. Miss Jean will always and forever love her daughter. But Kathleen isn't here anymore. She's . . . she's gone to another place, so Miss Jean had to go on with her life. That doesn't mean Miss Jean lost her love for Kathleen.

"That's a lot like my feelings for Etienne and Raoul . . . except I'm the one who's come to another place, and I believe they have happily gone on with their lives without me.

Edna squeezed Penelope's hands. "I like it here, Penelope. I have no intentions of leaving Pine Cove . . . or you."

Penelope sniffled. "Even if ya had a whole lot o' money?"

For a few moments, Edna envisioned the resumption of her privileged life in New Orleans. Certainly, she missed a few modern conveniences her home provided there. She then reflected on the previous months since arriving on the island . . . of the people she had come to know, of those who helped her adjust, in discovering she could take care of herself. Above all, she savored the awakening of her inner spirit. Even if it were possible to return, she could not imagine sacrificing the richness her life had come to value in Pine Cove.

Hugging Penelope tighter, Edna said with conviction, "Even if I had a whole lot of money." Chuckling, she added, "Not that there's much chance of that happening. I'm quite content here, Penelope. I will resume my artwork, and perhaps I'll see about working at the hotel again. In any case, I can't imagine living anywhere else." She raised her shoulders in an expression of apology. "I guess I thought you knew that."

Penelope settled into Edna's embrace. A few minutes passed before she finally spoke. "Do you love me?"

Edna's heart swelled. "Yes, I do. I love you very much. I thought you knew that, too."

Quiet for a few moments, Penelope finally asked, "Will you always love me . . . no matter what?"

Edna chuckled again. "Of course, silly goose. I'll love you forever no matter what."

Penelope took a deep breath. "Promise?"

Something in Penelope's voice troubled Edna, and she looked into her eyes. "Yes, I promise. But why would you ask me that?"

Penelope sighed again and swallowed. "'Cuz I've got somethin' ta show you."

***

Only the clatter from the kitchen and the never-ending cry of gulls over the island broke the heavy silence in Penelope's bedroom.

Edna stared at her open palm. She lifted her gaze to Penelope's downcast head as the child stood in front of her. Looking back to her palm, she pressed her lips together and closed her hand. Searching her mind for something to say, she took hold of Penelope's arm and steered her to sit next to her on the bed.

When at last Edna spoke, all she could say was, "Why?"

When Penelope finally spoke, all she could say was, "I'm sorry."

In thinking through their myriad conversations over the past several months, Penelope often dwelled on the brilliant glitter of the sun's rays dancing on the Gulf water. When out in her little boat, she imagined millions of sparkling diamonds floating around her. She spoke often of her princess book and longed for a pink ruffled dress trimmed in sparkles like the princess character's dress.

More than once, when walking on the beach, Penelope pointed out how the sun's rays made grains of sand glitter, how the stars twinkled in the night skies, and more recently, the dazzling sparkle of candlelight on the chandelier in Mrs. Peck's dining room.

In the dullness and sadness of Penelope's existence, Edna's understanding of Penelope's need for "sparkle" in her life grew. She imagined a time when she could provide Penelope with a pink ruffled dress with sparkles.

More thoughts coalesced... of Penelope's peculiar, guarded behavior when spending time together at her safe place, particularly around her mother's memorial marker. Edna now understood Penelope's recent distancing from her and refusing to look Edna in the eye. Her somber facial expression and far-off stares now made sense. Penelope had been wracked with worry and guilt.

Sorting through a multitude of reeling emotions, Edna remained quiet for several moments before finally speaking.

"So, to be clear, when you found me on the beach last summer and you thought I was dead, you pulled my ring off my finger because you liked how it sparkled."

Penelope nodded and mumbled, "Yes ma'am."

"And because you thought I was dead, you didn't think it would matter if you took the ring."

Once again, Penelope nodded. "Yes ma'am."

"Then you buried it beneath your Mama's grave marker at your safe place."

Again, Penelope nodded.

Edna opened her palm and stared at the diamonds circling a gold band . . . her wedding ring she thought was lost in the sea as she battled for her life. "And you didn't return it to me when you discovered I was alive because . . . ?"

Her head still hanging low, Penelope shrugged her shoulders. "When you started moanin', I got scared an' I guess I forgot I put it in my pocket until later. Then I was afraid ta tell anybody I took it.

She at last looked at Edna. "I knew it was wrong ta take it, and I'm sorry I took it. But then I . . . well, I wanted ya ta stay here, an' I was afraid if I gave it back to ya, maybe you'd sell it an' go back where ya came from." Penelope hung her head and mumbled again, "I'm sorry."

Edna contemplated the situation. She could not bring herself to scold Penelope.

What would be the point? She knows it was wrong and she's apologized. What if I'd had the ring all along? What would I have done with it? Sold it for passage back to New Orleans while carrying this child?

The baby's movement, perhaps a foot or a fist, poked Edna's rib. She sat up straighter and pressed against her round belly.

Not likely.

The rising sun's rays brightened the room and the dark shadows on the floor and walls evaporated.

Wrapping her arm around Penelope's shoulder, Edna nudged the child's arm. "You need a bath."

Penelope sniggered. "Yes ma'am."

Resting her cheek on top of Penelope's mud-crusted head, Edna whispered, "I have a question."

Penelope whispered back, "What?"

"What color shoes would you like to go with your pink dress?"

Chapter Twenty-Five

Edna picked up a cardboard box from a kitchen chair and set it on the table. Pulling out another chair, she dropped onto it with a groan. "This might be a good time to sort through this box. Jean's finishing up Mrs. Peck's bedroom, and I want to help Penelope with her school work when she gets home."

Glory Bee replaced the broom and dustpan in the pantry. Returning to the kitchen, she opened the weathered house door. Sunshine spilled across the worn plank floor. A cool February breeze blew through the screen door carrying with it the distant screech of gulls. She pulled out a chair and sat down, the aged wood creaking under her weight.

"Good o' time as any." Glory Bee peered into the box and scowled. "Look like a whole lot o' nothin' ta me."

"It might be, but who knows? Jean had to pry open the lock to the top drawer, so there might be something important here. It won't take long to sort through it."

Edna removed a few items collected from Mrs. Peck's desk . . . a Bible, a box containing many pencils, and a stack of stationery. She set them in the middle of the kitchen table.

Glory Bee slid the Bible to Edna. "I got one. Maybe you'd like ta have this one."

"I would like that very much. Thank you."

Opening the cover, Edna turned to the genealogy page. It was blank. Flipping through the tissue-thin pages, she noted comments along the margins of certain passages.

"I feel like I'm invading Mrs. Peck's privacy," Edna said. She closed the worn, cracked covers and laid the Bible aside.

"I can use this stationery," Glory Bee said. "Never have enough paper ta write ta Olivia."

Edna continued to empty the varied unremarkable-looking remains of the box.

"I bet the ladies from the church would like these lace-trimmed handkerchiefs." Edna studied the red, yellow, and blue flowers. "I wonder if Mrs. Peck embroidered them. The detail of the flowers is exquisite." She set the handkerchiefs aside.

Incidentals included hair pins, hair nets, a key chain, gloves, an ink well, fountain pen, and a shoe horn.

Edna set aside the two most notable items, a sealed envelope and a small black box engraved with the letter "W" in gold script. She handed the box to Glory Bee.

"This is lovely. Looks like a gift box. You should open it."

Glory Bee turned the box upside down and side to side. Turning it face-up again, she unhooked a tiny catch on the front and lifted the cover. A tightly folded piece of paper fell on the table revealing a gold locket lying on a bed of black velvet.

"Will ya look at that!" Glory Bee exclaimed.

Edna leaned forward. "How beautiful! That looks like a 'W' engraved on the locket as well." She grew thoughtful. "Funny. I don't ever remember Mrs. Peck wearing it."

"Me neither," Glory Bee replied as she lifted the locket from the box and opened it.

Edna turned her attention to the box of pencils. "There must be two dozen or more pencils here. I'm sure Penelope's teacher will appreciate them. She said they're always short of . . ."

Interrupted by Glory Bee's muttering, Edna set the box of pencils on the table. "Is something wrong?"

Glory Bee stared at the open locket in apparent bemusement. "I dunno." Frowning, she looked up at Edna. Again, she said, "I dunno."

Handing the locket to Edna, Glory Bee picked up the folded paper.

With its delicate gold chain dangling between her fingers, Edna laid the locket in her hand. She expected to look upon a photograph perhaps of Mrs. Peck's husband, Walter, or even her son, Jeremy. Instead, she was surprised to be looking at the face of a stunning Colored woman perhaps in her early twenties.

Edna glanced up at Glory Bee then back to the locket. "She's lovely." Her eyebrows raised, she asked, "Is this Olivia?"

Shaking her head, Glory Bee unfolded the paper that had fallen out of the gift box and began scanning its contents.

Edna tried to read Glory Bee's rapidly changing facial expressions . . . from scowl, to pursed mouth, to bulged eyes, to dropped jaw. "What is it?" she asked.

Overhead, furniture scraped across the floor as Jean continued cleaning Mrs. Peck's bedroom. Outside, palm fronds rattled in a rising wind. Chilly gusts rushed through the screen door blowing dishtowels off the drying rack.

Edna rose from the table and closed the door. Picking up the towels, she placed them back on the rack.

Returning to her chair, Edna ventured. "You're obviously baffled by something, Glory Bee. Is it some kind of document that goes with the locket?"

"It goes with the locket alright," Glory Bee muttered. Continuing to absorb the paper's contents, she whispered, "Bless my soul."

A hint of a smile on Glory Bee's face proceeded to grow into a grin that erupted into a chuckle. A soft rumble from her throat then expanded into her chest. Within moments, she exploded into a howling caterwaul while tears streamed down her cheeks.

Having never seen Glory Bee react this strongly over anything, Edna stared at her wide-eyed and somewhat concerned.

Jean clamored down the stairs. She ran into the kitchen, dust cloth in hand, her face flushed with exertion.

"Jesus, Mary and Joseph! Glory Bee, are ye a'right?" Jean's widened green eyes looked to Edna. "Wha' happened? Is she laughin' er cryin'?"

Edna shook her head. "I'm not sure. I think she's laughing, but I don't know why." Edna handed the locket to Jean. "It started while she was reading that paper she's holding. It was inside the box that locket came in."

Gazing at the opened locket, Jean's eyebrows shot up. "Who in baldy notion is this?"

"I've no idea," Edna replied, "but Glory Bee apparently knows after reading what's in that paper."

By now, Glory Bee had regained control of her hysteria and dabbed her eyes with a handkerchief she pulled from her apron pocket. She laid the paper on the table and sat in apparent bewilderment. After several moments, she reached out to Jean for the locket and stared again at the picture inside.

"Never in all my days . . ." Her voice trailed off.

Jean pulled a chair from the table and sat down. "Are ye gonna tell us wha' sa funny about this picture and . . ." She pointed to the paper. "An' whatever's in that . . . whatever it is?"

A tenebrous shadow gradually crept across Glory Bee's face. She stared up at the ceiling and whispered. "Forgive me fer cursin' ta m'self, Lawd. An' God fergive her."

As if a new dawn had arrived following days of violent weather, Glory Bee's eyes widened once again. In a voice filled with pure joy, she cried out, "Oh my sweet Jesus!" Looking from Edna to Jean, she clutched her hands to her bosom.

Completely perplexed, Edna and Jean turned their puzzled faces to each other then back to Glory Bee. Anticipation and impatience finally won out. The Irish in Jean erupted.

Pushing herself from the table, Jean stood up, placed her hands on her hips, and said in her thickest brogue, "If'n ye don' tell us wha' in bloody hell's in that paper, the two o' us is gonna bust!"

Jean's outburst brought Glory Bee out of a near trance. She wilted against the back of her chair, her cheeks plumped with a broad smile.

"I can't b'lieve it! Long as I been prayin', I never thought it'd happen!" Unable to contain her excitement, Glory Bee shouted, "My babies can come home!"

***

Pummeling waves of emotion had left Glory Bee spent. When she finally was able to reply to Edna's and Jean's questions, her voice quivered.

"Don't know whether ta laugh or cry." She picked up the paper again and stared at it. "Pains me so ta think o' the hurt Miz Peck caused . . . hurt ta Jeremy, hurt ta Olivia and Priscilla, hurt ta me an' Tom . . . an' all the while . . ."

Tossing the paper back on the table, Glory Bee pointed to it. "That there is a letter ta Miz Peck from her daddy thirteen years ago. Seems Miz Peck's daddy had ta clear his conscience befo' he died.

Glory Bee's voice escalated. "He says in there that the woman he got married to up in North Car'lina . . . the woman that raised Miz Peck from a baby and who Miz Peck believed was her Mama? Turns out that woman weren't her real Mama a'tall."

Several moments passed as Glory Bee stared into space.

"Well?" Edna finally coaxed with raised eyebrows. "Then who was her real Mama?"

Scowling, Glory Bee shook her head and muttered. "I can't b'lieve it."

A few more moments passed before an exasperated Jean raised her arms. "Glory Bee! Can't b'lieve what?"

Returning from wherever her thoughts had taken her, Glory Bee picked up the locket, opened it, and stared at the picture again before looking up at Edna and Jean.

"Turns out Miz Peck's daddy got hisself involved with a woman what worked at a neighborin' estate from the one where he worked as a gardener." With a petulant look on her face, she turned the picture toward Edna and Jean.

"This picture here? This Colored woman? This was Miz Peck's Mama." Glory Bee paused then raised her voice. "Her *birth* Mama!"

Time crawled and lingered at a near stop before the revelation . . . and the implications . . . of Mrs. Peck's birth origins registered with Edna and Jean. They stared at Glory Bee stupefied.

"Jesus, Mary and Joseph," Jean finally whispered.

Staring at the clutter of Mrs. Peck's belongings on the table, Edna mumbled. "I can't believe it. Who would have guessed . . . ?" She frowned. "All that pretense, the way she treated me." She looked at Glory Bee and exploded. "The way she treated *you*!"

Following Edna's outburst, the heavy silence in the kitchen hovered until water boiling over the side of the kettle on the stove hissed.

Jean scrambled for a pot holder to lift the lid. "Eggs'r done," she muttered as she set the kettle aside and sat back down.

Glory Bee closed the locket and ran a finger over the engraved "W." She stared at the letter laying on the table.

"Her daddy says Miz Peck's birth Mama was called 'Winnie,' short fer Winifred. Winnie died givin' birth ta Miz Peck. The daddy named the baby after the Mama and him . . . his name bein' Robert, so he named the baby Winifred Roberta. A year er so later, he married the woman Miz Peck grew up believin' was her Mama. That woman . . . name o' Hortense . . . never knew she wasn't raisin' a white girl.

Glory Bee inhaled deeply before continuing. "Letter says he decided ta tell Miz Peck all this 'cause with her bein' so white like him, if she had any child'ern or gran'child'ern who might show signs o' bein' Colored, he didn't want her wonderin' where it come from.

Glory Bee studied the picture. "Thing is, I can see Miz Peck and Jeremy takin' afta' this Winnie. In the eyes and the high cheek bones, Jeremy's dark curly hair, chocolate marble eyes... Miz Peck said he took after her own daddy. Once he died, she didn't hafta' worry he'd show up ta prove otherwise."

Glory Bee snorted. "Hated her hair. Complained one time 'bout it bein' coarse. When I said somethin' about my frizz, she let me know right off she didn't have no frizz." She closed the locket and set it on the table.

Edna's head buzzed with myriad recollections of Mrs. Peck's behavior. "She was always so angry." She looked at Glory Bee. "Or maybe she was simply afraid... afraid someone might find out."

People will do awful things when they're afraid.

Nodding in agreement, Glory Bee's recollections mounted. "Oh, I sees it now. Remember I tol' ya she'd lay up there in that bed howlin' and bawlin'? Said nothin' was wrong an' ta jus' leave her be?" She bobbed her head at the locket. "Looks ta me like we found out what was ailin' her. An' I 'member way back..." She picked up the letter. "Guess it would be when she got this letter, she tol' ever'body ta stop callin' her 'Winnie.' That's when she started callin' herself 'Birdie.'"

Jean finally broke her silence. "Might explain why no family pictures 'r hangin' anywhere in the house." Scowling, she drummed her fingers on the table. "That locket box... it was in plain sight in the top desk drawer. She had ta know somebody was gonna open it. She could o' thrown it away. Wonder why she kep' it."

Ruminating over the startling revelations, Edna reflected on her past misguided actions.

Maybe everybody reaches a point when they feel a need to unburden themselves of regret . . . dead or alive.

"It could be it was her way of . . . you know . . . baring her soul and relieving herself of guilt without having to face her family and friends."

"S'pose so," Glory Bee said, "but that don't excuse sacrificin' her family . . . and mine all this time. Drove away her own son an' my daughter an' our gran'baby 'cause she wouldn't own up ta where she come from.

Glory Bee's eyes widened. "Come ta' think of it, if anybody had o' known Miz Peck had Colored blood runnin' in her veins, it's her an' her white husband would o' got run out o' town on a rail."

"Jesus, Mary, and Joseph," Jean said. "Gotta' be why she dinna tell anybody. S'pose he knew?"

"Don' know," Glory Bee said. "They got married up in North Car'lina. Met him while she was in boardin' school. Moved ta Pine Cove couple o' years later ta start his accountin' business. Town was busy then. Hortense . . . the only Mama she knew . . . had already died. Miz Peck got this letter long before Mr. Peck died eight years ago." Glory Bee grew thoughtful. "Maybe he found out and that's what drove him ta drink."

"She lived with this secret a long time," Edna said. She picked up the envelope that also had been retrieved from Mrs. Peck's desk. She slid it across the table to Glory Bee.

"It might be nothing, Glory Bee, but it's sealed, so you should be the one to open it in case . . ." Edna lifted her shoulders. "You know. In case it's something important."

With a measure of apprehension, Glory Bee unsealed the flap and slipped two folded pages from the envelope. When she unfolded them, a picture fell on the table. She scanned the contents of the first page. "It's a letter from Jeremy to his Ma from two years ago."

Turning her attention to the picture, her eyes watered as she stared at the faces of Jeremy, Olivia, and Priscilla. She held the picture to her chest then set it on the table.

After silently reading Jeremy's letter, Glory Bee folded it and placed it back in the envelope. She unfolded the second page, glanced over it, refolded it, and placed it back in the envelope. She slipped the picture into her apron pocket.

"They won't be comin' home," Glory Bee said, crestfallen. "Says he'd keep his Ma's secret 'bout her an' him havin' Colored blood, but he'd never fergive her fer what she done when him and Olivia got married knowin' they didn't break no law."

"He knew all along," Edna whispered. The sadness of it was too much. "I could weep," she whispered again.

Jean scowled. "Poor wee things. For Miz Peck ta . . ." She was at a loss for words until struck with a thought. "But now with his Ma dead, why canna' he and Olivia come back?"

Glory Bee shook her head. "Says he wants nothin' ta do with Pine Cove or this house, that me an' Tom deserve it more'n his Ma ever did. Besides, if the town don' know he's got Colored blood, it still looks like they broke the law. An' he says he'd keep his Ma's secret.

Glory Bee nodded at the envelope. "That other piece o' paper's the deed ta this house."

Edna nor Jean could think of any comforting words to say to Glory Bee. The obvious conclusion was that she might never see her family again.

Her voice filled with dejection, Glory Bee dabbed her eyes with her handkerchief. "Maybe someday me an' Tom can take a trip up north." She gazed out the window as she stuffed the handkerchief into an apron pocket.

A smile slowly spread across her face and she chuckled. "Wonder what the town folk would say if they knew Miz Peck's buried in the wrong cemetery." Her eyes crinkled with laughter. "An' I'd sure like ta see the looks on them church ladies' faces if they knew who was hostin' their Bible study every week."

The mood lightened over the avalanche of eye-opening revelations during which Edna's discomfort became evident. She dabbed perspiration from her forehead with a handkerchief.

"I'd like to go up to my room now if you don't mind. Sitting on this hard chair so long . . . my back is . . . well, I do need to lie down awhile."

She smiled with compassion at Glory Bee. "Have faith. Maybe one day, Jeremy and Olivia will relent and come back to Pine Cove for a visit. After all, no law was broken when they married."

Jean sniggered. "Miz Peck'll be rollin' over in her grave when the town folk find out about this."

Edna peered at Jean. "You wouldn't."

"Oh, wouldn't I?" Jean replied. "Some things need ta be made right. Like ye said, Miz Peck might o' needed ta bare her soul. Don't see any reason we shouldn't help her out."

"Well, I can't argue with that," Edna said with a strained smile.

Jean pushed herself from the table. "Let's leave Glory Bee ta decide what ta do with Miz Peck's things. I'll go upstairs wi' ye. Still have a few things ta tidy up in her bedroom." She picked up the empty box. "May as well take this back up. Might find some more interestin' things before I'm through.

Bobbing her head at Glory Bee, Jean glanced at the stove. "Don't be frettin' with those eggs. Be back down shortly ta peel 'em."

"I'm sure I'll be able to help after I rest awhile," Edna said. "There's a chicken to debone, and I can do that sitting right here."

Pushing herself from the table, Edna stood up with a groan. Before taking a step, water from beneath her skirt dribbled and puddled onto her shoes and the kitchen floor.

Chapter Twenty-Six

At the slam of the kitchen door, Glory Bee turned from the kettle of water steaming on the stove. She tossed her potholders on the table and perched her fists on her broad hips.

"Penelope Worth, I done tol' ya ta stay down yonder! This ain't no time or place fer a young'un!" She pointed to the door. "Now ya git on back to Miz Lydia's and stay there 'til afta' this baby's been born! You hear?!"

Following a bellowing howl from overhead, Jean shouted down the stairway, "Glory Bee, ye gotta gi' on up here! An' bring more towels if ya can!"

Wide-eyed, Penelope looked at Glory Bee with defiance. "No! I ain't stayin' at Miss Lydia's! I wanna be here . . . with Miss Edna.

Tears filled Penelope's eyes and trickled down her cheeks. "Miss Lydia's mean! Makes me sit in a chair with my ankles crossed an' holdin' a Bible! Keeps tellin' me ta pray!" She wiped her tears away with her coat sleeve. "An' I already told her I don't wanna eat supper there. Please, Glory Bee. I gotta stay here. I gotta know . . . I gotta know Miss Edna's alright and that her baby's alright."

Glory Bee shook her head and turned back to the stove. "You are one stubborn chil'." She took a deep breath and turned back around. Shaking a finger at Penelope, she spoke with a warning tone.

"Alright then, but you stay up in yer own bedroom. An' keep yer door closed!" She glanced at a lower cupboard. "Now, git all the towels out o' that there cupboard and bring 'em upstairs."

More howls and yells reverberated throughout the house. Glory Bee clutched the kettle's handles and hustled to the stairway, grateful her arm and leg had healed from her fall down the stairs months before. She called over her shoulder, "An' yer gonna haf'ta git yer own supper, hear?"

"I ain't . . . I'm not hungry!" Penelope dropped to her knees in front of the cupboard, gathered up an armload of towels, and trotted close behind Glory Bee.

At the top of the stairs, Jean was wringing her hands. "Ye gotta see ta Edna! I don't know . . . Penelope! What'r ye doin' here?!"

"Never you mind. She's stayin'," Glory Bee said as she headed to Edna's room. "Penelope, remember what I tol' ya. Stay in yer room with the door shut 'til we say so. Miz Jean, bring along them towels. Oh, an' go git a couple o' sheets from Miz Peck's bedroom closet."

Penelope scooted out of Jean's way as she darted into Mrs. Peck's bedroom. Returning with a stack of bed sheets, Jean hastened into Edna's bedroom. Before closing the door, she turned to Penelope and whispered, "Gw'on now. Do as yer told."

Penelope tiptoed to her room and gently closed the door. After taking off her coat, she went straight to her window and pushed up the sash. A chilled February west wind off the Gulf raised goose bumps on her arms as it pressed her yellow muslin dress against her small frame. Her hair whipped around her face. In the distance, the ocean shimmered and glittered in the orange glow of the setting sun. Overhead, gulls soared, their ceaseless cries blending with the whine of the wind.

A howl jolted Penelope, and she yelped. Shoving down the window, she scrambled onto the bed. She covered herself with Tepkunset's blanket then pulled the pillow over her head. She thought about praying. Prayers had always disappointed Penelope, but now she had a new reason to try.

Squeezing her eyes shut, Penelope pressed her small hands together. "Please God. Please don' let nothin' bad happen ta Miss Edna. Or her baby."

Over and over, Penelope prayed the same prayer. Before long, the warm cocoon of the blanket and pillow and the moan of the wind drowned out the now muffled sounds coming from Edna's room, and she fell asleep.

***

"Miz Jean, quick, go git a lamp from Miz Peck's bedroom. I need mo' light." Glory Bee smacked the side of Edna's bare leg. "Don' be holdin' yer breath now, hear? Ya got ta breathe!"

Gripping the bed sheet with both hands, Edna ran her tongue over her dry lips. As the relentless pressure against her lower extremities mounted to unforgiving pain, she cried out, "I can't! I can't!"

Glory Bee shouted from the foot of the bed. "Yes, ye can! Come on now! Yer crownin'! Next one, give it a good push!"

Jean set the lamp from Mrs. Peck's bedroom on the bureau. Turning it on, she hastened to the head of the bed and took hold of one of Edna's hands. "Edna, look at me. Yer doin' grand. Try ta relax. Yer almost there."

Panting, Edna turned to Jean with pleading eyes. "Water," she whispered. "I'm so thirsty. Please, just a . . ." The grip of another contraction cut Edna's breath short. Her groan escalated to an animal-like howl.

"Push!" Glory Bee yelled. "Miz Jean, sit 'er up!"

Reaching behind Edna's shoulders, Jean raised her into a near sitting position. "Push, Edna! Push!"

Weakened from nearly seven hours of hard labor, Edna's endurance had waned. Her head wobbled and flecks of light blinked behind her closed eyelids. Mustering her last bit of strength, with an explosive gasp, she pushed then collapsed against her pillow. Her head buzzed as if overtaken by a hive of bees. From somewhere, water sloshed. She was thrashing in the sea. Muffled voices drowned out her cries for help. The voices faded then were gone. She was drowning.

***

Reverend Albright swallowed the remains of lemonade and set his glass on the kitchen table. "Seems a bit soon for a visit. Baby came middle of the night, you say?"

Glory Bee nodded. "Yessir. Right about midnight."

"Well, if you're sure it's alright, I'll go up and see what I can do." Stepping away from the table, Reverend Albright turned back around. "When's Dr. Bartlett coming?"

"Tomorra's Wednesday, so I 'spect he'll be here," Glory Bee said as she handed Jean a stack of dirty dishes.

Reverend Albright headed for the hallway then turned back. "Is Penelope alright?"

"Yessir," Jean said, pouring hot water from a kettle into the sink. "Penelope's jus' fine. Sent her off ta school kickin' and hollerin' wantin' ta stay home."

Reverend Albright adjusted his collar. "School will keep her mind busy. Best place for her."

"Just a minute, Rev'rend," Glory Bee said as she poured a fresh glass of lemonade. "Take this up to her. Might make her feel a little better."

The Reverend bobbed his head as he took the glass. "Might so." He headed for the kitchen doorway again.

"Oh, wait," Jean said, drying her hands on her apron. She rummaged in the box sitting on a kitchen chair containing Mrs. Peck's belongings. "Take her these handkerchiefs, too. We were gonna give 'em to the church ladies, but, well, Edna might need 'em more."

With lemonade and handkerchiefs in hand, Reverend Albright began a slow climb up the stairs. At Edna's door, he slipped the handkerchiefs into his jacket pocket and tapped lightly. "Edna, it's Reverend Albright. May I come in?"

In a nasally voice, Edna replied, "Yes, of course. Please, come in."

Reverend Albright opened the door and stared at Edna propped against her pillows, tears streaming down her face. After stepping inside, he closed the door, set the glass of lemonade on the bedside stand, and handed the handkerchiefs to Edna. He dragged the chair from the far side of the room, set it next to her bed, and sat down.

Leaning forward, Reverend Albright smiled. "First, let me say congratulations."

Sniffling, Edna wiped her tears and mumbled, "Thank you."

"Now, let me have her." Taking the sleeping baby in his arms, Reverend Albright loosened the pink blanket. He stroked the baby girl's head covered in a white-blond fuzz then hooked a finger in her tiny hand. The furrows between his bushy, graying eyebrows deepened.

"You've brought a perfectly healthy, beautiful child into the world, Edna, yet Glory Bee and Jean say you're inconsolable." He began rocking side to side as the baby began to squirm. "What could possibly be wrong?"

Edna sniffled and wiped more tears from her face. "I don't know. I . . . I wasn't like this with the birth of my sons." She dabbed her eyes. "Of course, I'm overjoyed with her. Beyond words.

She closed her eyes for a few moments. When she opened them, fresh tears spilled down her cheeks. "I can't seem to stop crying." She blew her nose with one of the handkerchiefs. "I feel like . . . like I don't deserve her . . . after the terrible thing I tried to . . .

Recalling her walk into the Gulf off Grand Isle and later asking Dr. Bartlett how she might terminate her pregnancy, Edna muttered, "When I look at her now, how could I have even . . ."

Reverend Albright scooted the chair closer to the bed. Cradling the baby in one arm, he took one of Edna's hands. "Listen to me," he said in a stern voice. "It's very simple. By the grace of God, you and this baby were intended to live."

Turning to the window, Edna dabbed her eyes and wiped her nose. "But so much . . . so much of what I've done was so wrong." She brushed away another tear and scowled at Reverend Albright. "I left my sons, Reverend. What kind of mother does that?"

Reverend Albright pursed his lips. "At the time, you had your reasons. I'm not going to pass judgment on anything you . . . or anybody, for that matter . . . have or haven't done. What I will tell you is we all make decisions, whether right or wrong, based on our circumstances. We all have to figure out how to live with those decisions. And we all . . . hopefully, I'll add . . . we all learn from them." Smiling, he let go of Edna's hand and patted it. "It's what builds character."

Edna's mouth hinted at a smile. "You're just trying to make me feel better."

"Well, of course, I am!" Reverend Albright leaned forward. "But this isn't all about you, you know. Your sons are still there. Don't rule out that you might see them again. For now, I want you to think about how you've affected some folks in Pine Cove." He raised his voice. "Think of the effect you've had on Penelope, for Heaven's sake, and what that child's life would be like if you weren't here. You've breathed new life into some folks . . . and this island.

Reverend Albright gazed down at the baby. "And now this child is going to bring much-needed joy to this house that's been missing for a very long time." The baby began to fuss, and he handed her back to Edna.

Having gained control of her tears, Edna stroked the baby's head and rocked side to side. "I suppose you're right. You've given me a lot to think about.

She gazed across the room. "Glory Bee insists I use her granddaughter's clothing and other infant things she'd stored in that trunk."

"You don't say." Reverend Albright followed her gaze and shook his head. Sadness spread across his face. "Well, at least something good came out of her loss.

He tilted his head and raised his eyebrows. "You remember the first time I met you right here in this room . . . the night of Birdie's Bible study?" He chuckled. "You nearly tumbled down the stairs if you recall. I told you then there's a lot of family history on this island . . . ties that bind if you will. Take Glory Bee and Birdie. Their ties have bound them forever. Whether Birdie was happy about it or not doesn't matter."

Leaning against the chair's back, Reverend Albright crossed his arms. "You've begun making your own history on the island, Edna." He nodded at the baby. "I'd like to think you've made a life for yourself in Pine Cove and now for her, too."

Edna grew thoughtful. "I could never go back to that . . . that other life."

"Well, never say 'never,' but there would be some very disappointed people if you did." Reverend Albright leaned forward. In a commanding voice, he said, "Stop your sniveling. You've moved on. That's what matters now."

Growing weary, Edna rested her head against the pillow and whispered, "Yes. I believe I have."

Edna's mind drifted for a moment.

I wonder if he knows about Mrs. Peck's secret history.

Gazing at the blanket's monogram, Edna caressed the baby's head. "Almost everything in the trunk has the initials 'PPP' . . . for Priscilla Porter Peck. The monogram works out perfectly for the name I chose for her." She kissed her daughter's forehead. "Did Glory Bee or Jean tell you what I named her?"

Reverend Albright shook his head. "No. Assuming I'll be

baptizing her, guess I ought to know what to call her. And then I'll be going. You need your rest."

Edna giggled. "It's a mouthful for such a little one." She beamed at her daughter's peaceful face. "Her name is Paulette Penelope Pontellier."

* * *

In the early morning's lamplight, Glory Bee tucked a blanket around Edna's legs. "Like I tol' ya, Miss Edna, I been birthin' babies long as I can remember. Even birthed Priscilla when Olivia's time come."

Edna rested her head against the pillow and scowled. "What date was Paulette born? I've lost track of time."

Glory Bee folded an afghan and laid it at the foot of the bed. "Well, t'day's Wednesday, Feb'rary 14. She was born right aroun' stroke o' midnight, so could o' been Mond'y, the 12th, er Tuesd'y the 13th. Docta' Bartlett be here later. He'll have a birth certificate, so y'all can decide which date ya want on it.

With a groan, Glory Bee straightened her torso and pressed her hands against her back. "I'll tell him how ya passed out at the end. Like ta scare Miss Jean an' me half ta death yellin' ya were drownin' an' all. Sure glad ya come to not long afta'."

Edna whispered, "I thought I was going to die."

The bedroom door opened. "Here's yer wee girl," Jean said as she handed the swaddled infant to Edna. The newborn squirmed and puckered her tiny mouth. "All bathed and changed."

Jean tilted her head, a hint of melancholy in her smile. "She's a beautiful babe, Edna. Rosy cheeks . . . like me Kathleen when she was born." Her mouth twisted with a scowl. "Don' know 'bout that white hair though. S'posin' it'll lean t'ward yer dark brown when she gets grown."

Edna felt her face warm. She brought Paulette to her breast and stroked the baby's head. "It's . . . it's her father's coloring. He's quite fair."

The awkward moment passed. Overcome with exhaustion, Edna pressed her head further into the pillow.

"Thank you both," she muttered. "I knew it wasn't likely Dr. Bartlett would be here when my time came. Thank goodness my water broke when you both were here."

Exhausted in their own right, Glory Bee and Jean beamed with pleasure as they hovered over Edna and her newborn daughter. Yawning, Jean picked up a stray towel from the bedroom floor while Glory Bee collected water glasses and an empty water pitcher.

Glory Bee hesitated at the door as Jean left the room. "Imagine ya gotta be hungry. I'll be back up in a while with some breakfast." She grinned. "Miss Jean's goin' back ta the hotel this mornin'. Tol' her ta tell Lloyd Blauers she won't be needin' that room no more. She'll come back here later with as much as she can carry this trip. Hopin' Docta' Bartlett can carry the rest in his carriage when he gits here. No reason she can't move into Miz Peck's room.

A skeptical look crossed Glory Bee's face. "O' course, she needs ta earn a livin', so she's gonna ask Sylvester if she can work in the café. An' if she can do some housekeepin' at the hotel or work in the kitchen with Miss Molly, she ought'a be able ta earn a pretty good livin'. No tellin' if that'll fly with Mista' Blauers givin' her . . . well, what she's been doin'. All's she can do is ask."

"Oh, I do hope that will work," Edna replied. "I can't imagine getting along without her here."

"She'll be a big help and lovin' every minute she can spend with that baby. It'll take a load off o' my mind, too." Glory Bee chuckled. "Tom's wonderin' if I'm ever comin' home. Now git some rest. Penelope'll be wakin' up soon. Good thing she's got school. That child's gonna wear you out wantin' ta hold that baby. Proud as a peacock you givin' Paulette 'Penelope' for her middle name.

Before closing the door, Glory Bee popped her head into the

room. "Oh, an' I got a cradle an' a rockin' chair up home. I'll git Tom ta bring 'em t'day."

In the pre-dawn glow through her window, as the baby suckled, Edna reflected on the births of her children.

I barely remember my pregnancies with Etienne and Raoul ... or their births. That tiny bit of chloroform Dr. Mandalet gave me ... it was over before I knew it had started. Then the nurse whisked them away to the nursery.

Léonce had insisted on a wet nurse. "You'll want to regain your figure soon," he had said right after their second son was born. "Don't forget our trip to Europe is scheduled for next month."

Edna recalled feeling completely numb following the births of her sons. Physically and emotionally removed from them, she grew indifferent to their care. She performed daily tasks in perfunctory fashion as if she were made of wood. Even visits to the nursery did nothing to boost her spirit.

The boys looked at me as they looked at all visitors.

Breathing in her mother's milk smell, Edna gazed at Paulette's now sleeping face. Memories of her battles in the sea back in August surfaced, of the overwhelming odds that prevented her drowning. As Edna gently ran her hand over the spot pulsing on Paulette's tiny head, the miracle of it all struck her.

I feel a lifetime has passed. What a journey we've had, my sweet. I thought I would die with you. Three times ... twice in the sea and again when you were born ... I truly believed we would die.

The first streams of sunlight spread throughout the room turning the faded yellow walls a vibrant gold. Humming *Brahms Lullaby*, as Edna teetered on the edge of sleep, a blank canvas took shape behind her closed eyes. Her mind's paint brush ushered forth a genesis of images in subdued hues. Pastels of blue, lavender, pink, and creamy white ... of a woman lounging on a chaise cradling an infant, a tow-headed child sitting cross-legged on a lush green lawn, her head resting against the chaise as her pink dress floated around her. Beyond the lawn, white foam skirted dazzling turquoise water in a sun-soaked blue sky.

An overwhelming sense of calm and peace that comes with understanding overcame Edna. No longer would she brood over the mysterious adoration she observed between mothers and their children in Mary Cassatt's paintings. No longer would she feel excluded from the venerable bond of motherhood, convinced she was incapable of tenderness and compassion.

Everything I've longed for . . . that unconditional binding love and instinctive need to protect that eluded and bewildered me for so long . . . lay right here in my arms.

Another face coalesced, and Edna whispered, "Penelope. Darling child, you stirred these feelings in me as if you, too, had formed in my womb . . . as if I had given birth to you as well."

Edna breathed a sigh of contentment that reached into the depths of her soul. Beyond her bedroom window, the distant surf's ebb and flow lulled Edna further toward sleep.

In a near chimerical state, she muttered, "I have never felt more . . ." The images from her mind's canvas resurfaced, and she smiled. "Alive. I have never felt more alive."

Chapter Twenty-Seven

Four weeks after Birdie Peck's death on January 27, Pine Cove residents packed the Congregational Church for the February town council meeting. Having learned of Birdie's true heritage, they had gathered to cast their votes by private ballot on whether or not to relocate her grave to the Colored cemetery.

Council Leader Chester Smith oversaw two other council members as they documented the "yeas" to relocate and "nays" to leave Birdie where she was interred. When the counting concluded, a hush fell over the crowd.

The Council Leader pulled a wadded handkerchief from his pants pocket, blew his bulbous nose then shoved the handkerchief back in the pocket. Scowling, he crossed his arms on the lectern and panned the crowd. Having gained command of his audience, he spoke in a stern voice.

"Now, if the votes is in favor o' diggin' up the deceased's body an' movin' it up yonder to the Colored cemetery, I'm here ta tell ya it ain't gonna be that easy. Might hafta' git the sheriff involved. Maybe the Levy County coroner. Messin' with graves don't sit well with the law." Smith looked around at the eager faces waiting to hear the results. "Jus' sayin'."

The Council Leader held out his hand for the tally. After scrutinizing the numbers, he looked up at the deathly quiet crowd. "Hun'erd an' seven 'yeas.' Nine 'nays.'"

Feet shuffled over the worn wood floor amid a kerfuffle of chatter.

Banging the gavel on the lectern, Smith shouted, "Order!" He waited for the crowd to settle down before speaking. "Like I said, y'all. I'm forewarnin' ya. This might not be as easy as some o' ya think."

A man's voice bellowed from the rear of the crowd. "Don' see what the sheriff or the coroner haf'ta say 'bout this, Chester! Whites is buried with Whites an' Coloreds is buried with Coloreds!"

Smith banged the gavel again. "Yer out o' order, Willis. Sit down." He addressed the crowd. "Now, we'll call a special meetin' soon's we git this fig'ered out." He banged the gavel one last time. "No further business. Meetin's adjourned."

Less than a week following the meeting, an unknown contingency of Pine Cove residents took it upon themselves to right what they saw as a wrong. In the dark of night, Birdie Peck's casket was dug up and deposited in a grave in the Colored cemetery. She would spend eternity far from her husband, Walter, surrounded by the spirits of those she rejected in life.

Standing behind the lectern at the next meeting, Council Leader Smith spoke to the dozen or so residents in attendance.

"Unless any one o' ya wants ta claim responsibility or make any accusations, this matter is closed." Following a few moments of silence, Smith banged the gavel. "No further business. Meetin's adjourned."

The following day, as Edna poked holes in a pie crust preparing it for a peach filling, she whispered to Jean. "You let the secret out, didn't you?"

Jean shook her head and whispered back. "Wa'n't me." She tossed more chicken pieces into a bowl of flour.

At the stove, humming *Carry Me Back to Ol' Virginny*, Glory Bee stirred a kettle of peaches bubbling over a hot grate.

Edna's and Jean's eyes met and they smirked.

Setting the knife in the sink, Edna wiped her hands on a damp towel and cleared her throat. "So, Glory Bee, now there's nothing preventing Olivia and Jeremy from coming home, is there?"

Glory Bee set the ladle aside. "S'pose they could, but they'd be takin' a awful risk. Best they stay put least ways fer now."

"Have you heard from them? Have they said whether or not they'll ever come home?" Edna asked.

Perching her fists on her broad hips, Glory Bee pursed her lips. "Olivia wrote me back they'd think about it. Fer now, we got our satisfaction knowin' their names is clear, that they didn't do nothin' wrong when they married.

At the pantry door, she turned back to Edna. "Most of all, it's gratifyin' knowin' they *could* come home instead o' bein' told they *can't*."

***

Thanks to Dr. Bartlett's handling of the sale of Edna's ring to a jeweler in Tampa, Tom gradually made repairs to the house. He fixed the front porch railing and patched a leak in the roof. Bit by bit, he scraped flaking and peeling paint off the exterior of the house.

From the top rung of the ladder, Tom called to Edna watching from below. "Need ta tighten up the outside first, Miss Edna, so be thinkin' what color ye want this house painted. Come colder weather, we'll tackle the inside."

With the approach of summer, in anticipation of the dwindling tourist season, Edna spent as much time sketching at the dock as the few hours between Paulette's feedings and daily tasks would permit.

Glory Bee admonished Edna for fretting over the handling of larger household chores. "Gettin' up ev'ry few hours in the night, ya got ta be bone tired, so don' be worryin' 'bout chores fer now.

"Penelope's learned how ta make her bed an' change the

sheets, an' you been takin' care o' yer own room. Miss Jean an' me can handle the rest o' the chores jus' fine. You go on an' take care o' business while the gettin's good."

Sylvester happily hung more of Edna's sketches on his café walls. "Brightens up the place," he said as he surveyed the dozen or so pictures. "An' people'r stayin' in here longer 'n longer eatin' an' lookin' at 'em."

A comfortable communal routine fell into place in Birdie Peck's house. For Edna, waking to the sound of Paulette gurgling and cooing in her cradle each morning brought a level of joy she could not have imagined. For Penelope, her delight with her "baby sister" grew by the day. When she was not in school, doing homework, or playing with Paulette, she pitched in to help Glory Bee and Jean with simple cooking and cleaning tasks.

Once Paulette adjusted to an occasional bottle feeding, leaving her in Jean's care, Edna and Penelope would row the small boat to Penelope's safe place. After clearing away pine cones and pine needles that had accumulated around the two graves and repairing the crosses, they would lounge on Tepkunset's blanket a short while to eat their picnic lunch.

Through an encounter with Joseph while fishing the Gulf, Nathan learned that Tepkunset had passed away.

"Joseph said she died middle o' April," Nathan told Edna on the dock one day. "Took her body up to a big Seminole encampment north o' the Suwannee for burial. Lot o' swamp land up that way, but they've been buryin' their dead up there a long time. Guess they know what they're doin'."

Edna and Penelope made a visit to Joseph to offer their condolences.

"My grandmother loved you very much," Joseph said as he wiped tears from Penelope's face. "Don't grieve for her. She lived a good life on this island. Many came to our tribal ceremony and brought gifts to assure her spirit arrived safely at its destination."

With her hands on Penelope's shoulders, Edna smiled at Joseph. "Tepkunset was very special to Penelope."

Reaching behind his head, Joseph removed a leather cord with a round woven circle of beads with feathers attached to it.

"This was my grandmother's dream catcher," Joseph said as he placed it over Penelope's head. "It was a gift to her from a Cherokee woman many years ago. I would like for you to have it to remember her by."

Penelope smiled through her tears. "I will always remember her, Mr. Joseph. Thank you."

* * *

On the first Saturday of May, as Penelope played with Paulette in her pram, her ears perked up to the sound of voices . . . lots of voices . . . laughing and shouting. Hopping off the kitchen chair, she ran to the back porch.

Around the corner of the house, a dozen of her classmates ran into the back yard shouting "Happy Birthday" at the tops of their lungs. Not far behind, Penelope's bespectacled young teacher, Miss Treeter, hustled to keep up with the children.

Bowled over with surprise, Penelope could only stare at the throng of well-wishers. Edna and Jean, who had coordinated the get-together with Miss Treeter, appeared on the porch with pitchers of lemonade and cookies.

Under Miss Treeter's supervision, the children played tag, kick the can, and pin the tail on the donkey. Nathan showed up with several lengths of rope and Tom with a board and a ladder. In no time, a sturdy swing hung from a branch of the tree outside Edna's bedroom window. The game was on as to who could swing the highest.

At lunch time, the women brought out platters of strawberry jam sandwiches along with more pitchers of lemonade. In the center of it all, Penelope beamed with happiness.

Watching from the back door with Jean, Edna shook her head. "The only other time I can recall seeing Penelope this happy was when she asked if she could call me 'Mum'."

Jean squeezed Edna's shoulder. "Aye. Grew on her hearin' me talk so much 'bout me own Mum." Jean giggled. "Dinna forget when she found all them pennies under her pillow when the tooth fairy came."

"Oh, yes!" Edna said. "I can still hear that scream when she came running down the stairs!"

With the platters of sandwiches emptied and the children worn out from playing, Edna stepped out to the porch. "Who wants birthday cake?!"

A chorus of children's voices yelled, "Me!"

Holding open the screen door, Edna called into the kitchen, "Miss Jean, we're ready!"

Jean emerged from the pantry carrying a layered chocolate cake topped with a flaming wax candle.

Penelope's jaw dropped. She could not take her eyes off the cake the whole time everyone sang the "Happy Birthday" verse to *Good Morning to You All*.

"Make a wish, make a wish!" Penelope's friends shouted.

Penelope's face glowed. At last, she inhaled a deep breath and blew out the flame while her classmates cheered and clapped. When Miss Treeter and the children said their good-byes, Penelope hugged them all, a chocolate smile spreading from ear to ear.

Later, Edna called Penelope to her bedroom. She pulled the chair to the middle of the room and pointed to it. In a lilting voice, she said, "Have a seat, sweetheart. I have something for you."

Puzzled as to Mum's chirpy behavior, Penelope did as she was told.

"Now, close your eyes," Edna instructed. "And no peeking." She paused. "Promise you won't peek?"

Penelope squeezed her eyes closed. "Yes! I promise!" When she heard the closet door open followed by a rustling sound, she teased, "Can I open my eyes now? Please?!"

"Not yet. One more second."

At the sound of more rustling, Penelope stomped her foot. "Mum! Please!"

"Okay! You can look now!"

When they opened, Penelope's azure eyes fixated on the most beautiful pink dress she had ever seen in real life. In slow motion, she stood and reached out to touch the dress's delicate fabric.

Edna held the dress against Penelope's slender body. "It probably doesn't have as many sparkles like the dress in your story book, and it might be a little big." She chuckled. "But if you keep eating like you have been, it should fit you perfectly before long."

Penelope ran her fingers over the taffeta ribbon circling the waistline. Taking the dress from Edna, she turned the dress around and back again taking in every detail . . . from the layers of pink chiffon to the sequined pink lace around the neckline to the numerous pink satin-covered buttons down the back.

Looking up at Edna, she whispered, "Is it really mine? I get to keep it?"

Edna held Penelope's face between her hands. "Of course, it's yours, silly. Who else would it belong to?"

Penelope groped for words. "But Mum, there aren't no . . . aren't any stores in Pine Cove that's got anything like this." She raised her eyebrows. "How . . . ? Where did it come from?"

Edna touched the tip of Penelope's nose. "Well, nosy, if you must know, it didn't come from a store." She sat on her bed and patted the quilt. "Come sit."

Penelope sat next to Edna holding the dress against her as if she feared it might evaporate.

"So," Edna began, "Miss Jean learned from Reverend Albright that the family of one of the church ladies, Mrs. Yost, owns a millinery shop in Tampa. They decorate hats using all kinds of material. We told Mrs. Yost, who is a seamstress, what we wanted. A few weeks ago, when Dr. Bartlett went to Tampa, he picked up this material from the millinery shop and took it to Mrs. Yost for her to make the dress for you."

Stroking the delicate fabric and trims, Penelope sighed. "It's the prettiest dress I've ever seen." In somber voice, she added with a shrug, "But where can I . . . ?"

Before Penelope could finish her question, Edna wrapped an arm around her shoulder. "But where would you ever wear it, right?"

Nodding, Penelope glanced up at Edna. "Sure can't wear it ta school. Not sure I'd even wear something this nice ta church."

Edna nodded her understanding. "Well, the dress isn't the only surprise. I promise there will be opportunities for you to wear it.

Taking a deep breath, Edna shared the rest of the surprise. "One Wednesday, hopefully soon, when Dr. Bartlett comes, we . . . you, Paulette, and I . . . will leave Pine Cove with him. He and Mrs. Bartlett have invited us to spend a night at their home in Otter Creek. The next day, we will travel with him to Tampa where the three of us will spend a few days sightseeing, eating at fine restaurants, and shopping, of course. We need to find shoes to match your dress. Dr. Bartlett will then return to fetch us and bring us home."

Penelope . . . a child brought up in the most deprived of circumstances, who had never known anywhere beyond Pine Cove Key and a few surrounding islands . . . could only gape at Edna.

When at last she could speak, her voice filled with awe, Penelope asked, "Who'r we stayin' with in Tampa?"

A smile blossomed over Edna's face. Reaching into her dress pocket, she withdrew a picture post card Dr. Bartlett had given her. The card showcased the ornate intricate design of the sprawling Tampa Bay Hotel. Domes, cupolas, and thirteen giant minarets, topped with crescent moons, spiraled skyward from the rooftop above the magnificent five-story building's colossal arches.

"Well," Edna said, "we aren't exactly staying *with* anybody."

Handing the postcard to Penelope, Edna squeezed Penelope's shoulder and pulled her close. "We're staying in a castle."

Chapter Twenty-Eight

On a sunny and warm Saturday in early June, with meager requests for sketches due to a single tour boat carrying only a few passengers, Edna strolled the dock with Paulette snuggled in her pram. Penelope skipped along and chatted with the fishermen. In the rising heat of the afternoon, Edna undid the top button of her cotton gingham dress. After putting on a pair of sunglasses, she lowered the brim of her straw hat against the sun's glare.

All around, boat rigging clanged and hammers banged amid the ever-present screech and squawk of gulls. Pelicans plodded along the dock and perched on boat hulls patiently waiting for fishermen to toss morsels into their gaping bills.

A few yards ahead of Edna, two little boys clad in knickers and visor caps ran helter-skelter around the dock before a smartly attired man collared them. Beige linen suit, fedora hat, walking cane . . . he struck quite a pose as the threesome hovered over the side of the dock watching the fishermen's activities.

Catching her breath, Edna stopped in her tracks.

Spotting Nathan toward the end of the dock, Penelope waved her arms and yelled as she ran. "Nathan!"

Edna opened her mouth to call her back. Too late.

An attractive woman Edna estimated to be in her early thirties and outfitted in handsome travel apparel called from the café doorway.

"Darling! You must come inside and see the most stunning autographed sketches hanging on the walls. The café owner says a local artist drew them." She pointed in Edna's direction. "Look! There's her table!"

The two boys ran to the woman and wrapped their arms around her skirt.

"I'm hungry!" the older of the two shouted.

"Me, too!" shouted the littler one.

"I know you are, Sweets," the woman said, patting the youngsters' backs. She shielded her eyes from the sun's glare. "The children are hungry, dear. We have some time before the boat leaves for Tampa. Let's have a bite to eat. Afterwards the four of us can sit for our portrait while we wait to depart. It would make a lovely souvenir of our trip!"

As the foursome disappeared into the café, Edna retreated to her table and began shoving her art materials into her satchel.

Penelope, having returned from chatting with Nathan, swung the satchel over her shoulder. "But Mum, why are we leaving so early?"

"Paulette is hungry, dear." Edna gripped the handle of the pram and swung it around. "It's time to go home."

***

As Edna lay on her bed, she mulled over the effect the near encounter had evoked. She could not say she was shocked that Léonce and the boys were there. Throughout the year, throngs passed through Pine Cove Key from various ports along the Gulf of Mexico on their way to Tampa and other destinations.

Nor could she say she was surprised Léonce had developed a relationship with another woman. Believing his wife was dead, he was free to do as he pleased.

Edna considered her feelings over Etienne and Raoul's display of affection with Léonce's companion.

They could have been posing for a Cassatt painting. The boys never would have embraced me like that. Why would they? It was never encouraged . . . by me or Léonce . . . yet there it was with this woman.

Something about the woman's depth of tenderness toward the boys she could not yet define puzzled Edna. Still, she felt no resentment toward her. On the contrary, she felt gratitude.

She was so patient with them, and the boys appeared comfortable with her . . . and quite happy. Perhaps this is someone, other than a nanny, who will comfort and rear them as a mother should.

In the quiet of her room, Edna recalled her close proximity to her husband, his companion, and her sons. Few people roamed the dock, so Edna was quite visible. At one point, the boys nearly collided with Paulette's pram as they chased one another around the dock.

Léonce had hastened toward Edna, his glance at her lingering but a few seconds as he took the boys by their arms.

Edna recalled wondering briefly what his reaction would be if she said something to him.

Léonce, it's me, Edna.

Shielded beneath her hat's brim, her sunglasses concealing her eyes, Edna had remained stoic . . . and silent.

Whisking the boys away, Léonce had called over his shoulder, "My apologies, Madam."

Mounting revelations aroused Edna. Leaving her bed, she stared out the window . . . at the giant oak tree, at Penelope's swing, at the sparkling water in the distance.

Of course, he hadn't recognized me. The fashionably dressed, polished, lofty socialite he once knew doesn't exist anymore. She's dead, gone forever from his consciousness. The plebian woman he came in contact with on the dock, a mere commoner attired in a simple cotton dress and straw hat pushing a pram, was someone to be disregarded.

Her arms crossed over her bosom, Edna walked the length of her bedroom and back again, squinting into the looking glass at her marriage. She recognized obvious signs that her relationship with her husband had waned.

He essentially ignored my willful behavior. He never suggested how we might overcome whatever forces had driven us apart. When I moved out of our home, why wouldn't he have sought me at the lodging I moved into?

Another thought goaded Edna into scrutinizing the displays of affection between Léonce and his companion. Less than a year had passed since she disappeared . . . drowned as far as her husband knew . . . a relatively short grieving period for a spouse typically concerned with appearances. Léonce seemed to have fallen into a new relationship fairly quickly with apparent ease.

Back at the window, as the church bells tolled noon, Edna faced a truth.

I was dead to him long before I walked into the Gulf. I had fulfilled my obligation in producing two sons, thus securing Léonce's legacy. And if the woman's affectionate and familiar endearments toward Léonce and my sons are any indication, my guess is her relationship with my husband has been going on much longer than I've been gone from their lives.

Watching a blue jay dart from limb to limb, Edna mused over her life since arriving on Pine Cove Key. Fear, loneliness, despair . . . all gradually replaced with a sense of confidence and purpose that no matter the challenges she might encounter, she would face them head on.

Immersing herself in Penelope's dreadful circumstances certainly had driven Edna toward a sense of purpose and meaning. As for her self-assuredness, maybe it started subliminally when she first began sketching at the dock. She knew her signed artwork would accompany travelers back to various ports, including New Orleans, and that her sketches might be shared among the travelers' friends and family.

Edna could have discouraged Sylvester from hanging her portraits on the café walls. But the autographed display . . . of Lloyd and Annie at the hotel, Fred at the mercantile, Jean, Glory Bee, Nathan, Sylvester, Elmer and many others . . . represented affirmation and a statement of empowerment. In less than a year,

Edna had learned to thrive in Pine Cove . . . as an artist, as a valued member of a community, as a mother, and a friend. Having overcome unimaginable obstacles to attain these achievements, she would not allow anyone to take them away from her.

Paulette began to fuss in her cradle. Edna turned from the window and undid the top buttons on her dress. Sitting in the rocking chair the Porters had kindly loaned, she brought Paulette to her breast.

Humming *Brahm's Lullaby*, Edna rested her head against the top of the chair. As she rocked, the chair runners clicked over the hardwood floor a mesmerizing ticking in time with the hour. A warm breeze buffeted the curtain panels at her open window. A squirrel chattered on a tree branch.

Downstairs in the kitchen, voices murmured amid the clatter of dishes, silverware, pots, and pans. The mouthwatering aroma of chicken vegetable soup and baking bread rose up the stairs.

When the knock came at the front door, Edna pulled a sleeping Paulette from her breast and buttoned her dress.

Penelope shouted from the kitchen. "I'll get it!"

Cradling Paulette, Edna stood and glanced in her bureau mirror. After tucking a loose curl into her chignon, she smoothed the wrinkles of her dress and stepped into the hallway.

By the time Edna descended the stairs, Jean and Penelope had reached the door. Edna stood behind them as Glory Bee strode up the hallway to join them.

When Penelope pulled open the door, Léonce Pontellier stared in stunned silence at the cadre of women before him. He then focused on his wife's face in apparent bewilderment.

Edna lifted Paulette to her shoulder and patted her back. An audible burp broke the silence.

As Penelope giggled, Edna smiled at her husband. "Hello, Léonce. Won't you come in? I'd like you to meet my family."

Acknowledgments

I believe it's safe to say every author is grateful to a host of individuals. I certainly am. For over three years, members of Tall Tales Writers Group of Gainesville, Georgia, have inspired me with their invaluable insights and critiques toward publication of *Islands of Women*. To each of you, Charlene DeWitt, the group's organizer and leader, Evelyn Asher, Gina Dyer, Wanda Fuller, Jane Hemmer, Doug Jones, Marsha Patterson, and Candis Stephens, I cannot thank you enough for the time and thought invested in this book. Additionally, the knowledge gained through my affiliation with the Northeast Georgia Writers and Northeast Georgia Literary Society related to the art of writing and publication is immeasurable.

Thanks also to my first readers for taking time out of their busy lives to read my manuscript: my husband, Rick Smith, and my sister, Lorabeth LeWorthy, both avid readers; authors Candis Stephens and poet Evelyn Asher; to Gina Dyer for contributing her poignant poem at the beginning of the book; to my talented visual arts grandson, Dylan Stevens, for his design of my book cover; to long-time friend, Jim Freeman, for his help with traditional Irish expressions; and to BookLogix Publishers in Alpharetta, Georgia, for their outstanding professionalism, guidance, and patience with me through the publication process.

Last but not least, I thank my cherished family and circle of friends for their support and belief that this book would come to fruition. To my husband, who never complained if meals, house cleaning, and laundry took second place, thank you for your ongoing encouragement each and every day. I love you for many reasons and especially for your trust in me in countless ways.

About the Author

Eileen A. O'Hara has worn several hats throughout her life including administrative and entrepreneurship. She owned a flower shop in Florida for several years and currently operates a specialty food business that she and her family started over twenty years ago.

She earned her B.A. in English and Creative Writing from Eckerd College in St. Petersburg, Florida, in 1999. Upon completing her M.A. in English at the University of South Florida/Tampa in 2002, she was employed by Eckerd College as an adjunct professor where she taught research writing. Her inspiration to write *Islands of Women* came from reading the classic novel *The Awakening* by Kate Chopin.

Eileen and her husband, Rick Smith, are now retired among the tranquil foothills of the north Georgia mountains with their obscenely spoiled felines, Griffin and Hannah. *Islands of Women* is Eileen's first novel.